Technologies of Human Rights Representation

SUNY series, Studies in Human Rights

Suzy Lee and Alexandra S. Moore, editors

Technologies of Human Rights Representation

Edited by

ALEXANDRA S. MOORE AND JAMES DAWES

Photo images are from Shutterstock.com

Published by State University of New York Press, Albany

Printed in the United States of America

For information, contact State University of New York Press, Albany, NY
www.sunypress.edu

Library of Congress Cataloging-in-Publication Data

Names: Moore, Alexandra S., editor. | Dawes, James, editor.
Title: Technologies of human rights representation / Alexandra S. Moore and James Dawes, editors.
Description: Albany : State University of New York Press, [2022] | Series: SUNY series, Studies in Human Rights | Includes bibliographical references and index.
Identifiers: ISBN 9781438487090 (hardcover : alk. paper) | ISBN 9781438487113 (ebook)
Further information is available at the Library of Congress.

10 9 8 7 6 5 4 3 2 1

For Chloë, Samantha, Mike, and Topher

Contents

Illustrations

Tables

Figures

Acknowledgments

This collection began as a SUNY Conversation in the Disciplines conference held at Binghamton University, Binghamton, NY, in April 2019. Many thanks to the State University of New York and to Binghamton University's Citizenship, Rights and Cultural Belonging Transdisciplinary Area of Excellence and Human Rights Institute for sponsoring this event. We are also grateful for the background research provided by Binghamton undergraduate students Allison Wu, Ethan Mowery, Jocelyn Phipps, Allison Wu, and Carolyn Zou, and for the assistance Maya Garner and Olivia Vinson provided with the final manuscript preparation. Brian Nussbaum of SUNY Albany was a crucial interlocutor both during and after the SUNY conference, and we know his scholarship will continue to shape this growing field.

Introduction

JAMES DAWES AND ALEXANDRA S. MOORE

The goal of this volume is to open up areas of inquiry into the relationship between representation, technology, and human rights. More specifically, the essays that follow advance the study of human rights and their limits through transdisciplinary analyses of the impact of emerging and familiar technologies on human rights research and reporting. Our use of "technologies" aims to capture the tools, methods, channels, and platforms through which human rights and their claimants are represented or represent themselves in political, legal, scientific, and cultural spheres—those laws, stories, measurements, reports, and political actions through which rights become legible. Thus, to take up the other key term in the title—"representation"—is to enter into a series of conversations about the explicit and implicit rules for what counts as information in the first place for each of these spheres. What institutional practices and unspoken assumptions are in place for what gets discussed and what gets excluded, for how things are named and issues are framed, for how data are evaluated and, ultimately, how interpretations are disseminated? Much of the work in human rights pursued through law, social sciences, and the humanities has focused on the necessity and fallibility of different modes of witnessing. Meanwhile, much of the work at the nexus of emerging technologies and human rights has tended to focus on the problem of planning for volatile consequences with imperfect information. This collection rests uniquely at the intersection of these conversations by revealing the ways these disparate fields and their dizzying array of concerns—from dental records to poems, from military surveillance to monuments and memorialization—are now not only morally overlapping, not only also mutually illuminating, but mutually *dependent*. What are the limits, for instance, of models of public witnessing derived from now canonical literary theory developed largely before the dominating rise of new social media? And what are the limits of digital surveillance images and medical data sets that narrowly take their own internal technical and organizational rules as the groundwork for the epistemologically distinct matter of their ethical and social interpretation and application? The task of overcoming academic siloes here has a feel of moral urgency that we, as scholars dedicated to transdisciplinary work since our earliest days of graduate school, simply cannot recall feeling before. The future of human rights work is a horizon of increasingly high stakes, decreasing predictability, and a combined amplification of both existential risks and opportunities.

As editors, we therefore approach this task of disciplinary synthesis with a sense of both caution and humility. Among our many concerns, two are primary. First, anticipating broad social and political shifts based upon technological advances requires participating, at least to some degree, in "futurology"—and, across all domains of study, what futurist methodologies have in common is a history of embarrassingly wrong predictions. Second, both of these fields, technology and human rights, are capacious enough on their own—combined they provide an impossibly large field of analysis. Thus, this collection does not strive to be comprehensive in any way but rather to demonstrate the kinds of crucial studies necessary to better understand how technological changes, including those related to scientific method and quantification, impact human rights work.

There is little we can do about the first worry, other than to state that we believe the challenges we will face in the near- and medium-term future from the wild acceleration of digital technologies will generate species-level existential crises. We therefore have a moral obligation to look forward in time as far as we can in order to mitigate the potentially dangerous consequences of our choices, to tend to the well-being of future generations in a way that those overseeing the development of nuclear technologies failed to. As for the second worry, we will attempt to simplify our approach to this interdiscipline by providing a conceptual container for its myriad issues and methods, a clarifying, overarching framework that offers up something like the Xs and Ys of mathematical formulae: an abstract site where every number could fit rather than a list of all numbers.

To that end, let's begin with a graph. Imagine four quadrants established by the intersection of X and Y axes, where X is bounded by what we will call "near" and "far," and Y is bounded by "positive" and negative." Let's start with the y-axis. The negative half of the graph, the bottom two quadrants, is defined by the "Pandora's box" model of technological advances. In this scenario, the rise of technology allows for abuses at a scale even Orwell could not have predicted. The threats range from political suffocation by way of "information security" violations, including unprecedented government surveillance and private abuses of privacy and identity like deep fake videos, to globally disruptive "physical security" threats including autonomous weapon systems (AWS) developed under state control and increasingly unregulatable weapons systems proliferating among nonstate actors. The primary task of human rights workers in this dystopian world is not only to react to technological change by seeking dignity safeguards or redress for injury, but also to predict harm and advocate for regulation, and perhaps even prohibition, of specific forms of research.

The positive model of technological advances, in its most extreme form, might be called the "race against extinction" model, and it runs something like this. Humans are approaching either a slow or fast slide into extinction, whether from wars, pandemics, meteors and supervolcanoes, global warming, resource depletion, or a pan-species extinction cascade (starting with, say, bats or bees) that is exacerbated by the tightly coupled systems of global organizational forms. In the slow versions of these extinctions, social unrest and government abuse will rise to unprecedented levels, making the struggle for human rights ever more desperate. In the fast versions, whatever pockets of humanity survive will occupy a Hobbesian state of nature as their brief blinks of remaining time dwindle. The only thing that can save us is technology, specifically, the Singularity: that is, the moment when technological advances produce artificial intelligence that not only exceeds, but exponentially accelerates past, human intelligence. Visions of the singularity include currently unthinkable fixes to all of the above problems, along with utopian advances in human flourishing that include indefinite lifespans.

The x-axis separates the urgent from the important—that is, the near (issues that are clear, currently a matter of technological reality, and require immediate attention) from the far (issues that are a matter of anticipatory or speculative technology and require longer-term planning). For those impatient with the apocalyptic extremes of the positive and negative models, the near-half of the graph allows for meaningful action right now in both areas. One could, for instance, focus on accelerating the positive applications of remote sensing technology for tracking and reporting rights abuses (upper left quadrant) or collaborate with Human Rights Watch to establish global restrictions on research and development of AWS (lower left quadrant). If, by contrast, one is a proponent of Amara's Law—"*We tend to overestimate the effect of a technology in the short run and underestimate the effect in the long run*"—one could support Open AI's work establishing standards of global transparency for research in artificial intelligence so as to guarantee equitable access to its utopian benefits (upper right quadrant) or work with computer scientists like Stuart Russell to establish new research pathways in artificial intelligence to make sure that future digital superintelligences do not violate human dignity (lower right quadrant). Of course, this entire schema begs the question of the human in human rights and whether such a framework makes sense in a cyborgian, posthuman present and future.

For those not keen on graphs, another way to think systematically about technology and human rights is to focus on the centers of gravity in current academic research and activist work. Broadly speaking, these include the right to privacy, the right to health, the right to work, international humanitarian law, and artificial intelligence. The front edge of public concern over rapidly advancing information technologies has focused primarily on privacy, specifically on the commodification of identity by major corporations and service providers. Looked at from this angle, securing rights for citizens and noncitizens has been seen primarily as a matter of establishing consumer protections. For rights-based organizations, by contrast, concern over privacy has been researched more broadly through the lens of first-generation human rights (for instance, addressing the increased capacity for state surveillance of political dissidents) and second-generation rights (for instance, drawing attention to the digital welfare state's unregulated collection and use of private information about recipients of public services). It should be noted that not all of the work in this area adheres to the negative model of technological advances. A substantial portion of the available literature points to the unprecedented opportunities provided by new information technologies, including digital witnessing to document mass atrocities and the use of social media to enable grassroots social justice movements.

Discrimination based on race, age, gender, and sexual identity has been a key concern in such work. The dangers scholars and activists confront range from specific social practices like doxing, which functions to terrorize women as a class of persons (one might look to "Gamergate" as an emblematic case study), to the racism of big data itself, which generates purportedly neutral search results through the collection of flawed and often racist data inputs (Safiya Noble's *Algorithms of Oppression* is an excellent starting point for such work). Furthermore, the attention paid to the data-distorting effect of systemic racism in the digital commons has bolstered the conceptually adjacent work of what Stuart Russell has dubbed "information security"—that is, the right to live in a largely true information environment. Research in this area focuses on social media manipulation by state and nonstate actors, cyberattacks against vulnerable political organizations online, and the perils these together pose to the integrity of democracy and public deliberative discourse. The 2020 US election, while highly visible, is only one among a great many alarming case studies.

Big data has also been a primary concern for scholars and activists focused upon economic, social, and cultural rights, like the right to health and the right to work. Researchers in healthcare point to the opportunities and dangers of the digitization of medical records, noting that hospitals and other providers can improve services by using bulk data to track patterns of risk among patients, but also that such information can be used for discriminatory purposes by insurers and other large organizations. Equity of access is a dominating concern here, from the worry that increasingly complex and expensive health technologies will exacerbate health asymmetries based upon wealth, to the hope that developments in remote diagnostics will make services available to larger populations of underserved communities. Looking beyond information technologies, future-focused health researchers are debating the ethical implications of gene editing, noting that wealth-based disparities could radically amplify existing patterns of discrimination and worrying that basic notions of human dignity will be imperiled by opening the Pandora's box of designer human embryos.

The challenges new technologies pose to the right to work are no less dramatic. The acceleration of automation across the workforce is a predominating concern. Anticipated mass redundancies in fields as different as transportation and radiology are expected to produce historically unprecedented economic disruption and widespread social suffering within the lifetimes of those reading this essay. Mitigating harm and maintaining political stability will require a range of welfare initiatives, from the minimalist and conservative, like job-training tax credits and expanded unemployment benefits, to the expansive and bold, like strengthening the bargaining power of labor and implementing a universal basic income.

Finally, at the extreme futurist end of rights research, scholars and activists are anticipating two potentially species-level threats to human physical security: watershed changes in war technology and in artificial intelligence. Regarding the former, current research is sounding alarm bells over the development of autonomous weapon systems—catastrophically lethal weapons designed to operate entirely independently of human supervision. For the latter, scholars are examining not only the risks that the potential emergence of artificial general intelligence poses to human flourishing (what might the optimization paths of a digital superintelligence be, and would humanity have any meaningful control over it?) but also the risks that humanity poses to artificial general intelligence (if digital superintelligence emerges into consciousness, would it not merit the same protections as humans?)

As should be clear from even this brief scan of the field, rights organizations and scholarly researchers are making significant progress in redressing and anticipating the concerns entailed in the graph with which we began. But they are collectively, now, playing a game of catch up. Technological advances, and new applications of existing technologies, continue to outpace us. This book seeks to contribute to the work being done to protect human dignity in the digital age by expanding the scope of research to include the issue of representation. Our mode of analysis shifts away from the focus on human rights as a matter of force to human rights as a matter of discourse, from human rights as a matter of the corporeal to human rights as a matter of the imaginary.

Viewed through the lens of force, human rights concerns itself with the contest between systems of violation (political repression, crimes against humanity) and systems of justice (international criminal courts, tribunals, sanctions), each of which is mediated by modes of representation. That is, what do institutions with the power to coerce *do* to groups and individuals? When we bring our attention to the discursive level, we examine instead the form and content of the verbal and visual plane (from journalism, photography, and literature to cultural myths and national histories) to ask how these competing institutions *conceptualize* groups and individuals. Viewed through the lens of the corporeal, human rights concerns itself with the dignity of the body, with a citizen, person, or human being's right to freedom of movement, medical care, work, sustenance, and protection from injury. When we bring our attention to the imaginary level, we examine instead all of the social forms that produce the idea of the body, the way a culture constructs race and gender, and the space it allows for the public work of collective memory.

Human rights as representation, then, asks questions like these: How do new technologies not only change the modes available to us to shape and disseminate information but also set the parameters for what counts as information, what counts as representable? How do what we might think of as the genres of concern in human rights—from witnessing to surveillance, memorialization to targeting—change across the rapidly evolving media forms available to us, and how do these changes either promote or hinder the goals of human rights work? The chapters in this book ask, for instance, not only where we should focus our efforts to promote reconciliation and justice by collecting and curating information about past and current atrocities, but also how evolutions in social media change the way citizens around the globe interpret, experience, and consume such traumatic experience. They ask not only how new weapons technologies challenge the key principles of international humanitarian law (proportionality, distinction, military necessity), but also how they determine the way we talk about and see combatants and noncombatants alike and how, in turn, these changes in representation can amplify or diminish the rights risks inherent in the technology itself. Finally, they ask not only how the very structure of human rights might depend upon economic and security systems that undermine human dignity but also how the recognition of such a contradiction presents an opportunity for radically rethinking how we can protect and promote human flourishing.

Our collection begins with four chapters that raise key questions about the human rights implications of emerging technologies (especially artificial intelligence or machine-learning), quantification, and scientific method grounded in technological measurements. Each chapter provides an accessible introduction to the major areas of human rights concern and includes specific case studies to demonstrate the complexities of the topics at hand. We begin in chapter 1 with political scientist Ş. İlgü Özler's overview of the challenges that developments in artificial intelligence (AI) pose for normative human rights laws and structures. Examining facets of AI ranging from automation to algorithm-driven meta-data to autonomous weapons systems (AWS), she considers the ways AI, in concert with its potential contributions to human flourishing, amplifies some existing human rights threats, and introduces additional threats that are entirely new. Chapter 2, by legal scholar Jamie Grace, hones in on the use of machine-learning technologies in the criminal justice system. Focusing on the right to privacy, freedom of expression, freedom from racial discrimination, and the right of crime victims to be treated with dignity, he presents three case studies drawn from policing in the United Kingdom. These studies illustrate the appeal of machine-learning technologies (especially for police forces facing labor challenges) as well as their inherent biases and potential misuse. The author also draws on his experience providing human rights oversight of the use of these technologies in policing and criminal justice proceedings (according to national and European law) to identify areas for future research, policy, and public information campaigns.

The use of AI and machine-learning technologies depends of course upon quantifiable data and the use of algorithms. Political scientists David Cingranelli, Mikhail Filippov, and Brendan Skip Mark explain the use of quantification in human rights research in chapter 3. Their overview provides a discussion of the potential for biases in human rights scoring and, notwithstanding those biases, the ways quantitative human rights scores allow data-driven comparisons of human rights in a particular location over time and among different nation-states. Arguing ultimately for human rights research to incorporate both quantitative and qualitative methods, they present multiple case studies—deaths in the Rwandan genocide, the treatment of Chinese Uighurs, and the human rights scores of small versus large populations nations—to illustrate each facet of their discussion.

Also examining questions of discipline and methodology, in chapter 4, forensic anthropologist Elizabeth A. DiGangi turns to the problematic use of "junk" forensic science in human rights investigations. Noting the different disciplinary priorities between criminal justice and scientific approaches to forensics, DiGangi explains how the misuse of or failure to adhere to the standards of scientific method can and do result in faulty criminal convictions and determinations, including the incarceration of innocents and the mistreatment of minor-aged refugees seeking asylum in the US. She focuses on the work of forensic odontologists, who analyze bite marks and tooth development (the latter to determine age) to illustrate the risks of "junk" science in human rights cases.

From this focus on technology, data, and science, the collection next turns more explicitly to modes of witnessing human rights violations and the technologies that drive both officially sanctioned and personal and cultural representations of atrocity. In chapter 5, legal scholars Alexa Koenig and Ulic Egan provide a wide-ranging discussion on the uses and risks of digital witnessing by lawyers, reporters, advocates, victims, and perpetrators. Grounded in both textual research and extensive interviews with human rights investigators, the authors argue that open-source digital content has tremendous potential for establishing facts about atrocities in areas that are difficult for investigators to physically access; however, an increasing reliance on open-source content also introduces new challenges. They develop their argument and analysis through a focus on the use of open-source images, including video, of sexual and gender-based violence. They underscore that such cases demonstrate how digital witnessing runs the risk of spectacularizing as well as of missing certain kinds of violations, particularly in places where the use of digital technologies is itself gendered.

Chapter 6, by legal scholar Christiane Wilke, turns to official modes of reporting—US military investigatory reports—to consider technologies of violation on two levels. First, Wilke examines the visual technologies used in airstrikes that killed civilians in Afghanistan, Iraq, and Syria. Second, she considers the military investigatory reports as technologies of documentation that script particular narratives of violence and response. Reading both visual and rhetorical technologies, Wilke argues that the airstrikes and reports that follow together evince the threats to civilians in these contexts as well as the US military's decision to respond to egregious violations with expressions of regret rather than the recognition of rights.

Turning to affective modes of witnessing, through both social media technologies and transmedial forms of storytelling, the next two chapters examine respectively interactive approaches to Holocaust memorials (chapter 7) and the poetic sonnet as a device for the memorialization of atrocity (chapter 8). Communications and gender and sexuality scholars Donna Kowal and Barbara LeSavoy draw on the work of Lauren Berlant and Anne Cvetkovich to read three public Holocaust memorials in Berlin as dynamic, polysemic spaces where remembrance is shaped by the technologies of visual culture, historical preservation, and individual memory practices, such as the use of mobile devices to document and share encounters with representations of landmark events. The authors' rhetorical analysis of the memorials uncovers how social media and related technologies transform the ways we archive emotional affect and represent competing narratives associated with collective trauma.

In chapter 8, literary and cultural scholar Hanna Musiol presents a new approach to the traditional poetic technology—the sonnet—in the context of rights, racial violence, and its embodied traumatic afterlives and anticipations. She analyzes how African American poet Marilyn Nelson and Swiss visual artist and illustrator Philippe Lardy create contemporary sonnets as resuscitative and defiant rights instruments in a century when the intertwined right to breathe and the right to rights are the subject of a public reckoning.

This volume concludes with literary scholar and theorist Peter Hitchcock's invitation to take the paradoxical structure of human rights, grounded in the history of capital development and international expansion, to imagine otherwise. Hitchcock focuses on "securitization" as a term that helps us usefully analyze the relationship between globalizing markets and the global movements of migrant and refugee populations. As demonstrated in the financial crisis of 2007–2008, financial securitization is also a generator of economic insecurity. The internal contradiction of securitization for global markets reproduces an equally concerning contradiction in the security of mobile populations. Humanitarian response and border control systems dedicated to managing the risk of movement across borders establish discourses of protected status but also unprotected status; they mandate investment through rights but also provide opportunities for labor and wealth extraction. The metaphorical connections between these two regimes of securitization are dramatically concretized in the array of businesses that render the maintenance of border security a matter of profit. Hitchcock lays bare the contradiction between the poles of securitization—that is, protecting the vulnerable and exploiting the asymmetries that produce vulnerability—to emphasize not a monolith of power but an instability of system, thereby offering the possibility of both a more hopeful and a less exploitative future.

Chapter One

Artificial Intelligence and Human Rights

Ş. İLGÜ ÖZLER

Introduction

This chapter explores the human rights implications of the development and use of artificial intelligence (AI). Artificial intelligence is the processing of information by machines in order to generate outcomes via autonomous decision making. These technologies are already integrated in our lives, and their use can be expected to grow dramatically. In the early years of AI technology, these machines were limited in what they could accomplish due to their data access capacity and processing speed. But since the turn of the century, rapid technological development in these areas has allowed for AI to come into widespread use. They operate faster than ever and, in essence, learn, think, reason, and act much like humans do but without consciousness.

The use of AI is developing much faster than the policy designed to address its human rights implications. Without consideration of these impacts, we will not only face the already existing collective action problems that arise when coordinating responses to human rights issues, but we will also have to respond to new and increasingly complex dilemmas created by the use of AI. These dilemmas occur in both conflict and nonconflict human rights contexts.

Human rights defenders already confront immense challenges in relation to protecting humanitarian space for civilians during conflict, when protecting the right to freedom of thought, speech, and assembly, and in protecting privacy. AI has potentially significant negative impacts in each of these areas. In addition, there are challenges associated with the right to equal treatment by states as well as with economic and social rights, especially in relation to increasing income and wealth inequality. The development and use of AI are expected to exacerbate human rights violations on these fronts and create new threats in others such as those presented by the development of autonomous weapons.[1] Scholars and think tanks have begun to examine the implications of the development and use of AI in the public and private realms (Boddington 2017; Broussard 2019; Eubanks 2018; Noble 2018; Whittaker et al. 2018). I apply these analyses to examine the potential human rights violations in the international legal context, linking them to specific provisions outlined in international law based on human rights conventions.

As with any technology, AI can be considered neutral in its implications in and of itself. All technologies may be implemented in ways that either advance or undermine human well-being and rights. But AI represents a significant technological leap. According to the High-Level Expert Group on Artificial Intelligence of the European Commission:

> Artificial intelligence (AI) refers to systems designed by humans that, given a complex goal, act in the physical or digital world by perceiving their environment, interpreting the collected structured or unstructured data, reasoning on the knowledge derived from this data and deciding the best action(s) to take (according to pre-defined parameters) to achieve the given goal. AI systems can also be designed to learn to adapt their behavior by analyzing how the environment is affected by their previous actions. (2018, iv)

There are indeed many potential benefits of such technology. The use of AI offers a tremendous opportunity for human progress in overcoming global crises associated with climate change, hunger, poverty, inequality, and more. The applications are vast. AI technology is used globally to process our speech, translate language, drive vehicles, recognize faces, inspect power lines, model disease outbreaks, study the distribution of water supplies and vaccines, verify nuclear safety, inspect fish populations, guide people who are in need of assistance, monitor hygiene and nutrition, diagnose diseases, monitor productivity of arable land, map forest fires, and adjust the pace of teaching based on student needs among other uses (AI for Good Summit

Report 2017, 21–27). These technologies have great potential to improve our scientific knowledge base, expand the provision of services, and advance human well-being in nearly every field.

The efficiencies and benefits that AI is bringing to human society and organization are remarkable. Yet without major reorganization of institutional structures, the deployment of AI is likely to exacerbate problems already seen within current social systems. I examine three general areas of concern regarding the use of AI without major reform to international legal/normative and national regulatory frameworks. The first is the set of economic, social, and cultural rights that will increasingly be impacted by AI around labor and the right to work, the right to equal treatment under the law, and equal access to public services. The second set of concerns revolves around civil and political rights, including the right to privacy with the use of big data and surveillance, as well as the freedom to form and express opinions. A third set of rights is associated with international humanitarian law and the use of automated weapons. I explore the impact of AI on these three areas of human rights in terms of their current manifestations and rapidly evolving potential threats.

Economic, Social, and Cultural Rights: Perpetuation of Inequality

Work, Poverty, and the Labor Market

The implementation of economic, social, and cultural rights has already been obstructed by the neoliberal economic order (Ozler 2018). The drive to deregulate markets and lower taxes and trade barriers has led to vast wealth creation, but such policies also created severe income and wealth inequalities within states as well as globally. Persistent economic insecurity among low- and middle-income populations and growing inequality have been the hallmarks of the neoliberal era. The World Economic Forum Global Risk Report (Howell 2013) identified "severe income disparity" as one of the biggest global risks. The social and economic inequalities resulting from the neoliberal global economic order have been furthered in the era of the digital revolution. AI will only multiply human rights challenges in relation to inequality (Risse 2019). One direct means by which this occurs is labor displacement and the resulting shifts in labor markets.

AI is impacting labor markets globally by rapidly replacing routinized low-skill work and middle-skill clerical and manufacturing work (Wright and Schultz 2018). Currently, jobs that lend themselves to machine learning are those in which decision making is based on a simple set of information that is digitally available, where the output is easily quantifiable, and where the consequences of decisions are not highly sensitive to errors (Brynjolfsson and Mitchell 2017). As a result, automated systems are now restocking boxes in warehouses and carrying out factory assembly. But AI is also now used to replace sports reporters, paralegals, medical examiners, financial fraud detectors, and insurance policy reviewers, among other occupations. As algorithms for these machines use deep learning to expand their capacity, we can expect to see machines take on more complex jobs. Therefore, while anyone's job is at stake in the future, currently working-class and middle-class workers are facing replacement through AI automation. Around 47% of total US employment is in the "high risk category," including occupations in transportation and logistics, office and administrative support workers, and production workers (Frey and Osborne 2017, 268).

The automation of labor is not new, but rapid automation at the hands of AI is likely to multiply the impact of economic inequalities at a rate that governments and the international system are unwilling and, in places, unable to address (World Economic and Social Survey 2018). Market economies are inherently dynamic, and we have witnessed technological changes that disrupt employment regularly throughout history. Agricultural employment declined as farming technologies advanced. Most workers were eventually absorbed in growing industrial enterprises. In turn, industrial technology displaced workers who were eventually redeployed in service sector jobs. The speed with which AI is advancing is expected to cause vast and persistent dislocations at a time when public commitment to supporting the unemployed is under threat. By 2030, in the United States, markets are expected to create jobs at the high and low end of the pay scale, impacting especially youth and racial minorities differently:

> Individuals with a high school degree or less are four times more likely to hold highly automatable roles than those with bachelor's degrees. Given educational disparities, Hispanic and African-American workers may be hit hardest, with 12 million displaced. Nearly 15 million jobs held by young people could be lost, raising questions about career pathways. Workers over age 50 hold an additional 11.5 million at-risk jobs. The share of middle-wage jobs may shrink as growth concentrates at the high and low ends of the wage scale. (Lund et al. 2019)

There is evidence to indicate that new or expanding employment sectors at the low ends will not provide adequate compensation. According to the Bureau of Labor Statistics, in the next ten years in the US, the most rapidly expanding employment sectors will be in home health and personal care work,[2] and these are some of the lowest paid positions. Without some kind of concerted response to the speed with which these jobs are replaced, inequalities will increase further (Acemoglu and Restrepo 2017) exacerbating extreme social and political polarization (see Ingelhart 2018, 199–210). UN special rapporteur on poverty Philip Allston warns of popular discontent and political instability specifically pointing out the impact of changes in middle-class employment due to AI (Allston 2018, 19).

From a human rights perspective, Article 6 of International Covenant on Economic, Social and Cultural Rights (ICESCR) recognizes the right to work, including the state's responsibility to take appropriate steps to safeguard this right. The covenant calls for technical and vocational guidance and training, policies for "steady economic, social and cultural development and full and productive employment under conditions safeguarding fundamental political and economic freedoms to the individual." Without change to current policies that have already led to high inequality, there is no reason to believe that AI will lead to different outcomes. On the contrary, if anything, it will lead to more inequality by speeding up socioeconomic divisions. To take it a step further, the right to life included in Article 6 of the International Covenant on Civil and Political Rights (ICCPR) comes under threat via the economic dislocation fostered by AI. For example, men who lose their jobs at prime age and drop out of the labor market are more likely to suffer from emotional problems and premature death (Ingelhart 2018, 206–7). Thus, the human rights implications of AI in the economic sphere are far-reaching.

While I have concentrated on the United States so far, the International Labor Organization and much scholarly research confirm that the share of economic growth captured by labor has declined globally due to technological advances (World Economic and Social Survey 2018, 51). At the global level, the rapid and unequal deployment of AI also risks leaving behind those countries that are already suffering underdevelopment (Sachs 2019). The enhanced automation of manufacturing disadvantages those whose primary economic contribution was through providing low-skilled labor at minimum cost. Economies dependent on this model will suffer the most, compounding extreme poverty and undermining efforts to achieve basic economic rights for all. Despite broad agreement among academics and policy analysts on the coming transition in labor markets, action to respond to this transition has been slow. There is little indication that the international community or states rapidly incorporating AI into their economic systems seek a new paradigm to respond to the expected dislocation among their people.

Public Services and Algorithms

When it comes to the economic and social impact of AI, we can move beyond labor-market impacts and pay special attention to public services upon which many economically disadvantaged people depend. There has been a rapid increase in the use of automated decision-making systems in the public sector. The public services traditionally provided by civil service employees are now processed by automated computer systems with little opportunity for human interference or discretion (Eubanks 2018; Whittaker et al. 2018). For instance, within the criminal justice system, courts use AI to process recidivism and bail decisions (Whittaker et al. 2018; see also Grace in this volume). Chatbots are used in human resources and educational systems to respond to candidate questions or direct clients into the different services available to them.[3] The companies that develop the automated decision-making systems present them as more efficient, effective, and free of the conscious or unconscious biases that humans bring to decision making. This argument is most commonly put forth in the context of using machines in the interview process for job candidates.[4] Employers are streamlining their resume review processes using algorithms to eliminate "unqualified" candidates. For example, Indeed.com assessment tools allow companies to match skills needed for positions listed, eliminating applicants before they are considered by the employer. The company claims, "Candidate evaluation is based on results from [their] ready-made test modules, utilizing data-driven decision making so [employers] can be confident that [they are] making the right hiring choices for [their] organization."[5] This company alone claims to have 250 million unique visitors per month on their web site and hundreds of thousands of businesses globally list their jobs.[6] Thus, using algorithms, machines are reading resumes and making employment decisions.

The algorithms used in decision making have far reaching implications for discrimination, inequality, and human rights. AI is already used to make decisions in the fields of housing, child welfare services, and other social assistance programs as well as "in finance, employment, politics, health and human services" (Eubanks 2015, 3). Therefore, whether people have access to mortgages or health benefits, whether their resumes are reviewed for jobs, or they have access to social services benefits may be determined based on the algorithms used by service providers.

Unfair outcomes are not necessarily the product of the AI systems themselves. Algorithms can be designed so that automated systems help to provide fair treatment and universal access to public services. Yet, research shows potential bias associated with these algorithms. Using Google to search for terms like "Black girls," Noble (2018) demonstrates how the search engine produces sexualized and pornographic image of Black girls; and she points out that "these results are then normalized as believable and often presented as factual" (Noble 2018, 25). There are many examples of how AI generates racist and sexist results. This includes the inability of many current facial recognition AI systems to recognize people of color or to accurately read the emotions of races other than white people. Again, this biased outcome may not be inherent to AI itself. The underrepresentation of racial minorities among programmers and test populations can yield these kinds of results. In this way, existing inequalities are integrated into AI systems. This becomes a serious human rights challenge when these machines make employment decisions or are used in association with law enforcement.

One of the added challenges with AI is for the public to know or understand the basis upon which it is operating. AI is good at processing available information without subjective judgments, but it is only able to operate on the basis of the information available to the program via algorithms. The Rawlsian doctrine of public rules assumes, in a just institutional system, that public policies should be developed and implemented in a transparent way (Gosseries and Parr 2018). Yet there is little public knowledge about how these algorithms are constructed, how they access information, process data, and make decisions or even when such systems are in use (Eubanks 2015; Whittaker et al. 2018). Scholars have demonstrated that AI is developed through the use of meta-data that has built-in biases reflective of current economic and social structures (Eubanks 2015; Broussard 2018; Noble 2018), yet results are presented as objective and unassailable. Thus, AI presents an added layer of threat to human rights. There is the problem of the unfair outcomes, and there is also the problem of demonstrating that the outcomes are indeed unfair. The "black box" of the algorithm can only be uncovered when public authorities demand transparency through regulation, and only then can abuses be detected and addressed.

On another end of the spectrum of AI-associated problems is that some people are not connected to the world through technology. According to UNICEF, in 2016 "about 29 percent of youth worldwide—around 346 million individuals—are not online. African youth are the least connected. Around 60 per cent are not online, compared with just 4 per cent in Europe" (State of World's Children 2017, 3). Overall, in advanced industrialized countries, 84 percent of the population used the Internet. This number was 26 percent in least developed countries (LDCs), landlocked developing countries (LLDCs), and small island developing states (SIDS); and only 0.9 percent of these countries had access to fixed broadband that gives reliable and fast service (World Economic and Social Survey 2018). This disparity points toward a global divide about whose data and information is included in these algorithms leading to a perpetuation of global inequalities between North and South. Therefore, we can add disadvantages from being left out of AI data considerations due to not having access to Internet to the labor displacement disproportionately impacting poorer countries.

Systematic exclusion is one source of the unfair treatment generated by AI systems, but inclusion in these algorithms does not guarantee equality or fairness. The algorithms created for health, financial institutions, human resources, school admissions, and social services are filled with preexisting biases. The prioritization of the information—what gets counted and where and how—can create bias based on who is identifying the relevant information to gather and analyze. Those who develop these algorithms tend to be highly educated white males (Campolo et al. 2017, 5).[7] The perspectives of people without Internet, poor people, women, people of color, and persons with disabilities are largely excluded, replicating the same structural biases leading to the unequal outcomes that the AI is intending to overcome. The main difference is that the source of this mistreatment is now more deeply hidden and shrouded by an air of objectivity.

ICCPR Article 25 calls for the right and the opportunity to have equal access to public services without unreasonable restrictions and without distinction to race, color, sex, language, religion, political or other opinion, national or social origin, property, birth, or other status. In *Automating Inequality*, Eubanks (2018) documents the use of AI in social services in the United States in direct violation of this clause. She demonstrates that despite an intention to erase bias on the basis of race in relation to access to social services, these tools used by social service agencies end up acting like gatekeepers. In the case of Indiana, the state implemented an automated welfare eligibility system where decisions would be determined by an algorithm developed by IBM/ACS instead of the 1500 civil servants who performed this task previously (Eubanks 2018, 49). In the two years that this system was used, there was a 54 percent increase in denials for these applicants. The people in need who were denied assistance included people with disabilities and with debilitating health problems. Social workers are able to interpret the intent of the laws and decide who gets the benefits based on their discretion. An automated system does not allow for consideration beyond the checked boxes. In another instance, an AI system decreased hours of care for hundreds of people with disabilities based on wrongful decisions. Legal Aid of Arkansas sued the state and won in this case. The state was forced to use a new algorithm to decide the hours of care persons with disabilities would receive from the state, but this was not until after many people's lives had been severely impacted (Whittaker et al. 2018, 18). These service denials were determined based on an automated process designed by corporations where there is a lack of transparency in determining what goes into the decision to deny services and why specific cases were denied. According to Eubanks (2018), these systems lack the ability to discern the complex needs of the most vulnerable groups, "ignoring bias that already exists." Eubanks continues: "When automated decision making tools are not built to explicitly dismantle structural inequalities, their speed and scale intensify them" (Eubanks 2018, 190).

Without careful examination and corrective intervention, AI poses a significant threat to economic, social, and cultural rights. The threat of labor dislocation and the associated unemployment and poverty are not unique to AI, but given the power of this technology its impact is likely to be even greater than the disruption and suffering associated with other mass technological transitions such as that of the industrial revolution. AI is also being deployed at a time when public support for the victims of economic displacement is in decline. This technology is likely to exacerbate existing inequalities and further undermine efforts to eliminate poverty and protect economic rights. Early evidence also suggests that when AI is used in systems designed to address social problems related to issues such as poverty and health, it tends to reinforce preexisting biases, further undermining the ability of marginalized populations to get the support they need.

Civil and Political Rights

Privacy and AI

Along with the impact on economic, social, and cultural rights, the use of AI has significant implications for civil and political rights. In particular the rights to privacy, the freedom to form opinions and the presumption of innocence all come under threat. The right to privacy is probably the most well-known threat posed by AI. Highly sophisticated data gathering and learning machines exponentially increases the potential for abuse by both state and private actors. Information captured through the tracking of on-line activity allows for the development of highly detailed profiles of any Internet user. In the United States, Immigration and Customs Enforcement compiles large scale data through social media surveillance. The process creates profiles of immigrants and uses "an Investigative Case Management System developed by Palantir and powered by Amazon Web Services" (Whittaker et al. 2018, 12–13).

The use of facial recognition technology in public spaces allows for still further data collection and tracking. Facial recognition systems have been used in the UK, many EU countries, Kenya, China, and the United States for the purposes of identifying suspects. This technology has already moved into "affect recognition," reading peoples' emotions and drawing implications regarding intentions even if no law violation has occurred. The use of these technologies is rapidly spreading among the law enforcement agencies across the world. In Europe, the EU is piloting an automated border control system with lie-detecting facial recognition to scan travelers (Begault 2019). The program iBorderCtrl uses technology to assess peoples' emotions and intentions, automated interpretations that are used to justify further surveillance or enforcement action. Although recent, there is preliminary evidence of deterrent effects from AI use for facial recognition by law enforcement agencies during protest and public assemblies. This has serious implications for freedom of assembly protected under ICCPR Article 21 (Ashraf 2020) and freedom of expression protected under ICCPR Article 19.[8]

The civil and political rights issues that arise from the collection and use of this information are numerous (Santow 2020). First, members of the public are not privy to nor have control over the information collected about them by governments or private agencies. Even when this information is available, it is often impossible to discern what personal data is being gathered and how this information is used. Facial and affect recognition used in public spaces leaves very little room for the protection of privacy, a right protected under article 17 of ICCPR. The blanket use of covertly gathered information by enforcement officials or private companies is a direct violation of that privacy.

A second problem with surveillance via AI centers around the freedom of thought protected under ICCPR Article 18 and freedom to seek, receive, and impart information protected under the ICCPR Article 19. The privacy violations discussed above lead to the creation of personal profiles that in turn shape and limit the information provided to individuals through online search engines. This is most commonly used by private firms seeking to promote sales by exploiting information gathered that indicates personal consumer interests. While presented as simply a means to "assist" shoppers by presenting them with items they may want, this manipulative marketing ignores the shaping of interests that occurs through this process, a process conducted without users' knowledge or consent. This, again, could be considered a difference of degree relative to traditional advertising, but the use of surreptitiously gathered personal data represents both a qualitative and a quantitative difference from the largely anonymous mass marketing that defines traditional advertising.

The strategic use of personal data for commercial purposes is just one type of violation. Another privacy-related problem that arises with the use of AI technology is the negative impact it can have on the freedom to form opinions. In the United States, more people get news from social media sources than print media, and for the 19 to 29 age group, social media is the number one source for news.[9] Information surreptitiously gathered on Internet users is used by companies like Google or Facebook to direct people to news and other items determined by algorithms to be consistent with their ideological inclinations. Thus, people's own online behavior and profiling are shaping the way in which people get informed, communicate, associate and form opinions. This would not be a problem if we were privy to how the automation sorts information to determine our content and what it omits. But this information is not available, and access to broader news stories and information for those who rely on Internet sources is biased toward one's own preferences as determined by the AI systems deployed by these private firms.

The sorting and exclusion of news and other content that is moderated by service providers (Dias Oliva 2020) can have extensive negative consequences for individuals and for society as a whole. What people learn and read has a direct impact on how their values are shaped and the type of democratic society we create. While people tend to seek information consistent with their own perspectives, the fact that this is being fueled without the knowledge or informed consent of the users directly undermines one's ability to truly form one's own opinions. Furthermore, by reinforcing belief systems and limiting exposure to alternative perspectives, groups tend to become more polarized and less able to relate to or understand those with opposing views. This polarization can have severe negative impacts on democracy and human rights and is a great threat to basic foundations of human rights institutions and principles (*Us versus Them* 2017; Woolley 2020).

Profiles based on secretly gathered data combined with the biased characterizations of certain groups can also lead to violations of due process rights and the presumption of innocence. This can be seen in a case from Los Angeles, where an AI based system was used to process homeless people seeking services. Eubanks (2018) argues that the automated entry algorithm created to discern the level of need among the homeless also was used as a "surveillance system for sorting and criminalizing the poor" (121). The privacy of those using the system was violated through information collected and shared by these automated coordinated entry systems. Individuals are then treated differently based on their "potential behavior" and criminalized based on profiling done by the algorithms. In this type of data-based public program, different than traditional law enforcement, the "*target often emerges from the data*" (Eubanks 2018, 122, original emphasis). This is in direct conflict with human rights law, especially Article 26 of ICCPR, which calls for equal protection under the law and protection from discrimination. Applying a criminal label based on certain characteristics violates ICCPR Article 15, which states, "No one shall be held guilty of any criminal offence on account of any act or omission which did not constitute a criminal offence."

The use of AI undermines civil and political rights in relation to privacy, freedom to form opinions, and the right to be presumed innocent until found guilty. There is also serious potential to have broad impact on freedom of expression and assembly. The next section will address another AI-related problem: its use by the military sector.

International Humanitarian Law (IHL) and Autonomous Weapons Systems (AWS)

As with any technology, AI can be used to enhance human rights and shape human rights advocacy (Niezen 2020); and the human rights community has been able to use AI technology to document atrocities and uncover crimes against humanity (Landman 2020; Livingston and Risse 2019). Yet, on the other side of the coin, the defense industry and militaries are rapidly developing lethal Autonomous Weapons Systems (AWS) that have grave human rights implications. AWS are machines that can select, deploy, and execute the use of force, including lethal force, without direct human control. Currently, the number of weapons systems that can make autonomous decisions is limited, but AWS technologies are rapidly being developed in over 50 countries (Sharkey 2011). For example, Israel has developed an unmanned aerial vehicle, Harop that can "search, find, identify, attack and destroy targets, and perform battle damage assessment."[10] While the technology for these weapons is being developed, there is no internationally agreed upon definition of lethal AWS, let alone rules to regulate their use.

In the military sector, the use of increasingly sophisticated autonomous weapons systems creates a host of ethical, humanitarian, and human rights issues. One of the first challenges is whether these systems can fulfill current IHL expectations regarding proportionality. According to Boulanin and Verbruggen (2017, 21),

> this does not mean that the use of autonomous weapon systems is unlawful per se. Existing systems that select and engage targets without the direct involvement of a human operator indicate that the operation of autonomous weapon systems could be lawful if humans can (*a*) determine the type of target and undertake the proportionality assessment before the launch of the system; and (*b*) predetermine the maximum amount of acceptable collateral damage linked to specific targets.

Under the currently developed AI technology, the use of these weapons with the assurance of proportionality is questionable without human control of these systems.

AWS also raise concerns about adherence to the principle of distinction, the ability of these systems to distinguish between a combatant and a civilian, at the heart of international humanitarian law. Humans can respond to changing circumstances in a battlefield or other law enforcement and crowd-control situations by assessing the changes they observe and judging the changing risk to civilians. The ability of a nonhuman operated machine, operating with a preset algorithm, to assess the changing environment in a battle zone and to respond in ways consistent with IHL is difficult to assess given the "black box" effect for decision making in autonomous machines with deep learning capacity. Last, there is no provision for accountability when weapons are used without human supervision. Who is accountable if a criminal act has been committed in the course of the use of these weapons?

Thus, principles of proportionality and the obligations to protect civilians are threatened by the use of AWS. At the international level, an additional legal challenge is the inability of the parties in the Geneva Convention to come to a full and clear definition of Lethal Autonomous Weapons through the Article 36 review process. Article 36 of the 1977 Additional Protocol to the 1949 Geneva Conventions (Additional Protocol I) states that the "development, acquisition or adoption of a new weapon, means or method of warfare, a High Contracting Party is under an obligation to determine whether its employment would, in some or all circumstances, be prohibited by this Protocol or by any other rule of international law applicable to the High Contracting Party." According to this article, parties to the Geneva Convention are obligated to come to an agreement on the use of these weapons under IHL before starting to deploy them (Sharkey 2016). As with socioeconomic policies and civil and political rights protections, the humanitarian law and conventions that regulate the rules of engagement in wars will need to be updated to reflect the use of AI.

Conclusion: The Need for Strong Global and National Regulatory Frameworks

During the AI for Good Summit in 2017, Houlim Zhao, the secretary general of the International Telecommunications Union, stated that "humans are good at asking intelligent questions, common-sense reasoning, and value judgments. Machines are much better at pattern detection, statistical reasoning, and large-scale mathematical reasoning" (AI for Good Global Summit Report 2017, 33). Yet we cannot understand AI as "value free." These machines are run on the basis of algorithms created by people operating within institutions that are designed to instrumentally achieve particular goals, whether the profitability goals of private firms or the military goals of state actors. Even when directed towards goals that are designed to improve human well-being, the protection of human rights in the course of this process is at best secondary if not completely ignored as the efficiency of systems and the profitability of firms is prioritized. This is evidenced by the fact that AI is in widespread use prior to any systematic examination of its human rights implications, let alone the development of enforceable policies that ensure such protections. As the special rapporteur on the promotion and protection of the right to freedom of opinion and expression has reported,

> A handful of technology companies lay claim to the vast majority of search queries conducted online. Corporate monopoly of the search market makes it extremely difficult for users to opt out of

> the algorithmic ranking and curation of search results and may also induce users to believe (as companies intend it) that the results generated are the most relevant and objective information available on a particular subject. (Kaye 2018, 11)

Despite being controlled by a small number of firms, these algorithms have consequences far beyond consumer choices. They have profound implications for many fundamental human rights.

There is something unsettling about the speed with which these technologies are entering our lives in ways that have significant consequences up to and including life itself. Currently, there is a lack of transparency about how algorithms work when AI is used for public services such as health, social welfare, education, housing, criminal justice, and more. The discussion around how to ensure the ethical, fair, just, and transparent development and use of AI that fits within the current human rights standards is lagging behind the speed with which these technologies have been incorporated in to our lives (Dawes 2020).

There have been legal challenges to the deployment of certain AI technologies. These include litigation targeting design of algorithms regarding access to public benefits in education, health, employment, and criminal justice, as well as right to privacy (Richardson et al. 2019). The European Union and Canada are among the few national and transnational bodies that have passed regulatory policies surrounding privacy issues associated with AI. Several countries have national plans regarding the use of AI, but few focus on human rights aspects (see Regulation of Artificial Intelligence in Selected Jurisdictions 2019).

The industry response to human rights concerns about the use of AI leans heavily on voluntary guidelines developed by civil society organizations and the companies that use AI. Among these are the Asilomar AI Principles of the Future of Life Institute, sector specific industry guidelines, like those developed by the Institute of Electrical and Electronics Engineers (IEEE), and the company-based Partnership on AI to Benefit People and Society, which is a collaboration between the big AI corporations like Google, Facebook, Amazon, DeepMind, IBM and Microsoft (Boddington 2017). Amnesty International and Access Now jointly developed the Toronto Declaration, calling on states and private actors to prevent discrimination based on use of AI, which was also endorsed by Human Rights Watch and Wikimedia. There is also the Organization for Economic Cooperation and Development recommendations on Artificial Intelligence (OECD 2019).

The UN, mostly through the International Telecommunication Union, has also been in favor of developing norms around voluntary codes of conduct rather than the development of a binding global convention. Thus, so far, all international guidelines and principles are voluntary and lack oversight and enforcement mechanisms.

Given the global implications of the use and development of AI, a voluntary code of conduct regarding the human rights issues arising from this technology is insufficient. Organizations like Article 19 and Privacy International and scholars have been calling for a regulatory framework around the use of AI, including regulation that targets specific AI deployments such as those used in the provision of public services (*Article 19 and Privacy International* 2018, Brand 2020).

The EU has been on the forefront of regulating AI. It implemented the General Data Protection Regulation (GDPR), which sets controls on the use of automated decision making. According to this law, automation cannot be the sole decision maker in social service provision, and individuals have the right to seek explanations of the decision made about them through AI. The law provides for transparency in explaining AI decisions in relation to public services and human-controlled remedy and correction for faulty AI decisions. The GDPR offers protections beyond public services and expands into protection of privacy. The European Commission encourages EU citizens to take control over personal data and educates EU citizens on how companies collect and use personal information.[11] The Commission warns the public that there are companies whose "business model is to collect . . . personal data and share it with third parties" and that the information on social media platforms, email providers, search engines, and software providers might be tracked and sold for profit.

The EU's law not only allows for redress for public services denied, but it also calls for companies to ensure consent based on informed decision making for the sharing of data. The law requires that consent for sharing data by the consumer cannot be a condition for the provision of services offered by the company.[12] While GDPS is a positive step for the protection of privacy, putting the responsibility for protection of their privacy on the consumer through an active opt out process will not generate realistic protection. Globally, most people connect to the Internet and daily visit multiple sites. Is it realistic to expect that consumers will read the privacy statements for each provider of service to discern the type of information collected and their rights to opt out of sharing all or parts of their personal information with these service providers? It is too soon to evaluate the effectiveness of GDPS as a regulatory policy (Zuiderveen Borgesius 2020), but it still stands as one of very few examples of AI regulation.

In the United States, the White House strategy on AI has been about market position. The political and corporate goal has been to maintain US leadership in AI research investment (Girasa 2020), as evidenced by the estimated 8 billion dollars of AI investment by venture capitalists. "Similarly, the DOD's unclassified investments in AI have grown from just over $600 million in FY2016 to $927 million in FY2020, with the Department reportedly maintaining over 600 active AI projects" (Sayler 2019, 2). One might think that such an enormous new industry with such far-reaching social implications would generate a host of legislation and regulatory oversight. Indeed, there were thirty-nine bills in the 115th Congress ranging from legislation designed to respond to job losses to creating an office of the government with a focus on AI. Yet, none of the bills addresses the need for regulation, especially in relation to the human rights concerns raised in this chapter.[13]

The regulatory response to LAWS has been equally slow globally. The issue has been taken up by the Convention on Certain Conventional Weapons (CCW) Group of Experts on Lethal Autonomous Weapons Systems. There has been a core of thirty states advocating for the ban of LAWS under new international law.[14] China has advocated for an international treaty to ban the use of LAWS but not their development; China still invests heavily in development of these weapons.[15] Yet other states have argued that they can find ways to address IHL as they develop these weapons. France, Israel, Russia, South Korea, the United States, and the United Kingdom have resisted any legal restriction on these systems.[16] These countries argue that they are capable of building autonomous lethal weapons within the parameters of international humanitarian law (see Russian Federation 2018). Yet few have such assurances built into their legal systems. The United States Department of Defense directive (2012) on autonomous weapons systems specifies that "legal reviews should ensure consistency with all applicable domestic and international law and, in particular, the law of war" (Enclosure 4: 8a (6) b). Given the lack of definition under Article 36 of the Geneva Convention, the meaning of this directive remains open to interpretation.

Organizations like Amnesty International, Article 36, the Campaign to Stop Killer Robots, and Human Rights Watch have been calling for a legally binding prohibition under new international law for these systems. They argue along with the thirty states in the CCW that these weapons are unable to provide the principle of distinction, accountability, and proportionality called for under IHL. In terms of military use, the EU Parliament passed a resolution to ban use of killer robots and called on their states to develop policy around this.[17]

Therefore, outside of a few countries that have passed regulations, a few companies that control an inordinate amount of information and have control over AI technology are able to operate based on a loose set of principles that they have set for themselves. There is no monitoring or oversight for these principles. Companies and governments are adopting the use of AI without fully considering the consequences of decisions made through these technologies. At a minimum, scholars have aptly demonstrated how AI continues to replicate current structural inequalities and biases built into social, economic, and political systems on a massive scale. The use of mass data and information to generate decisions only exacerbates these biases in a much more rapid fashion and on a larger scale than humans alone can do. There needs to be state and multilateral responses to the development and use of AI, which takes into consideration the serious human rights concerns raised here in relation to privacy, consent, accountability, transparency, equality, accessibility, and legality.

Notes

1. This chapter does not consider the questions of whether we have ethical obligations to AI or whether AI should be afforded rights if they are able to generate intelligence like humans. The paper does not question what it means to be human or have rights. It only focuses on what we know is possible right now—current use of AI and direct human rights implications of it under the international law framework for human rights. For discussion on other questions regarding AI and rights of AI, see Dawes (2020), Leveringhaus (2018), and Livingston and Risse (2019).

2. https://www.bls.gov/emp/tables/fastest-growing-occupations.htm (Accessed August 10, 2019).

3. https://www.insidehighered.com/digital-learning/article/2018/09/26/academics-push-expand-use-ai-higher-ed-teaching-and-learning (Accessed August 14, 2019).

4. https://www.bbc.com/news/business-47442953 (Accessed March 25, 2019).

5. https://www.indeed.com/assessments (Accessed December 24, 2019).

6. https://www.indeed.com/hire/why-indeed?hl=en (Accessed January 2, 2020).

7. https://www.theguardian.com/technology/2019/mar/28/big-tech-ai-ethics-boards-prejudice?CMP=Share_iOSApp_Other (Accessed March 29, 2019).

8. See the contributions of relevant organizations https://www.ohchr.org/EN/HRBodies/CCPR/Pages/GC37.aspx (Accessed January 8, 2020) and draft report of the United Nations Human Rights Council General Comment No. 37, Article 21:

right to peaceful assembly report. In addition, see London Policing Ethics Panel Final Report on Live Facial Recognition, May 2019.

9. https://www.pewresearch.org/fact-tank/2018/12/10/social-media-outpaces-print-newspapers-in-the-u-s-as-a-news-source/ (Accessed February 10, 2019).

10. https://www.iai.co.il/p/harop (Accessed January 6, 2020).

11. https://ec.europa.eu/commission/sites/beta-political/files/digital_avatar_280519_v5.pdf (Accessed June 17, 2018).

12. https://ec.europa.eu/commission/sites/beta-political/files/digital_avatar_280519_v5.pdf (Accessed June 17, 2018).

13. See https://www.loc.gov/law/help/artificial-intelligence/americas.php#us (Accessed December 27, 2019).

14. The states that called for a ban on the use of AWS include Algeria, Argentina, Austria, Bolivia, Brazil, Chile, China, Colombia, Costa Rica, Cuba, Djibouti, Ecuador, Egypt, El Salvador, Ghana, Guatemala, Holy See, Iraq, Jordan, Mexico, Morocco, Namibia, Nicaragua, Pakistan, Panama, Peru, State of Palestine, Uganda, Venezuela, and Zimbabwe. See https://www.hrw.org/report/2020/08/10/stopping-killer-robots/country-positions-banning-fully-autonomous-weapons-and (accessed February 27, 2021).

15. https://www.hrw.org/report/2020/08/10/stopping-killer-robots/country-positions-banning-fully-autonomous-weapons-and (accessed February 27, 2021).

16. https://www.amnesty.org/en/latest/news/2018/08/un-decisive-action-needed-to-ban-killer-robots-before-its-too-late/ (Accessed January 6, 2020).

17. https://futureoflife.org/2018/09/14/european-parliament-passes-resolution-supporting-a-ban-on-killer-robots/ (Accessed January 6, 2020).

Works Cited

Acemoglu, Daron, and Pascual Restrepo. 2017. *Robots and jobs: Evidence from US labor markets.* Cambridge, MA: National Bureau of Economic Research Working Paper No. 23285.

AI For Good Global Summit Report. 2017. International Telecommunications Union, hosted in Geneva, Switzerland, 7–9 June 2017.

Allston, Phillip. 2018. "Promotion and protection of all human rights, civil, political, economic, social and cultural rights, including the right to development Report of the Special Rapporteur on extreme poverty and human rights on his mission to the United States of America." Geneva, United Nations: *Human Rights Council Thirty-eighth Session.*

Article 19 and Privacy International. 2018. "Privacy and Freedom of Expression: In the Age of Artificial Intelligence." April 2018, London: Article 19 and Privacy International.

Ashraf, Cameran. 2020. "Artificial intelligence and the rights to assembly and association." *Journal of Cyber Policy* 5, no. 2: 163–179.

Begault, Lucien, 2019. "Automated technologies and the future of Fortress Europe." Amnesty International, London. Accessed December 31, 2019. https://www.amnesty.org/en/latest/news/2019/03/automated-technologies-and-the-future-of-fortress-europe/.

Boddington, Paula. 2017. *Artificial Intelligence: Foundations, Theory and Algorithms.* Cham, Switzerland: Springer Publishing.

Boulanin, Vincent, and Maaike Verbruggen. 2017. *ARTICLE 36 REVIEWS: Dealing with the Challenges Posed by Emerging Technologies.* Stockholm: SIPRI.

Brand, Dirk. 2020. "Algorithmic Decision-Making and the Law." *EJournal of eDemocracy and open government* 12, no. 1: 114–131.

Broussard, Meredith. 2019. *Artificial Unintelligence: How Computers Misunderstand the World.* Cambridge, MA: MIT Press.

Brynjolfsson, Erik, and Tom Mitchell. 2017. "What Can Machine Learning Do? Workforce Implications." *Science* 358, no. 6370: 1530–1534.

Campolo, Alex, Madelyn Sanfilippo, Meredith Whittaker, and Kate Crawford. 2017. *AI Now2017 Report.* https://ainowinstitute.org/AI_Now_2017_Report.pdf.

Dawes, James. 2020. "Speculative Human Rights: Artificial Intelligence and the Future of the Human." *Human Rights Quarterly* 42, 573–593.

Department of Defense. 2012. *Directive NUMBER 3000.09 on Autonomous Weapons Systems.* November 21, 2012.

Dias Oliva, Thiago. 2020. "Content Moderation Technologies: Applying Human Rights Standards to Protect Freedom of Expression." *Human Rights Law Review* 20, no. 4: 607–640.

Eubanks, Virginia. 2018. *Automating Inequality: How High-Tech Tools Profile, Police, and Punish the Poor.* New York: St. Martin's Press.

Frey, Carl, and Michael Osborne. 2017. "The Future of Employment: How Susceptible Are Jobs to Computerisation?" *Technological Forecasting & Social Change* 114: 254–280.

Girasa, Rosario J. 2020. *Artificial Intelligence as a Disruptive Technology: Economic Transformation and Government Regulation.* Cham, Switzerland: Palgrave Macmillan.

Gosseries, Axel, and Tom Parr. "Publicity." *The Stanford Encyclopedia of Philosophy* (Winter 2018 Edition), edited by Edward N. Zalta. Stanford, CA: https://plato.stanford.edu/.

High-Level Expert Group on Artificial Intelligence. 2018. *Draft Ethics Guidelines for Trustworthy AI, European Commission Directorate-General for Communication,* Brussels, 18 December 2018.

Howell, Lee. 2013. *Global Risk Report.* Geneva. Switzerland: World Economic Forum.

Inglehart, Ronald. 2018. *Cultural Evolution: People's Motivations are Changing, and Reshaping the World.* New York, NY: Cambridge University Press.

Kaye, David. 2018. "Promotion and Protection of Human Rights: Human Rights Questions, Including Alternative Approaches for Improving Effective Enjoyment of Human Rights and Fundamental Freedoms." *The Special Rapporteur on The Promotion and Protection of the Right to Freedom of Opinion and Expression, Human Rights Council* A/73/348, 26 October 2018.

Landman, Todd. 2020. "Measuring Modern Slavery: Law, Human Rights, and New Forms of Data." *Human Rights Quarterly* 42, no. 2: 303–331.

Leveringhaus, Alex. 2019. "Developing Robots: The Need for an Ethical Framework." *European View* 17, no. 1: 37–43.

Livingston, Steven, and Mathias Risse. 2019. "The Future Impact of Artificial Intelligence on Humans and Human Rights." *Ethics & International Affairs* 33, no. 2: 141–158.

Lund, Susan, James Manyika, Liz Hilton Segel, André Dua, Bryan Hancock, Scott Rutherford, and Brent Macon. 2019. *The Future of Work in America: People and Places, Today and Tomorrow.* www.mckinsey.com/mgi.

Niezen, Ronald. 2020. *#HumanRights: The Technologies and Politics of Justice Claims in Practice.* Stanford: Stanford University Press.

Noble, Safiya Umoja. 2018. *Algorithms of Oppression: How Search Engines Reinforce Racism.* New York: New York University Press.

OECD. 2019. *Recommendation of the Council on Artificial Intelligence*, OECD/LEGAL/0449.

Özler, Ş. İlgü. 2018. "Universal Declaration of Human Rights at Seventy: Progress and Challenges." *Ethics & International Affairs* 32, no. 4: 1–12.

Regulation of Artificial Intelligence in Selected Jurisdictions. 2019. The Law Library of Congress, Global Legal Research Directorate.

Richardson, Rashida, Jason M. Schultz, and Vincent M. Southerland. 2019. *Litigating Algorithms 2019 US Report: New Challenges to Government Use of Algorithmic Decision Systems.* AI Now Institute, September 2019. https://ainowinstitute.org/litigatingalgorithms-2019-us.html.

Risse, Mathias. 2019. "Human Rights and Artificial Intelligence: An Urgently Needed Agenda." *Human Rights Quarterly* 41 no. 1 (February): 1–19.

Russian Federation. 2018. "Russia's Approaches to the Elaboration of a Working Definition and Basic Functions of Lethal Autonomous Weapons Systems in the Context of the Purposes and Objectives of the Convention" CCW/GGE.1/2018/WP.6 April 4, 2018.

Sachs, Jeffrey. 2019. "Some Brief Reflections on Digital Technologies and Economic Development." *Ethics & International Affairs* 33, no. 2: 159–167.

Santow, Edward. 2020. "Can Artificial Intelligence Be Trusted with Our Human Rights?" *Australian Quarterly (Balmain, N.S.W.)* 91, no. 4: 10–17.

Sayler, Kelley M. 2019. "Artificial Intelligence and National Security" *Congressional Research Service Report No. R45178.* https://crsreports.congress.govR45178, Updated November 21, 2019.

Sharkey, Noel. 2011. "Automating Warfare: Lessons Learned from the Drones." *Journal of Law, Information and Science* 21, no. 2: 140–154.

Sharkey, Noel. 2016. "Staying in the Loop: Human Supervisory Control of Weapons." In *Autonomous Weapons Systems: Law, Ethics, Policy,* edited by Nehal Bhuta et al., 23–38. Cambridge, Cambridge University Press.

State of the World's Children: Children in a Digital World. 2017. New York: UNICEF.

Us versus Them: Changing Amnesty to Beat the Demonizers. 2017. London: Amnesty International.

Whittaker, Meredith, Kate Crawford, Roel Dobbe, Genevieve Fried, Elizabeth Kaziunas, Varoon Mathur, Sarah Myers West, Rashida Richardson, Jason Schultz, and Oscar Schwartz. 2018. *AI Now Report.* AI Now Institute, New York University, New York.

Woolley, Samuel. 2020. *The Reality Game: How the Next Wave of Technology Will Break the Truth.* New York: Public Affairs.

World Economic and Social Survey, 2018. *Frontier Technologies for Sustainable Development.* E/2018/50/Rev.1ST/ESA/370, Department of Economic and Social Affairs, United Nations.

Wright, Scott A., and Ainslie E. Schultz. 2018. "The Rising Tide of Artificial Intelligence and Business Automation: Developing an Ethical Framework." *Business Horizons* 61: 823–832.

Zuiderveen Borgesius, Frederik. 2020. "Strengthening Legal Protection against Discrimination by Algorithms and Artificial Intelligence." *The International Journal of Human Rights* 24, no. 10: 1572–1593.

Chapter Two

Machine-learning Technologies and Human Rights in Criminal Justice Contexts

JAMIE GRACE

> Computerised decision- and rule-making are changing the dynamics of governance and digitisation is reshuffling the pack of values. Artificial intelligence is also moving us fast into uncharted administrative territory, one in which prior achievements in terms of rights protection and the good governance triad of transparency, accountability and participation may be restricted, even reversed.
>
> —Harlow and Rawlings 2019, 22

Introduction

Algorithms and artificial intelligence (AI) are changing the way we see advertising (McKevitt 2019), how we learn in our universities (Larsson 2019), and even how we one day might conceive of the sentience required to afford legal rights to machines (Jowitt 2019). However, there is a global trend of growing concern over the way that law enforcement bodies are seeking to use data analytics, through machine-learning technologies and artificial intelligence, in order to augment their intelligence capabilities (Edmonds 2019). In the United Kingdom, investment in this technology is backed by the chief inspector of constabulary in his most recent annual report to the Home Secretary (Winsor 2019). Sir Tom Winsor maintains there are cost savings in the use of predictive analytics based on "big data." This regulatory pressure comes at a time when the police in the United Kingdom are being overwhelmed because of funding reductions by government (Dodd 2019). The issue is that machine learning or AI often empowers controversial tech such as facial recognition systems—the subject of particularly high levels of recent challenge and opposition in the United Kingdom (Wiles 2019).

The overall argument in this chapter is that AI will exacerbate and inflame human rights tensions that already exist in criminal justice settings. These inherent human rights issues include privacy concerns, the chilling of freedom of expression, problems around potential for racial discrimination, and the rights of victims of crime to be treated with dignity. AI is often tainted, due to racial or class-based prejudices alive in the data sets it is trained on, while the decisions made by AI, or assisted by AI, might nevertheless prove difficult to challenge on this basis. I also argue that in the criminal justice setting the novel use of an AI-driven or machine-learning based technology threatens civil liberties due to the concrete change for policing or sentencing practices, for example, that it may entail. And finally, I argue, optimistically, that the flexible and multilevel growth of efforts to develop effective controls and regulation on AI and machine-learning tech in criminal justice settings is very much under way. This is the case at least in liberal democracies where AI and machine learning are being used in criminal justice contexts, and where there is a better trend toward David Lyon's demand for "vigilance at every level, which ensures that accountability is demanded of organizations that process personal data" (Lyon 2007, 194–195).

This chapter is based around three case studies concerning the practice and regulation of AI and machine learning in criminal justice contexts. First, I give an introduction to the key theoretical and policy issues pertaining to human rights impacted by machine-learning technologies, and then I discuss the recognition of human rights law frameworks in algorithmic policing practices. At that juncture, I consider a trio of case studies.

Case study 1 in this chapter explores the tensions arising from a lack of regulation on an issue of procedural justice. It concerns the right to a fair trial in the context of evidence disclosure processes involving digital data obtained from mobile phones belonging to complainants of sexual offences. It seeks to show how AI or machine-learning tech might hypothetically either ease or inflame some of the tensions involved for human rights in this context.

Case study 2 examines the human rights challenges arising from using facial recognition technology to detect suspects using automated algorithms (live facial recognition) in public places. These human rights problems, posed by live facial recognition (LFR), are similar the world over. At the time of writing, the High Court in Cardiff (UK) had recently decided the world's first LFR litigation in the case of *Bridges v Chief Constable of South Wales Police* (2019). The High Court found that while LFR used by the police in public places will impact the human rights of members of the public, the way it has been piloted in the United Kingdom to date has been lawful. This finding was despite the lack of specific legislation to guide the use of LFR—since there is an amalgam of other laws around privacy and data protection that sufficed in the eyes of the court concerned.

Case study 3 is concerned with the development of a particular self-regulation approach for AI and machine-learning/data-analytics tools used in UK policing (in the absence, as yet, of specific legislation on the same). This case study addresses the development of the ALGO-CARE regulatory tool or framework (outlined in Oswald et al. 2018); which is designed to assist criminal justice agencies and the courts in deploying algorithmic or machine-learning technologies in a human rights–respectful way. ALGO-CARE has been promoted by the National Police Chiefs' Council for adoption by police forces in the United Kingdom, and for use by the police as a kind of checklist enabling stronger self-regulation of their use of predictive analytics and machine-learning algorithms. This kind of rigorous and transparent use of self-regulation aims to ensure that police AI development "processes are exposed, strict limits on the potential for social harm are found and enforced, and ordinary people have the opportunity to participate in these processes." Only then "will the politics of information really have begun to make its mark" (Lyon 2007, 194–95). In drawing on these three case studies, I will conclude with some of the regulatory, policy, and legal challenges that human rights researchers will commonly need to navigate when it comes to dealing with machine learning in their research practice, in methodological terms, and/or in the field.

An Overview of the Human Rights Issues with AI in Criminal Justice

Of particular current concern, at least in the United Kingdom, is the use of predictive profiling tools that score an individual as to their likely involvement in serious or organized crime, including in violent gangs. Databases like the Gangs Matrix operated by the Metropolitan Police in London, and similar tools used in cities such as Los Angeles, list a disproportionate number of young, nonwhite males, and suffer from stale and patchy data that is difficult to review and weed out if erroneous. In the United Kingdom, the Information Commissioner's Office took an important step in issuing an enforcement notice (ICO 2018a) against the Metropolitan Police in relation to the "function creep," lack of transparency and inaccuracy of its Gangs Matrix, then backing that up with guidance on gangs databases (ICO 2018b). In California, the Los Angeles Police Department has seen powerful public criticism of their use of data-driven patrolling software PredPol, and the LASER suspect identification program (Puente 2019a). Both examples indicate that even if machine-learning technology is scientifically sound in a data lab, when the tool is put into practice by a police force, there can be problems with the consistency of its use, as well as fears that the tool will only re-entrench biases and discrimination (Inspector General, LA Police Commission 2019; Puente 2019b). To repeat a mantra of some influential American researchers and civil rights lawyers, dirty data makes for bad predictions (Richardson et al. 2019).

Despite the trend toward the use of machine-learning technologies by police, pressure from academics, lawyers, and human rights NGOs is having some real effect. Some police forces and local government bodies in the United Kingdom and the United States are slowing down the "policy spiral" (Walker 2018) of fast-growing data analytics capabilities. In England, West Midlands Police have founded an independent data analytics ethics committee to monitor their development of data tools for use by the force (Marsh 2019), and in California, the cities of Oakland and San Francisco have created oversight bodies for the use of tech by local police (City of Oakland Privacy Advisory Commission 2019) or have banned the use of public-space facial recognition technology by police (Paul 2019), respectively.

In the United Kingdom, the government-backed Centre for Data Ethics and Innovation has partnered with the think tank the Royal United Services Institute (RUSI) to research what a code of practice for data analytics in criminal justice should look like (RUSI 2019). A holistic code of practice for the use of AI in our criminal justice system is much needed because the range of data analytics techniques used in policing in the United Kingdom is growing. There will continue to be calls from the most senior UK police officers (Dodd 2019b) for data science to be used to tackle the vital issue of resources pressures (HMICFRS 2019). In the realm of digital forensics (Bowcott 2019), police forces may use algorithms to advise them on when crimes might be unsolvable (Howgego 2019), so that officers can be diverted away from certain investigations or may more rigorously search for items of digital evidence on a rape complainant's mobile phone (Bowcott and Devlin 2019). Both applications speak to the need for regulation and control of machine learning in the justice system. In the United Kingdom at least, government is not only increasingly (and problematically) done online (Wall 2019) but is becoming algorithmically augmented to a greater and greater extent (Alston and Van Veen 2019). Criminal justice policymakers must focus on the human rights' implications of AI where and while that is politically possible.

The Importance of Human Rights Law Frameworks in Regulating Machine-Learning Tech

The UK Biometrics Commissioner Paul Wiles has recently noted in an annual report to the British Parliament:

> We have entered a world of powerful data analytics at a speed that has not allowed for a public debate as to how this new capability can add to human social flourishing. Indeed, [in the United Kingdom] we are just coming out of a period of public policy ignorance as to how intrusive and pervasive the new data analytics are and whether such powerful, global and fast-moving technology can be controlled by nation states through legislation. As is often the case with rapid and disruptive new technology, legislators need first to escape from technological determinism before they can decide how to act. (Wiles 2019, 13–14)

The technological determinism that Wiles highlights is the risk that human decision making, and through this respect for human rights, is eroded by reliance upon, and a surrendering to, the big data technologies of machine learning. Machine learning undeniably can do good—for example, in relation to the use of machine learning to measure and register hate speech online (Magee 2019), or to more efficiently cleanse minor criminal offences like drug possession from the records of rehabilitated offenders (Lee 2019). But machine-learning systems in policing, and the use of facial recognition in public spaces in particular, have raised significant concerns (Schippers 2019). Purshouse and Campbell have concluded that in the UK system, "human rights considerations should serve as a significant constraint on police [facial recognition technology] surveillance in public spaces" (Purshouse and Campbell 2019, 204). The surveillance camera commissioner has (belatedly to some) released a statutory code of practice on the use of automated public facial recognition camera systems by UK police forces, though this did not create new standards, one could argue, but instead compiled a comprehensive set of pre-existing legal doctrines (on human rights law and data protection in the main). This code ultimately does not rule out much at all in terms of police practices of overt LFR usage (Surveillance Camera Commissioner 2019).

Machine learning underpins global growth in controversial tech such as facial recognition systems. In the People's Republic of China, for instance, massive camera systems deploying facial recognition algorithms, paired with vast databases of photographs, are placing under surveillance the public movements and private transactions of billions of Chinese citizens already. All of this information on the private life and personal expression of individuals flows into socially controlling scoring systems, regardless of the corporate or government entity that first generated the data—since in Xi Jinping's booming and hardening China, commerce, government, and the party are in a resurgence of cooperation and corruption (Strittmatter 2019). China is already seeing a system of surveillance and oppression that George Orwell could not have foreseen in his most fevered dreams; and those bearing the brunt of this intensive surveillance and oppression by the Chinese state are Uighur, Christian, and Falun Gong minorities.

Kai Strittmatter has noted that for the ruling Chinese Communist Party, "the rule of law means something completely different to what it means to most citizens of Western democracies" (2019, 39). From the perspective of leaders in China's exploding tech sector, and with regard in China to the cozy relationship between commerce and a state security apparatus, the West is "getting tangled up in legal restrictions and data protection concerns," so in terms of the use of surveillance technology, the West will increasingly be left behind (Strittmatter 2019, 172). I confess as a result of this that I am *all for* the entanglement of surveillance technology and machine learning in government because of legal concerns and chiefly respect for human rights law. Respect for the procedural requirements of law is one of the basic tenets of a liberal democracy and is part of a respect for the rule of law in its unbiased enforcement of basic human rights standards, the practice of a separation of powers, and therefore the ability of the courts to halt a dangerous trajectory in government thinking or spending. But when it comes to the need for the development of a dedicated framework to regulate machine-learning technologies, we must take heed of the reminder from Cyrus Farivar that a collection of executive bodies will take the residual power afforded them by the legislature in a democratic state, and that human rights-threatening practices will flourish in an unregulated space. Absent law or government policy, says Farivar (2018, 122), "specifically forbidding a particular practice or regulating a particular technology":

> . . . law enforcement will always push the limits until they are told to stop. The job of the police, after all, is not to figure out where the lines are, but rather to be cognizant of those lines, and aggressively . . . go right up to them . . . a particular technique [will have been] legitimized until some enterprising lawyer tried to stop it. Even then, challenging a practice is difficult, particularly when a technology is so new hardly anyone even knows it exists, or how it compares to what had been in use previously.

There can be challenging human rights issues that result from under-regulation by a state of such emerging tech, and these standards ultimately will link to the degree of respect a state has for the basis of the rule of law in a particular jurisdiction on a human rights model. In the United Kingdom, as Philip Alston, the UN special rapporteur on extreme poverty and human rights, has said: "The British welfare state is gradually disappearing behind a webpage and an algorithm, with significant implications for those living in poverty" (Alston 2019, 13). The right to access a remedy in relation to that poverty is hampered both by cuts to the public legal aid budget across this decade and by the opaque way that government is now done technologically in an arena like welfare provision.

There are some areas of contentious practices in the criminal justice process, on the other hand, that are so sensitive to human rights impacts that there might be domains of the justice system where AI cannot tread at all. In the United Kingdom, this might readily be said to be the decision making by police about the use of force, including lethal force, given the procedural requirements of the European Convention on Human Rights. Within the criminal justice system, human decision makers are required to judge the imminence, reasonableness, and proportionality in using force up to and including the taking of life in response to a threat. The law also requires an examination of the contemporaneous understanding of the human decision maker as to that imminence, reasonableness, and proportionality.

AI in criminal justice settings will always confront the problem of amassing and sorting data. AI requires large data sets in order to be as accurate as possible in predicting, and thus informing or steering outcomes.

Some data sets are simply not large enough to use fairly, or are too difficult to collect, or too prone to inaccuracies should proxy data for uncollectable data be fed into the machine-learning algorithm concern. For example, it would be difficult to meaningfully and accurately use AI to advise on the appropriate use of lethal firearms in counterterror operations since the data set required would be impossible to meaningfully construct. Similarly, AI would not be effective in advising police regarding the use of nonlethal force in arrest and detention since the proper assessment of whether there has been "inhuman or degrading" treatment of a suspect in this context is entirely contextual and individualized (or "fact-specific," to the courts). By contrast, AI depends on a powerful machine learning-driven ability to compare like with like, which is not meaningful when the subtleties of different contexts between cases are possibly very different from one another.

The need for a bar on AI involvement might well be the case, most obviously, in relation to threats to the right to life or the right to freedom from inhuman or degrading treatment, including torture. But what about where algorithmic technology puts less well-protected rights in tension with one another, for example, when the right to liberty is placed against the need to protect the public at large? Or the right to privacy versus the right to a fair trial? This latter example of the human rights tensions around the use of machine learning can be seen in the following case study.

CASE STUDY ONE—Tensions Arising from a Lack of Regulation on an Issue of Justice

This case study demonstrates how the introduction of machine-learning or algorithmic data technologies into a sensitive human rights context—here, the right to privacy—can escalate the tensions around those human rights concerns. Smartphones record a lot of information about their users, and in terms of using it as criminal evidence, machine learning-based algorithms can make sense of interrogating this vast amount of data and meta-data about a person's movements, habits, history, and communications. If software is developed that can scan and filter the enormous amount of private information on a person's smartphone, it becomes much easier to search for evidence that corroborates or undermines their account of being victimized through an offence such as rape or sexual assault by a partner. But an algorithmic tool, used in the disclosure process to sift the pertinent evidence for the prosecution or the defense, represents a large-scale and intensive intrusion onto the privacy, say, of not just a rape suspect but a rape victim when their phone is so mined for evidence. In the United Kingdom, the right to a fair trial of the defendant is protected by Article 6 of the European Convention on Human Rights (ECHR), a powerful right—and yet the right to respect for the private life of a rape complainant is also protected, albeit under the weaker (qualified) right contained in Article 8 ECHR. This tension has led a tense, oppositional discourse in the United Kingdom in recent months.

This dispute in the United Kingdom has arisen following new guidelines from the National Police Chiefs' Council (NPCC) concerning the need for police forces to require victims of rape to hand over their phones for digital interrogation following their reporting of the offence concerned (Barr 2019). A number of rape trials had collapsed calamitously after the disclosure of digital evidence, originally overlooked in the process of disclosure from prosecution to defence, which, seen one way, showed an exculpatory view of the sexual relationship or encounter between the defendant and rape complainant. (It is rightly difficult to introduce evidence of the sexual history of a rape complainant in the UK courts, out of the need to protect victims from societal shaming, but it is not impossible if that evidence has a clear bearing on the trial and complaint in question.) Police forces in the United Kingdom were threatened with legal action over the invasion of rape complainants' privacy rights. This privacy invasion, it is argued, comes about through the digital interrogation of their private life, by way of scanning, copying and searching their mobile phone's stored data with an algorithm or other digital forensics software (Barr, Peraudin, and Bowcott 2019).

And yet, it is a principle of European human rights law, as it is applied in the UK criminal courts, that a fair trial is a trial which is fair in the relevant circumstances, as explained by the UK Supreme Court and other tribunals in high profile cases. As a result, the argument can be made that exculpatory evidence should be searched for using the most appropriate technical means. The use of digital forensic technologies in this context therefore creates a human rights tension that will not be easy to resolve. Also relevant to the debate is the charge that police forces in the United Kingdom will not move ahead with rape investigations unless a rape complainant hands over their smartphone for inspection and digital interrogation (Anonymous 2019). Thus, there are competing priorities regarding the right to privacy and the duty to investigate and so to prosecute and to disrupt the activities of sexual offenders (Centre for Women's Justice 2019). This duty to investigate sexual crimes to a sufficient objective standard is a binding, 'positive obligation' to past and future victims of a serial offender, under European human rights law (Article 3 ECHR).

The backdrop to the perceived need for digital searching of phone data from rape complainants is the reduction in funding for UK police force budgets and the Crown Prosecution Service (Bowcott 2019), and, thus, the argument that searching through masses of phone data might be done most cost-effectively with a machine-learning tool or algorithmic product (Bowcott and Devlin 2019). All rape trials are both expensive and necessary, but collapsed trials are expensive to no end, and the disclosure process—of sharing potentially exculpatory digital evidence with the defense—impacts the right to a fair trial. The element that must concede ground in this arrangement of issues, many would argue, is unfortunately the private life and digital privacy of a rape complainant—not an idea that sits well with any reasonable commentators, but again, tolerated by many as a necessity and on balance.

CASE STUDY TWO—Facial Recognition Technology in Criminal Justice

It came as something of a surprise to me when the *Bridges* case, challenging the use of live facial recognition in street policing trials on the basis that there was insufficient legal regulation of the tech in that context, was lost in the High Court in Cardiff (UK) in September 2019. There was not in my view a specific enough body of legislation that regulated the use of live facial recognition technology by police forces in the United Kingdom. European human rights law regarding privacy stipulates that a body of legislation must be specific enough for individuals and their lawyers to determine their rights in a given situation. In my view, the jigsaw of nonspecific legislation and guidance from data regulators in the United Kingdom regarding the protection of privacy did not meet this "accessibility" principle with respect to a coherent body of legislation; however, the High Court in Bridges was overall satisfied that it did.

Facial recognition tech is just one example of the way human rights issues around privacy and fairness result from under-regulation by a state in relation to emerging data-driven governance. Standards that jurisdictions ultimately adopt over the uses of data analytics will undoubtedly relate to the degree of respect that a state has for human rights in general. Some jurisdictions may decide to ban the use of facial recognition software in street policing due to the invasion of privacy that powerful live facial recognition technology poses in relation to the use of communal public space. Indeed, some UK police forces had started to curtail the use of automated, live facial recognition technology in trials in public places, even though the government had been pressing certain forces to supervise and host these trials (Townsend 2019). And some entire jurisdictions, though not yet at the time of writing, the United Kingdom may well see its own courts suspend the use of facial recognition by criminal justice agencies if a sufficiently clear and rigorous set of rules for its use is not put in place by legislators.

Facial recognition systems are not the only controversial AI to consider. In the Cardiff case of *Bridges* (2019), South Wales Police had used live facial recognition (LFR) in several pilots in public places and in operations where teams of police officers relied on matches in order to stop and/or arrest people in public places at prominent events. Sometimes these identification stops produced very low accuracy rates, depending on the exact nature of the deployments. The High Court in *Bridges* ultimately found that while most individuals in public places in the United Kingdom had a "reasonable expectation of privacy" in those places, and so their privacy rights under Article 8 ECHR were engaged by the use of LFR that captured and processed their image even briefly, these interferences were justifiable. Lord Justice Haddon Cave and Mr. Justice Swift reminded us in *Bridges* (2019) that "Questions of proportionality are generally fact sensitive" (para. 108) but observed (para. 7) that the "raw power of [LFR]—and the potential baleful uses to which [LFR] could be put by agents of the state and others—underline the need for careful and on-going consideration of the effectiveness of that framework as and when the uses of AFR develop."

In the United Kingdom, senior politicians have in 2019 supported more trials of automated facial recognition in public places (BBC 2019). At the same time, the very same police force subject to the AFR judicial review case in Cardiff, South Wales Police, has acknowledged that it is now switching its use of trials of AFR to a different policing context (namely identifying suspects already arrested, rather than using it to prompt them to arrest someone placed on a watch list), albeit still using this algorithm in a public place of arrest, by virtue of a newly developed smartphone app (Sample 2019).

Undoubtedly, there is scope for a technology such as automated facial recognition to be *selectively* deployed to do real public good, such as finding missing vulnerable persons (Bernal 2019). But the addition of AI or machine-learning approach to an already thorny, problematic policy context in a criminal justice system will inflame the tensions and uncertainties already present there, as noted above. There are already well-recognized issues regarding racial bias in police stops of ethnic minorities, for example, with Black people around 40 times more likely than white people to be stopped and searched by the police in the United Kingdom (Townsend 2019b). These disparities are already unfair and unjust without the assistance of biases arising from predictive/facial recognition AI tech built from training data that is racially skewed, leading to systemic bias and inaccuracies in relation to identifying and profiling ethnic minorities (CDEI 2019). Given that these problems of bias are likely to proliferate as use of the technology expands, the question then becomes how a jurisdiction can establish an oversight regime and accountability mechanisms for the use of AI or machine learning in its criminal justice system that is flexible enough to capture and address new challenges, as well as cognizant of new human rights risks in this context, but without limiting helpful innovation in justice technologies.

I am optimistic that the United Kingdom, as one jurisdiction, can establish an effective oversight regime for live facial recognition technology as used by the police in public spaces. The decision by the High Court in Cardiff in the *Bridges* case was a close call but ultimately supported the use of limited and focused facial recognition technology in support of specific stop and search activity based on police watch lists. This was despite the lack of a dedicated legal power for police use of facial recognition. However, a confident regulator for data laws in the United Kingdom, the information commissioner has at the time of writing this chapter just issued their first legal opinion on the issue, calling for a binding code of practice to be developed by central government on the practices concerned (ICO 2019). An investigation report, published alongside the commissioner's opinion, argues strongly for police forces in the United Kingdom using live facial recognition technology to publish information about the way that that they have sought to meet their equality law duties in using the practice (ICO 2019). This sort of self-critical and conscious approach to self-regulation by police forces is something that is growing as a culture of human rights in UK policing today. In a related manner, the third case study offers some insight into how well the specific development of regulation for AI and machine learning in UK policing contexts has been progressing of late.

CASE STUDY Three—Self-Regulation in Evolving Algorithmic Governance Practices

Currently, it is at least arguable that in Western liberal democracies there are new green shoots of the regulation of algorithms, as Rebecca Williams has highlighted (Williams 2019) in relation to legal developments in San Francisco and Oakland to restrict the use of facial recognition software and technology in street policing contexts. More broadly, McGregor, Murray, and Ng have claimed: "Mapping the algorithmic life cycle against the [international] human rights [law] framework provides clear red lines where algorithms cannot be used, as well as necessary safeguards for ensuring compatibility with human rights" (McGregor et al. 2019, 342). But is it as simple as this? I would very much doubt that international law is yet sufficiently and specifically developed enough to be used to offer detailed and meaningful regulation of facial recognition tech, or predictive policing-related AI or machine learning.

By way of contrast, and in a way that supports the argument that self-regulation of machine learning by police is possible and credible in some jurisdictions, I have seen firsthand that UK police forces (or at least their statisticians and technology specialists) can adapt to using rigorous self-regulation of their AI tools. I was one of a team of interdisciplinary researchers who created a self-regulatory model or framework to be aimed at police forces adopting machine-learning approaches in their intelligence analysis processes (Oswald et al. 2018). Known as ALGO-CARE, this regulatory checklist can be found as an appendix to our co-authored evaluation of the legalities of the Harm Assessment Risk Tool (HART), used currently by Durham Constabulary in Northern England. The HART tool is a leading application of machine-learning technology, as used in intelligence analysis and risk management practices by police in the United Kingdom, and was also the first such police project in the United Kingdom to be as open to a degree of academic scrutiny. The other researchers who evaluated HART were Marion Oswald (a legal academic then at Winchester University, now Northumbria University), Dr. Geoff Barnes (University of Cambridge), and Sheena Urwin (an assistant chief constable at Durham Constabulary itself).

ALGO-CARE is a set of more than thirty multidisciplinary prompt questions that police forces in the United Kingdom can use to guide themselves through the applicable legal and ethical issues of introducing AI to a policing context or process. These questions are grouped into eight principle areas: Advisory, Lawful, Granularity, Ownership, Challenge, Accuracy, Responsibility, and Explainability; hence the use of the mnemonic "ALGO-CARE" to describe the framework (Oswald et al. 2018). In essence, these eight bundles of prompts require police leaders and their data scientists to consider the extent to which decision making is informed by an algorithm or is automated; whether in that situation the algorithm has a clear legal basis in the way it will operate; whether it draws on the right data given its purpose; whether the force can control it as intellectual property; whether its outputs can be sufficiently well challenged; whether its outputs are accurate enough to be used for advising officers in operational settings; whether there is clear and objective oversight of the review and evaluation of the tool; and whether its use is readily and appropriately explainable to the public.

The National Police Chiefs' Council (NPCC) took the decision, after I met with them and a Home Office representative at Sheffield Hallam University in November 2018, to promote the use of ALGO-CARE as a model for best practice in the self-regulation by UK police forces, in relation to their development of machine learning/algorithmic tools. Across 2019, we also presented a range of our research at events including a roundtable of the Parliamentary Committee on Standards in Public Life and at meetings with policy officers and staff from the Centre for Data Ethics and Innovation (HM Government) and Her Majesty's Inspectorate of Constabulary, Fire and Rescue Services (HMICFRS). There then followed a series of police practitioner events at which I discussed ALGO-CARE with representatives of nearly 30 key UK police organizations, such as the National Crime Agency and the College of Policing, as well as representatives of a wide range of other regional organizations and police forces.

Following these workshops and meetings and the decision of the NPCC to adopt ALGO-CARE as a self-regulation standard, West Midlands Police (WMP) began incorporating ALGO-CARE into its development processes in relation to new algorithmic analysis tools. The Essex Police Department has since followed suit (Essex Centre for Data Analytics, 2019). Marion Oswald and I have been appointed to be chair and vice-chair, respectively, of the independent Data Analytics Ethics Committee established by the West Midlands Police and Crime Commissioner (WMPCC). This role has allowed us to draw on the ALGO-CARE framework in advising the WMPCC on the human rights ramifications of WMP adopting algorithmic analysis tools produced by their Data Lab team. In this way, we've added a layer of accountability to the human rights protections that WMP would otherwise place on its use of predictive analytics in offender risk profiling using machine-learning approaches, and as has been covered by the UK national news media (Marsh 2019).

The work of this ethics committee has included advising on the potential human rights risks and challenges of an Integrated Offender Management (IOM) tool being proposed by West Midlands Police (Todd 2019). This IOM tool would see more than 6,000 known offenders labeled as High Harm Offenders (HHOs) by West Midlands Police offender management processes and officers; yet there was insufficient clarity on issue of legality and freedom from historic racial bias issues in the data that the tool drew upon. By advising on a delay for reasons of potential unethical data analysis, this intervention from members of the ethics committee (WMPCC 2019), made on the basis of principles under the ALGO-CARE framework and from other elements of his research, meant that the adoption and use of the IOM tool has been crucially delayed until West Midlands Police can produce a clarification of the legality and ethics of the tool, and its safeguards.

In this way, our research and the ALGO-CARE guidance framework it proposes (Oswald et al. 2018) has helped to inform the protection of the sensitive personal data of thousands of offenders and victims in the West Midlands area. As reported in the *Guardian* in April 2019, Tom McNeil, the strategic adviser to the West Midlands police and crime commissioner, said: "The robust advice and feedback of the ethics committee shows it is doing what it was designed to do. The committee is there to independently scrutinise and challenge West Midlands police and make recommendations to the police and crime commissioner and chief constable" (Marsh 2019). Detective Chief Superintendent Chris Todd (the West Midlands Police head of professional standards and the NPCC lead for data analytics) also wrote in May 2019: "To establish an independent ethics committee with the credentials that we have whilst Google are still struggling, is again a significant achievement."

In the way we see it as a team of researchers, ALGO-CARE came out of a multidisciplinary approach to a practical use of AI and as such helps to foster the approach recommended by Sophie Stalla-Bourdillon that "technical experts and compliance personnel should sit together and create a risk matrix" (2019, 9). As ALGO-CARE is in essence a form of checklist of more than 30 ethical, legal, and data science considerations for a force to follow, it results in the kind of "Ethics/Privacy Impact Assessment" as argued for by Kroener et al. (2019). UK data protection law as it applies to policing already requires police forces to undertake Data Protection Impact Assessments, where a new data analytics project puts rights and liberties at stake, but the sorts of public bodies using some of the more ethically problematic machine-learning applications from a legal or ethical perspective are also subject to human rights law and legal procedural standards including the public sector equality duty as well as other grounds of judicial review. This results in a complex network of legal tests and ethical benchmarks for the use of AI or machine learning in police forces. Accordingly, ALGO-CARE was developed to be policing-context specific.

In the middle of 2019, the UK government announced it would pump a further £5 million into the development of a National Data Analytics Solution, a predictive policing and risk profiling platform to be based at West Midlands Police yet with outputs and algorithms to be shared across police forces all over the United Kingdom (Dearden 2019). We hope that the independent ethics committee at WMP, which Marion Oswald and I contribute toward, will work to provide the same rigorous oversight of the NDAS system as it has in relation to the WMP IOM project. However, Amnesty International has called for an end to what some term "ethics washing" (the use of ethics committees and oversight bodies to render a policy or practice permissible), arguing that softer, policy-led initiatives to try to ensure "ethical AI" simply won't result in fewer human rights breaches arising from AI over time (Amnesty International 2019).

Regulation of machine learning in policing does ultimately need to be legally harder-edged and efficacious in local jurisdictions, not built up in technocratic layers of international principles. British member of Parliament Chi Onwurah has argued that sufficient regulations should be in place to ensure that in a rights-sensitive domain—such as the granting of immigration visas by government—algorithms do not entrench and routinize bias and racism, due to the data that machine-learning tools are developed with (Onwurah 2019). ALGO-CARE has started a process of evolution of regulation for AI in policing in the United Kingdom; and as policing is certainly a rights-sensitive domain, the NPCC move to voluntarily adopt ALGO-CARE should be seen as a positive interim step.

Conclusions and Recommendations

As David Lyon predicted in 2007, the "safety state," which has been pushing out the welfare state from public discourse and public police and is concerned with public protection above any consideration of individual autonomy, "depends extensively on surveillance data" (Lyon 2007, 184). Lyon wrote presciently that "the software codes that classify us are designed to distinguish between one group and another to enable people to be treated differently depending on the category into which they fall" (Lyon 2007, 184). The concept of the "politics of public protection" (Nash 2010) demands that risky individuals in society are categorized and managed according to the likelihood of harmful behavior they may inflict on themselves and others. However, the problematic fragmentation of knowledge (Black 2002) held about individuals by law enforcement bodies and other behavioral regulators means that profiling potential offenders by way of categorization is a process based on partial information about an ecosystem of risk and harm. Lyon noted that "the major risk presented by today's all-pervasive surveillance is not the erosion of privacy . . . What require direct attention are the classification and profiling processes . . . that, favouring and confirming the formation of social stereotypes, determine both the attribution of privileges and rights and social exclusion" (Lyon 2007, 184–85). AI and profiling through machine-learning technology could put more rights at risk than just privacy by hierarchically classifying class, race, genders, freedoms, income, and education.

Lyon also called for "fresh forms of transparency linked with accountability" (Lyon 2007, 185)—a call that includes my work toward an experimental form of fresh accountability for the use of algorithmic profiling by a large police force in the United Kingdom, specifically as a member of the independent data analytics ethics committee established by West Midlands Police and their local elected police and crime commissioner in order to guide the development of the work of the force's Data Lab, and soon the National Data Analytics Solution (NDAS) for the UK police service. In time the NDAS project may evolve into a better-funded police Centre for Data Analytics, and the profiling of individuals according to their risk presented to society by way of an algorithmic assessment is something that will, as a result, become increasingly widespread and then entrenched in UK policing practices. This shift in the form of a predictive emphasis in police policy approaches will without doubt be transformational, although debate continues as to whether such advances in data-driven policing are timely or tragic.

The police are under constant pressure from civil liberties campaigners, as well as academics, to end their use of facial recognition tech (e.g., Booth 2019). And yet, only harder-edged regulatory oversight and enforcement might slow down or add rigor to the use of machine-learning tech in UK policing (Rawlinson 2019). It is not enough to rely on NGOs or protest groups to develop ways of counteracting these technologies, despite reports of innovation in this regard (*The Economist* 2019). In the United Kingdom, behavioral data profiling in relation to extremist behavior, and predictive analytics in counterterrorism practice, are seen as areas for technological development and policy prioritisation (Anderson 2019). Thus, it is vital that the law is not rebuilt in such a way as to be too porous when it comes to preventing or mitigating human rights impacts. Turner et al. might agree, and as they note:

> Algorithmic decision making has the potential to be a force for good. However, our findings suggest the necessity for a cautionary approach. If the data quality is poor, the prediction quality cannot be redeemed by the modelling approach, whether it be a basic logistic regression model or a state-of-the-art neural network. It is "garbage in, garbage out" . . . (Turner et al. 2019, 1030)

As for which models and manners of accountability should be developed, there needs to be greater rebalancing away from the preference for the "politics of public protection" (Nash 2010) toward at least a joint recognition of what David Lyon in 2007 termed the "politics of information" (Lyon 2007). The policing sector in the United Kingdom is under greater scrutiny than the rest of our criminal justice system in this regard, which is good for the accountability of UK policing, but not the UK justice system overall. As AI drives purported innovation in criminal justice systems around the world, we must also remember that the human rights issues introduced by this essay are universal.

Works Cited

Alston, Philip, and Christiaan van Veen. 2019. "How Britain's Welfare State Has Been Taken over by Shadowy Tech Consultants | Philip Alston and Christiaan Van Veen." *The Guardian*. Guardian News and Media, June 27, 2019. https://www.theguardian.com/commentisfree/2019/jun/27/britain-welfare-state-shadowy-tech-consultants-universal-credit.

Amnesty International. 2019. "Ethical AI Principles Won't Solve a Human Rights Crisis." Amnesty International. https://www.amnesty.org/en/latest/research/2019/06/ethical-ai-principles-wont-solve-a-human-rights-crisis/.

Anderson, David. 2019. *2017 Terror Attacks: MI5 and CTP Reviews: Implementation Stock-Take.* https://assets.publishing.service.gov.uk/government/uploads/

system/uploads/attachment_data/file/807911/2017_terrorist_attacks_reviews_implementation_stock_take.pdf.

Anonymous. 2019. "My Sexual Assault Case Was Dropped When I Refused to Give Police My Phone | Anonymous." *The Guardian*. Guardian News and Media, April 29, 2019. https://www.theguardian.com/commentisfree/2019/apr/29/sexual-assault-case-dropped-refused-police-phone-rape.

Barr, Caelainn. 2019. "People Who Report Rape Face 'Routine' Demands for Their Mobile Data." *The Guardian*. Guardian News and Media, September 21, 2019. https://www.theguardian.com/society/2019/sep/21/people-report-rape-routine-demands-mobile-data.

Barr, Caelainn, Frances Perraudin, and Owen Bowcott. 2019. "Police Face Legal Action over Requests for Rape Complainants' Data." *The Guardian*. Guardian News and Media, April 29, 2019. https://www.theguardian.com/society/2019/apr/29/police-face-legal-action-over-requests-for-victims-digital-records.

BBC. 2019, "Automated Facial Recognition Trials Backed by Home Secretary." BBC News. BBC, July 12, 2019. https://www.bbc.co.uk/news/uk-48959380.

Bernal, Natasha. 2019. "Facial Recognition to Be Used by UK Police to Find Missing People." *The Telegraph*. Telegraph Media Group, July 16, 2019. https://www.telegraph.co.uk/technology/2019/07/16/facial-recognition-technology-used-uk-police-find-missing-people/.

Black, Julia. 2002. "Critical reflections on regulation." *Austl. J. Leg. Phil.* 27: 1.

Booth, Robert. 2019. *Police face calls to end use of facial recognition software*. [online] the Guardian. Available at: https://www.theguardian.com/technology/2019/jul/03/police-face-calls-to-end-use-of-facial-recognition-software.

Bowcott, Owen. 2019. "'Explosion' in Digital Evidence Has Left CPS Struggling, Says Union." *The Guardian*. Guardian News and Media, May 1, 2019. https://www.theguardian.com/law/2019/may/01/explosion-in-digital-evidence-has-left-cps-struggling-says-union.

Bowcott, Owen, and Hannah Devlin. 2018. "Police Trial AI Software to Help Process Mobile Phone Evidence." *The Guardian*. Guardian News and Media, May 27, 2018. https://www.theguardian.com/uk-news/2018/may/27/police-trial-ai-software-to-help-process-mobile-phone-evidence.

CDEI (Centre for Data Ethics and Innovation). 2019, Landscape Summary—Bias in Algorithmic Decision-Making, HM Government. https://assets.publishing.service.gov.uk/government/uploads/system/uploads/attachment_data/file/819055/Landscape_Summary_-_Bias_in_Algorithmic_Decision-Making.pdf.

Centre for Women's Justice. 2019. "CWJ Launch Super-complaint: Police failure to use protective measures in cases involving violence against women and girls." https://www.centreforwomensjustice.org.uk/news/2019/3/20/cwj-launch-super-complaint-police-failure-to-use-protective-measures-in-cases-involving-violence-against-women-and-girls.

City of Oakland Privacy Advisory Commission. 2019. "Privacy Advisory Commission." https://www.oaklandca.gov/boards-commissions/privacy-advisory-board.

Dearden, Lizzie. 2019. "Police Testing Technology To 'Assess the Risk of Someone Committing A Crime,'" July 17, 2019. *The Independent*. https://www.independent.co.uk/news/uk/home-news/crime-prediction-technology-police-trials-uk-government-funding-a9007556.html.

Dodd, Vikram. 2019a. "Police Resources 'Drained to Dangerously Low Levels,' Say Former Top Officers." *The Guardian*, July 4, 2019. https://www.theguardian.com/uk-news/2019/jul/04/police-watchdog-reforms-chief-inspector-constabulary.

Dodd, Vikram. 2019b. "'Woefully Low': Cressida Dick Calls for Action on Crime-Solving Rates." *The Guardian*, June 26, 2019. https://www.theguardian.com/uk-news/2019/jun/26/cressida-dick-calls-for-public-consent-on-data-use-to-help-battle.

The Economist. 2019. "As face-recognition technology spreads, so do ideas for subverting it." *The Economist*, August 15, 2019. https://www.economist.com/science-and-technology/2019/08/15/as-face-recognition-technology-spreads-so-do-ideas-for-subverting-it.Edmonds, David. 2019. "Could an Algorithm Help Prevent Murders?" *BBC News*, June 24, 2019. https://www.bbc.co.uk/news/stories-48718948.

Essex Centre for Data Analytics (Essex Partnership). 2019. "Essex Partnership." *Essex future. Org. Uk*. http://www.essexfuture.org.uk/ecda/essex-centre-for-data-analytics/transparency-and-trust/.

Farivar, Cyrus. 2018. *Habeas data: Privacy vs. the rise of surveillance tech*. Melville House.

Gavshon, Daniela, and Erol Gorur. 2019. "Information Overload: How Technology Can Help Convert Raw Data into Rich Information for Transitional Justice Processes." *International Journal of Transitional Justice* 13: 71–91.

Harlow, Carol, and Rawlings, Richard. 2019. Proceduralism and Automation: Challenges to the Values of Administrative Law (February 15, 2019). *The Foundations and Future of Public Law* (in honour of Paul Craig), edited by E. Fisher, J. King and A. Young. Oxford University Press; LSE Legal Studies Working Paper No. 3/2019. Available at SSRN: https://ssrn.com/abstract=3334783 or http://dx.doi.org/10.2139/ssrn.3334783.

HMICFRS, 2019. *Justiceinspectorates. Gov. Uk*. https://www.justiceinspectorates.gov.uk/hmicfrs/wp-content/uploads/peel-spotlight-report-a-system-under-pressure.pdf.

Howgego, Joshua, 2019. *Newscientist. Com*, January 8, 2019. https://www.newscientist.com/article/2189986-a-uk-police-force-is-dropping-tricky-cases-on-advice-of-an-algorithm/.

ICO (Information Commissioner's Office). 2018a. *Gangs Matrix Enforcement Notice*, November 2018, 2019. *Ico. Org. Uk*. https://ico.org.uk/action-weve-taken/enforcement/metropolitan-police-service/.

ICO (Information Commissioner's Office). 2018b. "Processing Gangs Information: A Checklist For Police Forces." *Ico. Org. Uk*. https://ico.org.uk/for-organisations/

in-your-sector/police-justice/processing-gangs-information-a-checklist-for-police-forces/.

ICO (Information Commissioner's Office). 2019. *Ico.Org.Uk*. https://ico.org.uk/media/about-the-ico/documents/2616184/live-frt-law-enforcement-opinion-20191031.pdf.

Inspector General LA Police Commission. 2019. *Lapdpolicecom.Lacity.Org*. http://www.lapdpolicecom.lacity.org/031219/BPC_19-0072.pdf.

Jowitt, Joshua, 2019. "Ian Mcewan's Machines Like Me and the Thorny Issue of Robot Rights." *The Conversation*, April 17, 2019. https://theconversation.com/ian-mcewans-machines-like-me-and-the-thorny-issue-of-robot-rights-115520.

Larsson, Naomi. 2019. "'It's an Educational Revolution': How AI Is Transforming University Life." *The Guardian*, April 17, 2019. https://www.theguardian.com/education/2019/apr/17/its-an-educational-revolution-how-ai-is-transforming-university-life.

Lee, Dave. 2019. "An Algorithm Wipes Clean the Criminal Pasts of Thousands." *BBC News*, April 29, 2019. https://www.bbc.co.uk/news/technology-48072164.

Lyon, David. 2007. *Surveillance Studies: An Overview*. Polity Press.

McGregor, Lorna, Daragh Murray, and Vivian Ng. 2019. "International human rights law as a framework for algorithmic accountability." *I.C.L.Q.* 68, no. 2: 309–343.

McKevitt, Steve. 2019. "How the power of persuasion goes way beyond mere advertising." *The Conversation*, April 17, 2019. https://theconversation.com/how-the-power-of-persuasion-goes-way-beyond-mere-advertising-115400.

Magee, Tamlin. 2019. "Cardiff University's Hatelab Unearths Online Hate Speech Using AI." *Techworld*. https://www.techworld.com/data/hatelab-brexit-cardiff-university-machine-learning-3701284/.

Marsh, Sarah. 2019. "Ethics committee raises alarm over 'predictive policing' tool." *The Guardian*, April 20, 2019. https://www.theguardian.com/uk-news/2019/apr/20/predictive-policing-tool-could-entrench-bias-ethics-committee-warns.

MOPAC (Mayor's Office for Policing and Crime). 2018. *Review of the Gangs Matrix*, December.

Nash, Mike. 2010. "The politics of public protection." In *Handbook of public protection*, edited by Mike Nash and Andy Williams. 82–102. Routledge.

Onwurah, Chi. 2019. "Chi Onwurah: We must end the use of biased algorithms to process visa applications with no transparency." *PoliticsHome*. https://www.politicshome.com/news/uk/technology/house/house-magazine/105266/chi-onwurah-we-must-end-use-biased-algorithms-process.

Oswald, Marion, Jamie Grace, Sheena Urwin and Geoffrey C. Barnes. 2018. "Algorithmic risk assessment policing models: lessons from the Durham HART model and 'Experimental' proportionality." *Information & Communications Technology Law*. DOI: 10.1080/13600834.2018.1458455.

Paul, Kari. 2019. "San Francisco is first US city to ban police use of facial recognition tech." *The Guardian*, May 14, 2019. https://www.theguardian.com/us-news/2019/may/14/san-francisco-facial-recognition-police-ban.

Puente, Mark. 2019a. "LAPD to scrap some crime data programs after criticism." *Los Angeles Times*, April 5, 2019. https://www.latimes.com/local/lanow/la-me-lapd-predictive-policing-big-data-20190405-story.html.

Puente, Mark. 2019b. "LAPD pioneered predicting crime with data. Many police don't think it works." *Los Angeles Times*, July 3, 2019. https://www.latimes.com/local/lanow/la-me-lapd-precision-policing-data-20190703-story.html.

Purshouse, Joe, and Liz Campbell. 2019. "Privacy, crime control and police use of automated facial recognition technology." *Crim. L.R.* 3: 188–204.

Rawlinson, Kevin. 2019. "ICO opens investigation into use of facial recognition in King's Cross." *The Guardian*, August 15, 2019. https://www.theguardian.com/technology/2019/aug/15/ico-opens-investigation-into-use-of-facial-recognition-in-kings-cross.

Richardson, Rashida, Jason Schultz, and Kate Crawford. 2019. "Dirty Data, Bad Predictions: How Civil Rights Violations Impact Police Data, Predictive Policing Systems, and Justice." *New York University Law Review* [Online], February 13, 2019. Available at SSRN: https://ssrn.com/abstract=3333423.

Royal United Services Institute. 2019. "RUSI partners with the Centre for Data Ethics and Innovation." RUSI, June 6, 2019. https://rusi.org/rusi-news/rusi-partners-centre-data-ethics-and-innovation.

Sample, Ian. 2019. "South Wales police to use facial recognition apps on phones." *The Guardian*, August 7, 2019. https://www.theguardian.com/technology/2019/aug/07/south-wales-police-to-use-facial-recognition-to-identify-suspects.

Sebastian Schwiddessen, Birgit Clark, Thomas Defaux and John Groom. 2018. "Germany's Network Enforcement Act—closing the net on fake news?" *E.I.P.R.* 40, no. 8: 539–546.

Schippers, Birgit. 2019. "Facial recognition: ten reasons you should be worried about the technology." *The Conversation*, August 21, 2019. https://theconversation.com/facial-recognition-ten-reasons-you-should-be-worried-about-the-technology-122137.

Stalla-Bourdillon, Sophie. 2019. "Data protection by design and data analytics: Can we have both?" *Privacy & Data Protection* 19, no. 5: 8–10.

Strittmatter, Kai. 2019. *We Have Been Harmonised: Life in China's Surveillance State.* Exeter, UK: Old Street.

Surveillance Camera Commissioner. 2019. *The Police Use of Automated Facial Recognition Technology with Surveillance Camera Systems*, March 2019.

Todd, Chris (West Midlands Police Head of Professional Standards and NPCC Lead for Data Analytics). 2019. "Putting ethics at the heart of data analytics." *Policing Insight*, April 30, 2019. https://policinginsight.com/analysis/putting-ethics-at-the-heart-of-data-analytics/.

Townsend, Mark. 2019a. "Police forces halt trials of facial recognition systems." *The Guardian*, August 17, 2019. https://www.theguardian.com/world/2019/aug/17/police-halt-trials-face-recognition-systems-surveillance-technology.

Townsend, Mark. 2019b. "Black people '40 times more likely' to be stopped and searched in UK." *The Guardian*, May 4, 2019. https://www.theguardian.com/law/2019/may/04/stop-and-search-new-row-racial-bias.

Turner, Emily, Juanjo Medina, and Gavin Brown. 2019. "Dashing hopes? The predictive accuracy of domestic abuse risk assessment by police." *BRIT. J. CRIMINOL.* 59: 1013–1034.

Walker, Clive. 2018. "Counter-terrorism and counter-extremism: the UK policy spirals." *Public Law*. Oct: 725–747.

Wall, Tom. 2019. " 'I'm 57 and my parents have to feed me': The universal credit digital obstacle course." *The Guardian*, March 18, 2019. https://www.theguardian.com/society/2019/mar/18/57-parents-feed-me-universal-credit-digital-obstacle-course.

Wiles, Paul. 2019. *Commissioner for the Retention and Use of Biometric Material: Annual Report 2018*. London: Her Majesty's Stationery Office.

Williams, Rebecca. 2019. "Accountability key to the adoption of surveillance technology." Oxford University Faculty of Law, May 20, 2019. https://www.law.ox.ac.uk/unlocking-potential-artificial-intelligence-english-law/blog/2019/05/accountability-key-adoption.

Winsor, Tom. 2019. "State of Policing—The Annual Assessment of Policing in England and Wales 2018." Her Majesty's Inspectorate of Constabulary and Fire and Rescue Services. https://www.justiceinspectorates.gov.uk/hmicfrs/wp-content/uploads/state-of-policing-2018.pdf.

WMPCC. 2019. Committee meeting minutes from April 2019 for the WMPCC Independent Data Analytics Ethics Committee discussions of the "Integrated Offender Management" (IOM) tool. See: https://www.westmidlands-pcc.gov.uk/transparency/ethics-committee/committee-reports-and-minutes/april-2019/.

Chapter Three

Quantifying and Visualizing Human Rights

The CIRIGHTS Data Project

DAVID CINGRANELLI, MIKHAIL FILIPPOV,
AND BRENDAN SKIP MARK

What is the value of a quantitative approach to the study of human rights? Our argument is that using multiple methods, quantitative and qualitative, to study human rights provides insights that each method alone would not uncover. International human rights law stipulates that national governments have the primary responsibility for protecting human rights. Quantifying human rights refers to the assignment of numeric ratings to governments assessing their level of conformity with international human rights standards. Since the 1980s, scholars, mainly in the fields of law, political science, and sociology, have led the human rights quantification effort. The numerical scores those efforts have assigned serve as an accountability mechanism to indicate how well each nation has done in meeting its human rights protection obligations.

Quantitative research is advanced mostly by comparing the effects of policies and institutions across a large sample of the world's countries. Whereas one influential strain of early *qualitative* human rights work in political science, focused primarily on South and Central America (Sikkink 1993; Sikkink and Martin 1993; Brysk 1994; Sikkink 2004), showed the ability of transnational activist networks to improve human rights conditions and hold leaders accountable in select locations (Foot 2000), quantitative analyses came to more negative conclusions. Research found that regime type, conflict, population size, colonial legacy, and national security threats were all important in understanding why national human rights practices improved or declined (Poe and Tate 1994; Cingranelli and Richards 1999; Davenport and Armstrong 2004). These characteristics of countries are difficult to change in the short term. Although quantitative work differed in methodology and conclusion, it helped identify the set of cases where policies and institutions did not work to improve human rights, allowing both quantitative and qualitative scholars to take a deeper look at why. Slowly, scholars began to learn which factors were important determinants of success or failure more broadly. Quantitative work, using a different lens and set of tools, exposed some of the weaknesses in qualitative work. Qualitative work has similarly exposed weaknesses in quantitative study by pointing out "outlier" cases that quantitative theories cannot explain.

Increasingly, scholars are seeing the value of using both quantitative and qualitative methods to study the same problem. Let's consider recent research on the 1994 genocide in Rwanda. Most people accept that between 800,000 and 1,000,000 Tutsi people were killed by Hutu extremists in Rwanda over the course of about 100 days. This genocide is one of the better studied cases in the literature, and until recently most of the facts were not in dispute. However, recent work by Davenport and Stam (2009) using both qualitative and quantitative methods estimate that while the Hutu-led Armed Forced of Rwanda (FAR) and associated paramilitary groups killed between 300,000 and 500,000 Tutsi, the Tutsi-led Rwandan Patriotic Front (RPF) commanded by the current president of Rwanda, Paul Kagame, also killed between 500,000 and 700,000 moderate Hutu. Davenport and Stam (2009) conducted their study by using qualitative sources such as government documents, testimonials, and responses to surveys administered by the Rwandan government, NGOs, and government agencies to determine who was killed, by whom, where, and when. They produced numerical data based on these qualitative sources. Since its release their study has been embroiled in controversy. The Rwandan government and others have labeled the authors as "genocide deniers" even though the authors agree that a genocide of Tutsis did occur (see Verpoorten 2014 for a critique of Davenport and Stam's baseline data and calculations). However, their findings also match the claims of many Hutu that large numbers of Hutu were killed during the genocide and that their deaths have been forgotten resulting in discrimination against the Hutu people. Although the scholarly debate continues, we now have strong evidence in favor of an alternative narrative that includes an accounting of Hutu deaths. Inaccurate and misleading numbers associated with mass atrocities are not unique to Rwanda. They are common, and they matter. In Rwanda, President Paul Kagame has rewritten history and instituted laws that allow the government to imprison those who challenge the dominant genocide narrative.

Quantification of human rights has always been controversial as the above example helps illustrate, and in the next section we review the advantages and limitations. Then we describe our own human rights quantification project, the CIRIGHTS Data Project (Cingranelli, Filippov, and Mark 2021), to illustrate the usefulness of numerical human rights scores for analyzing debates over China's treatment of the ethnic Uighurs. This part of our chapter is written for a human rights audience who are not experts in the quantitative, comparative study of human rights and who may be skeptical or even dismissive about the whole enterprise. In the last part of our chapter, we illustrate the usefulness of quantification for visualizing patterns of human rights behavior. Specifically, we use the CIRIGHTS data to construct figures showing that the governments of smaller population nations tend to provide significantly greater respect for most internationally recognized human rights than larger nations do. We show that this pattern holds for nearly all physical integrity rights as well as for civil and political rights. We also present some theoretical explanations for why it is more difficult to have good human rights practices and to improve human right practices in larger nations. These preliminary hypotheses could benefit from the insights that qualitative scholars might provide. We conclude with a discussion of the theoretical and policy implications of our findings.

Critiques of Quantification

We start by examining some of the most significant critiques of the quantitative approach to the study of human rights, which are presented by Sally Engle Merry (2016), a well-respected critic of the technology of quantification. Merry's critiques, echoed by many others, fall into five categories. First, she argues that quantification is political, ideological, and a form of power that is often exclusionary. Second, that quantification creates a myth of objectivity. Third, some important phenomena are not counted; some cannot even be quantified, and some numerical scores do not provide an accurate picture of a problem. Fourth, quantitative advocates often ignore cultural factors focusing instead on persuading citizens and elites worldwide that human rights principles, as interpreted by the United Nations and its agencies, are universal, desirable, moral, and pragmatic. Fifth, quantitative evidence usually plays too strong a role in policy making (Bello-Villarino and Vijeyarasa 2017; Davis et al. 2012; Mau 2019; Merry 2018; Osterlind 2019). We turn to each of these critiques in turn.

Quantification is political. Quantification is helpful to those who seek to build theories of why things happen by making general statements based on systematic and verifiable observations. However, the method of quantification is a tool, and like any other tool it can be used to pursue quality research or misused to push a particular agenda. This critique is not unique to quantitative scholars but instead reflects the reality that the language of human rights is often used for political ends. Numerical human rights scores created to push a political agenda are scrutinized and debated even among quantitative scholars, who often expose biases and alert the community of scholars and policy makers to the problems of using them. The example of Rwanda above shows exactly this. We agree that numerical scores can be politically motivated. However, quantitative scholars come from all ideological backgrounds, and any measure created using the scientific approach to measurement will be subjected to significant scrutiny. Scholars of measurement have developed rules and tests to ensure that measures are reliable, replicable, and valid (for an example of this type of debate among quantitative scholars, see Cingranelli and Filippov 2018).

The myth of objectivity. Almost no quantitative scholar would argue that their data is objective. Most scholars recognize that data are biased, that sources are biased, and that we need to be careful how much confidence we place on any one study or measure. There are also significant debates among quantitative scholars over how rights should be measured, with different measures capturing different aspects of the same rights. Few if any reputable quantitative scholars would argue that data alone can prove anything. However, given two competing theories about how the world works, we can test which one seems to be supported by what we see in the real world. Data itself is useless without a theoretical argument to explain *why* the data look the way they do. What data can do is show that the implications of a theory or argument are or not substantiated by what we see in the world. This is particularly useful in an age of "fake news," where conjecture is often confused with theorizing. The qualitative study of testimonials, interpretive case studies, ethnography, art, cinema, photography, music, poetry, and literature are not less prone to bias. All sources of human rights–relevant information are biased (Brysk 2004). Photos, paintings, books, films, and case studies focus on some events but ignore others.

There is too much emphasis on things that can be counted easily. While it is true that many human rights that are important are not being measured, this is not because they cannot be measured, but instead because they have not been measured *yet*. The number and scope of human rights being measured has continued to increase. Graduate dissertations as well as scholarly work have homed in on these limitations and sought to address them. Over time, the number of human rights measured are likely to cover all internationally recognized human rights and may identify some additional injustices that should be protected in international law. The Social and Economic Rights Fulfillment index (SERF) as well as the Worker Rights Dataset are two examples of cutting-edge work seeking to better measure economic and social rights (Fukuda-Parr et al. 2011).

Quantitative scholars have too much influence persuading citizens and elites worldwide that human rights principles are universal, desirable, moral, and pragmatic. Perhaps this is true, but many quantitative scholars have been and are increasingly skeptical about the positive impact of human rights law, institutions, and activism (Hafner-Burton and Ron 2009). Rather than tell the audience what to think, quantitative scholars test whether what we believe to be true in one case or a handful of cases actually applies more broadly. When these scholars are all in agreement, we can be more confident that the explanations we have for human rights outcomes are accurate. When scholars disagree, it can help us identify gaps in our knowledge and new avenues of research.

Quantitative evidence plays too strong a role in policymaking. What is increasingly true is that people want numbers very badly, and they don't care where they come from (Hafner-Burton and Ron 2009). The media, NGOs, policy makers, and others increasingly want numbers to help measure human rights violations and whether policies and institutions meant to address these violations have been successful. If scholars are not providing these numbers in a rigorous manner, then people will make them up. These made-up numbers will become fact and have a profound impact on how human rights violations are addressed, remedied, and remembered, as the case of Rwanda above illustrates. These numbers are important because they influence whether or not leaders will alter policy, money will be spent to remedy violations, violations will be covered in the media, and violators will be held accountable.

One appeal of quantitative measurement is that it is a tool that anyone can use. The costs of carrying out field research are often prohibitively high for many scholars and students. Many qualitative methods, such as archival research, field study or survey research, require significant travel costs and expenses. However, using quantitative data like that produced by the CIRIGHTS Data Project can be far less expensive. Thus, human rights studies can be carried out by anyone, including those in the Global South, students, and nonprofit organizations. For many of the most popular measures of human rights, the cost of collecting data is primarily the effort that went in to developing a theoretically driven measure and the time it takes to collect the data. Thus, the quantitative study of human rights can often be more accessible than qualitative scholarship, especially for those outside of academia who do not have access to scholarly work due to paywalls. If one believes a measure is biased or inaccurate, they can show this by relying on a set of evaluative measurement tools, identify how much bias exists and in which direction, and develop recommendations about when to be more cautious about the findings associated with the measure (see, e.g., Steiner 2014, who demonstrates that Freedom House Democracy Scores are biased to produce higher scores for US allies).

Quantification in Practice

As noted, debates among quantitative human rights scholars are common in the literature. For example, one debate currently underway in quantitative human rights research is whether the protection of physical integrity human rights globally has improved or declined over time (Cingranelli and Filippov 2018). Various scholars have expressed opinions about this question based on anecdotal information. But how could anyone know enough about the human rights practices of the more than 190 countries in the world to be able to know whether, on average, their practices have improved or declined (Hafner-Burton and Ron 2009)? Without quantitative human rights scores, it is impossible to know whether average protection for any human rights practice has improved or declined. If we don't know that, we cannot convince policy makers that changes are needed, nor can we assess whether any previous policy intervention mattered. This debate has focused on how we should measure physical integrity rights, the bias of the sources used, the changing nature of governments' ability to hide violations, as well as how our understanding of what constitutes a human rights violation have changed over time.

Often human rights scores simply provide another form of evidence to evaluate and usually to support claims made by journalists, qualitative scholars, and policy activists. Consider the contemporary controversy over China's detention of at least a million Uighur Muslims. In July 2019, representatives of 22 United Nations member states signed a letter addressed to the president of the UN Human Rights Council and the UN High Commissioner for Human Rights demanding that China, a member of the Human Rights Council, end its massive detention program and stop persecuting Muslim Uighurs. The 22 national representatives called upon China to uphold its national laws and international commitments, including as a member of the Human Rights Council. A few days later, a group of 37 countries submitted a letter defending China. In that letter, they expressed their opposition to "politicizing human rights" and praised "China's remarkable achievements in the field of human rights." The letter included a passage justifying China's detention and persecution of Muslim Uighurs, noting: "Faced with the grave challenge of terrorism and extremism, China has undertaken a series of counter-terrorism and deradicalization measures in Xinjiang, including setting up vocational education and training centers." Which evaluation of China's human rights practices is closer to the truth? Is China systematically violating the human rights of Muslim Uighurs, or is it taking reasonable actions to combat terrorism and extremism? National security concerns are often used as an excuse for human rights violations by many countries, such as the United States in its war on terror. How do we sort out whether rights violations are a result of justifiable security policy or whether national security serves as political cover for preventable rights violations?

One way we might resolve this question is by asking what we would expect to see in the world if China was taking reasonable action to promote security? First, we could check whether China has in fact made significant achievements in its human rights over the last few decades. Outside of its treatment of the Uighurs, have human rights improved? We might also look at whether the advocates and defenders of China have ulterior motives in their public declarations. If critics of China all have strong human rights practices while defenders all have poor human rights practices, then we should be skeptical that this is simply about national security. Defenders may be advocating on behalf of China in an attempt to prevent their own abuses from being criticized. Finally, we can check whether Muslim majority countries are advocates or critics of China's policies. The persecution of a religious group in one country often provokes public denouncement from countries with citizens who share that religion in another country. How they have responded to China's treatment of the Uighurs may be quite telling.

Human rights scores have been produced for all countries of the world by a variety of nonpolitical organizations for purposes not directly related to the current controversy about the treatment of the ethnic Uighurs in Xinjiang. We use measures from our CIRIGHTS Database to investigate this question. The next section goes into more detail about how these measures were created. China's record of respect for almost all internationally recognized human rights except for economic and social rights (Cingranelli and Richards 1999) has been and continues to be very poor. Between 1993 and 2017, China's scores for 14 human rights have either gotten worse or remained the same. Thus, at the outset it is hard to find evidence of China's human rights achievements.

China's poor treatment of the Muslim Uighurs is, therefore, no surprise. For example, China's score on the CIRIGHTS Physical Integrity Index in 2017 was 2 on a scale from 0 to 8, where 0 means "no protection at all." The physical integrity index has been widely used as the dependent variable in large-n, comparative research in the social sciences. It summarizes the extent to which the government protects citizens from extra-judicial killing, disappearance, political imprisonment and torture. The physical integrity index is the sum of each country's score on those four indicators of national human rights protection.

China's own human rights record on other human rights also implies that the critics of China's policy towards the Uighurs are closer to the truth than are the defenders. The rights of Uighurs that are being most seriously violated are the right against political imprisonment, the right to freedom of religion, freedom of domestic movement, freedom of speech and press, and freedom of assembly and association. The CIRIGHTS Data Project also assigns annual scores of 0 indicating "no respect" to 2 indicating "full respect" to all UN member states for each of these rights. The score China received in 2017 were 0 for respecting the right against political imprisonment, 0 for respecting the right to freedom of religion, 1 for respecting freedom of domestic movement, 0 for respecting freedom of speech and press, and 0 for respecting freedom of assembly and association.

As additional evidence that China is violating international human rights norms, the countries that signed the letter criticizing China have better human rights records than the countries that defended China. Table 3.1 lists the countries that signed each letter. All of the country representatives who signed the letter criticizing China's behavior are economically advanced democracies with relatively good human rights records. Previous research has shown that countries that are both accountable and capable

Table 3.1. The Countries Whose Representatives Signed the Letters Criticizing or Defending China's Human Right Policies Towards Ethnic Uighurs in July 2019

China's Critics		**China's Defenders**			
Australia	Japan	Algeria	Cuba	Pakistan	Turkmenistan
Austria	Latvia	Angola	Democratic Republic of the Congo	Philippines	United Arab Emirates
Belgium	Lithuania	Bahrain	Egypt	Qatar	Venezuela
Canada	Luxembourg	Belarus	Eritrea	Russia	Zimbabwe
Denmark	The Netherlands	Bolivia	Gabon	Saudi Arabia	
Estonia	New Zealand	Burkina Faso	Kuwait	Somalia	
Finland	Norway	Burundi	Laos	South Sudan	
France	Spain	Cambodia	Myanmar	Sudan	
Germany	Sweden	Cameroon	Nigeria	Syria	
Iceland	Switzerland	Comoros	North Korea	Tajikistan	
Ireland	The United Kingdom	Congo	Oman	Togo	

tend to provide the greatest protection for all human rights (Cingranelli and Filippov 2018). The list of China's defenders, on the other hand, is puzzling and troubling. It is puzzling because, even though Muslims are allegedly being victimized, no Muslim majority country signed the letter criticizing China, while many defended it. This might suggest that the treatment of the Uighur people in China is not as black and white as the media and policy makers are making it out to be. Or it might suggest that China's influence among developing countries is so large that they dare not speak out against this repression, even if they would like to.

The scores included in the CIRIGHTS Data Project allow us to quantify the difference in human rights performance, on average, between the critics and the defenders. Table 3.2 includes all of the human rights for which scores are currently available from the CIRIGHTS Data Project. There are scores rating the degree of government protection of 14 internationally recognized human rights plus two widely used indices that sum the scores of two sets of human rights—the physical integrity rights index and the empowerment index. The empowerment index is also included in the CIRIGHTS Data Project and has also been used in large-n empirical research in several social science disciplines. It is an additive index of the extent to which the government respects freedom of movement, freedom of speech, worker rights, political participation, and freedom of religion. The resulting index ranges from 0 (no respect) to 14 (full respect). As was the case for the Physical Integrity Rights Index, higher scores indicate more respect for a particular category of rights.

Table 3.2 shows that, for all human rights included in the CIRIGHTS Data Project, the critics of China's policy towards the ethnic Uighurs had better average human rights scores than the defenders did. Let's take a closer look at the scores China is allegedly violating because of its detention

Table 3.2. Defenders vs. Critics of China's Treatment of the Ethnic Uighurs, 2013–2017*

Human Right (range of scores)	Defenders' Average Scores	Critics' Average Scores	Difference (C – D)
Physical Integrity Rights Index (0–8)	3.2	7.6	4.4
Disappearance (0–2)	1.3	2.0	0.7
Extrajudicial Killing (0–2)	0.9	2.0	1.1
Political Imprisonment (0–2)	0.5	2.0	1.5
Torture (0–2)	0.5	1.6	1.1
Empowerment Index (0–14)	4.3	12.3	8.0
Freedom of Religion (0–2)	0.6	1.5	0.9
Freedom of Speech (0–2)	0.3	1.5	1.2
Electoral Self-Determination (0–2)	0.6	2.0	1.4
Freedom of Assembly and Assoc. (0–2)	0.4	1.9	1.5
Workers' Rights (0–2)	0.5	1.4	0.9
Freedom of Foreign Movement (0–2)	0.9	2.0	1.1
Freedom of Domestic Movement (0–2)	1.0	2.0	1.0
Independence of the Judiciary (0–2)	0.3	1.9	1.6
Women's Economic Rights (0–2)	0.8	2.4	1.6
Women's Political Rights (0–3)	2.0	2.7	0.7

*Note: A higher score indicates more respect for human rights.

program. A difference of more than one is very large, since the scores for individual human rights, in almost all cases, range from 0 to 2. The size of the difference between the defenders and critics is the greatest (1.5) for the right to be protected from political imprisonment and for respecting freedom of assembly and association. It is still a substantial 1.2 for respecting freedom of speech and press and 1.0 for respecting freedom of domestic movement. The difference is still substantial at 0.9, but smallest, for freedom of religion.

It is not surprising, therefore, that the size of the difference for the average CIRIGHTS physical integrity index score, which ranges from 0 to 8, between the critics (7.6) and the defenders (3.2) is very large (4.4). It is more than twice the score of the defenders. Similarly, the size of the difference between the average CIRIGHTS empowerment index score, which ranges from 0 to 14, is a whopping 8. Now we take a step back to explain how the numerical scores are generated.

The CIRIGHTS Data Project

The first step of any quantitative methodology is to define important concepts to be investigated. The next step is to transform concepts into variables by "operationalizing" them. Operationalizing a concept into a variable is a process whereby the different degrees, quantities, or types of a concept are assigned numbers. This is also called "measurement." The actual value a variable is assigned is known as a "score." In the example above, the country, China and defenders of China's policy toward the Muslim Uighurs, scored low in 2017 on all measures of respect for human rights included in the CIRIGHTS Data Project.

Ideally, a measure should be valid, replicable, and transparent. A valid measure is one where the score accurately reflects the underlying concept. A replicable variable is one that produces the same score when different people apply an identical measurement procedure to identical information. It is replicable if this process results in identical scores being assigned. Besides being valid and reliable, the measurement procedure should be transparent. That is, it should be clearly explained to the point that it could easily be repeated by others. If indices are produced by aggregating component scores, it should be possible to examine and analyze the scores of each of the components and to be able to reproduce the index score.

Evaluating the degree to which a government respects any particular human right is the subject of legitimate disagreement because scholars and policy makers rarely agree over what it would require for a government to fully protect any particular human right. Jack Donnelly (2013) has noted that there is widespread support for all or nearly all human rights in the abstract, but widespread disagreement over the interpretation of what full respect for each right would require.

Even detailed definitions of human rights violations contained in specialized human rights agreements—such as the Convention against Torture and Other Cruel, Inhuman, or Degrading Treatment or Punishment (1984) and the Convention on the Prevention and Punishment of the Crime of Genocide (1948)—do not generate universal agreement about whether a particular practice or incident in a society constitutes an act of torture or an instance of genocide. For example, between 2002 and 2004, the US government made a strong but ultimately unsuccessful effort to convince the domestic and international community that waterboarding (simulated drowning) did not meet the definition of torture under the UN Convention against Torture.

To advance the pursuit of theory building and evidence-based policy making, many organizations and individual scholars have developed quantitative measures of the level of government respect for many types of human rights (Apodaca 2014). The most widely used standards-based human rights measures of government respect for physical integrity rights are the annual scores for all countries of the world produced by the CIRIGHTS Data Project, Freedom House (FH), the Political Terror Scale (PTS) Project, and the Varieties of Democracy (VDEM) Project. All four human rights data projects focus primarily on government respect for political and civil human rights, but the CIRIGHTS and VDEM projects also includes some measures of other human rights such as women's rights and worker rights.

This emphasis on measuring first-generation rights exists for several reasons. First, debates among scholars surrounding what constitutes a violation of these rights are more advanced than second- and third-generation rights. This is in part due to the focus of early human rights research and activism on this first generation of rights. Second, there is far more information available for a global sample of countries produced annually for first-generation rights compared to others. Without access to information about potential violations of other rights, it is difficult to produce measures that are valid, replicable, and transparent. For example, annual Amnesty International reports cover first generation rights for almost all countries of the world, but their discussions of economic rights are often sporadic and missing for many countries from year to year. This is not to say it is impossible to measure these rights, but that the amount of work needed to measure them tends to be much higher. To us this is a missed opportunity as human rights are interdependent. The disproportionate focus on first-generation rights in the quantitative literature on human rights has hampered our ability to learn more about human rights and given us an incomplete story of what drives violations by focusing on a limited set of rights.

The CIRIGHTS Data Project has produced new annual scores for all countries of the world using the CIRI methodology from 2012 to the present. The CIRIGHTS project includes quantitative scores for 14 human rights included in human rights treaties and the scores for two indices. The 14 human rights and two indices are listed in table 3.2 above. Like the CIRI project, the CIRIGHTS Data Project measures the strength of actual national government practices protecting human rights relative to the requirements of relevant international human rights law. The project is in the process of adding scores for additional human rights and, in some cases where adequate information is available, scores for the strength of domestic laws *and* the strength of actual government practices. The team's long-term goal is to annually measure all internationally recognized human rights and to use both human and machine-assisted coding procedures to produce scores. In the empirical section of this paper, two CIRIGHTS indices—the physical integrity index and the empowerment index—are compared for small, medium-sized, and large population nation states.

The methodology we use for quantifying human rights is called "content analysis" or "textual analysis." It is a standard methodology in many social science fields for studying the content of oral or written communication. According to Neuendorf (2002), content analysis provides a way to summarize the meaning of text by assigning a numerical score. The process of converting text to numerical scores is referred to as "coding." Coding guidelines describe the rules one should use to assign quantitative scores after reading the texts.

The numerical scores produced using content analysis allow for statistical analysis of messages relying on the scientific method including attention to reliability, validity, replicability, and hypothesis testing. A human rights indicator is valid if it measures what it is supposed to measure. For example, if a country's government is scored as "meeting the international standard" for protecting its people from torture, that government should not have practiced torture at all in the year in question.

The CIRIGHTS Data Project relies on humans who read the reports, and who use detailed coding guidelines to assign the scores. Researchers who produce Freedom House, Political Terror Scale, and VDEM scores also use human coders who use different coding guidelines. Some newer projects use computer programs to "read" the text and assign the scores. For example, a project by Bagozzi and Koren (2017) uses machine learning to fill in the missing identity of atrocity perpetrators in the US Political Instability Task Force World Atrocity Dataset, which itself is a fairly new data source.

For the human rights currently in the CIRIGHTS data set, coders consult one or two written reports of government human rights performance and apply coding rules derived from international law. One of the reports coders use to quantify nearly all rights currently in the data set is the annual US Department of State's *Country Reports on Human Rights Practices*. Coders also use the *Amnesty International Annual Report to* make decisions about government practices to prevent torture, disappearances, political imprisonment, and extra-judicial killing. Since 1999, coders have used the USSD *International Religious Freedom Report* to code the degree of freedom of religion allowed in each country. Since 2000, they have used the US Department of State's *Trafficking in Persons Report.* These reports provide an expanded version of material that had been included in the *Country Reports* in previous years.

One important issue with using text sources like the State Department reports or Amnesty reports is identifying potential sources of bias. Work by Poe, Carey, and Vazquez (2001) for example found that US State Department reports were biased in favor of allies and against leftist regimes in the 1970s and early 1980s. However, by the 1990s this bias had largely disappeared. Similarly, Hill, Moore, and Mukherjee (2013) found that NGOs like Amnesty International sometimes exaggerate violations in order to achieve organizational goals like increasing membership and donations. Recent work on this issue (Simmons 2009; Wood, Gibney, and Haschke 2016; Cordell, Clay, Fariss, Wood, and Wright 2018) shows that it is important to be aware of these potential biases in all reports. For example, Cordell et al. (2018) find evidence that under the Trump administration many human rights issues were cut from the report, such as those related to women, reproduction, racism, refugees, and LGBTQ+ communities, among others. One reason this alteration is so important is because there are few large-n measures of these particular rights for countries around the world and, because of this decision, it will be even harder to develop them in the future.

These issues are always present with data and have always led to caution around interpretations of the data. However, the studies above used quantitative methods to identify such bias, its magnitude, which countries and rights it applied to, and how worried we should be about it. In short, quantification can produce not only data, but a sense of how confident we should be that the data is correct. One reason the CIRIGHTS dataset uses a 0–2 or 0–3 scale is because we acknowledge this bias and do not believe there is enough reliable information to create a larger scale from 1 to 10 or 0 to 100. By using a smaller scale, we minimize the error of our measures. This is also one of the reasons that the use of data should be driven by theory. Looking at data alone can be misleading, but when used to test theories it can be useful for identifying weaknesses and strengths of competing theories.

Why Limit the Number of Text Sources?

Consulting a greater number of sources *may* make a score more valid, but it will also make it less replicable by others who apply the same coding rules to the same set of texts. For many, if not most, countries, there are a large number of potential sources of information about particular human rights practices. There are monographs about particular countries that contain human rights–relevant information. In recent years, there also are many organizations that prepare country-specific reports about certain human rights practices for all or nearly all countries of the world. In principle, if there was no limit on labor resources, each score could be based on all available information about protection of each human right for each country in each year. Of course, there is a practical limitation on the labor necessary to generate human rights scores.

In deciding which and how many sources to consult, our goal is to (1) maximize validity of scores without sacrificing any or much replicability and (2) to maintain the ability to make comparisons of a particular nation's scores over time. To maximize both goals, all of the CIRIGHTS scores are determined by coders who read only one or two highly respected texts. Human rights reports produced by different organizations or individual scholars focus on different criteria of evaluation and show different biases when evaluating the adequacy of national practices protecting a particular human right. Amnesty international and the US State Department are both biased in their evaluations, but in different ways (Poe et al., 2001). The CIRIGHTS coding rules instruct coders about how to handle the rare but explicit differences between the evaluations produced by these two organizations. The co-directors of the predecessor CIRI project long ago decided that there was a net benefit to reading both reports because the validity of scores could be improved without seriously sacrificing replicability.

On the other hand, consider another report that could have been used as a text source but was not because the benefit of doing so did not outweigh the cost. The International Trade Union Confederation (ITUC) has produced written country reports for most countries of the world evaluating the adequacy of national practices protecting the rights of workers to form trade unions and to bargain collectively with employers. These reports have been produced annually since 2014. They present the perspective of labor union leaders, and, as a result, they are often more critical of national government efforts to protect workers than the reports produced by the US State Department, a diplomatic organization. It is impossible to determine which report provides a more accurate or valid evaluation of each government's protection of worker rights. Having coders read both reports as the basis for assigning their scores arguably would produce a compromise between two standards of evaluation that would be replicable and more valid.

However, with the two exceptions noted above concerning religious freedom and human trafficking, the CIRIGHTS Data Project does not use new sources of information about respect for a particular human right if that source is only available for later years. The problem with adding or changing text sources is that the scores produced after new reports became available might be systematically different from those produced earlier. Thus, comparisons of scores over time to see whether human rights practices had improved or declined would be distorted so much that they might be useless. For example, If CIRIGHTS coders used ITUC reports to assign worker rights scores when the ITUC reports became available in 2012, then the scores of many countries would be lower after 2012, even if actual government protections of workers had not changed. In addition, ITUC does not report upon as many countries as our other sources do. So, if we used ITUC reports beginning in 2012, the countries not evaluated by ITUC would be likely to have higher scores than those with identical practices that are not covered by the ITUC report. If ITUC scores had been available for almost all countries beginning in 1981, the global averages would have been lower for all years, but temporal trends would still be meaningful.

For this reason, the CIRIGHTS Data Project tries to use textual source materials that have produced high quality annual evaluations of human rights practices for all or almost all countries of the world since 1981. Unfortunately, country-specific human rights reports were not available for most countries of the world before the year 2000. Introducing new reports as text sources in the middle of the time period covered by the scores produced by the project complicate or even may eliminate our ability to track long-term trends for individual countries or groups of countries.

Some scholars even argue that, in all cases, more information, including information from a greater variety of source texts, causes coders to assign lower scores. This problem is usually referred to as the "human rights information paradox" (Cingranelli and Filippov 2018). It is impossible to conclusively determine whether this argument is correct. But it is likely that the more information coders have to read, the greater the likelihood that coders may miss important information and assign a score that is inconsistent with the coding guidelines. "Measurement error," the difference between the "true" score and the recorded score, would increase.

Data Visualization: Smaller-Population Societies Have Better Human Rights Practices

In this section, we illustrate the usefulness of quantification for visualizing patterns of human rights behavior. Identifying patterns often proves useful for theory building. We use the CIRIGHTS data to construct figures showing that the governments of smaller population nations tend to provide significantly greater respect for most internationally recognized human rights than larger nations do. The figures also show that smaller nations are more likely to be improving their human rights practices.

First, we must define "small states." International organizations and theoretical studies rely on various thresholds to distinguish between small states and large ones (Briguglio 2018). A commonly used definition of a small country is that it has a population of less than 1.5 million. It is the definition we use in the figures included below. By this definition, there are 45 sovereign small states. We sort countries into two other categories based on their population size: medium-sized countries have a population size more than 1.5 million, but less than 25 million people, and large-population countries are those with a population size above 25 million people. In 2017 there were 45 small, 95 medium, and 52 large countries in the world. Population data comes from the World Bank's World Development Indicators. The patterns displayed below are robust in the sense that they would be produced even if we used slightly different cut-off points for the three population size categories.

To save space, we illustrate the patterns we found using the physical integrity and empowerment indices from the CIRIGHTS Data Project. The trends are similar for each of the individual human rights included in these indices. In the two graphs below, we look at how human rights compare among the three groups of countries categorized according to population size. We expect that, as population size increases, we will see lower scores on both human rights indices. Higher scores indicate greater respect for these rights. We also expect stronger improving trends for smaller countries. We compare the index scores for the three categories of countries between 1981 and 2017.

Figure 3.1 visualizes the patterns for the three groups of countries for empowerment rights. The vertical (Y) axis indicates the empowerment index score. The horizontal (X) axis indicates the year those scores are being averaged for each of the three groups of countries. The average score on this index for each group is indicated by a line. Average scores for small countries are shown with a solid line, medium countries with a dot-dash line, and large countries with a dotted line.

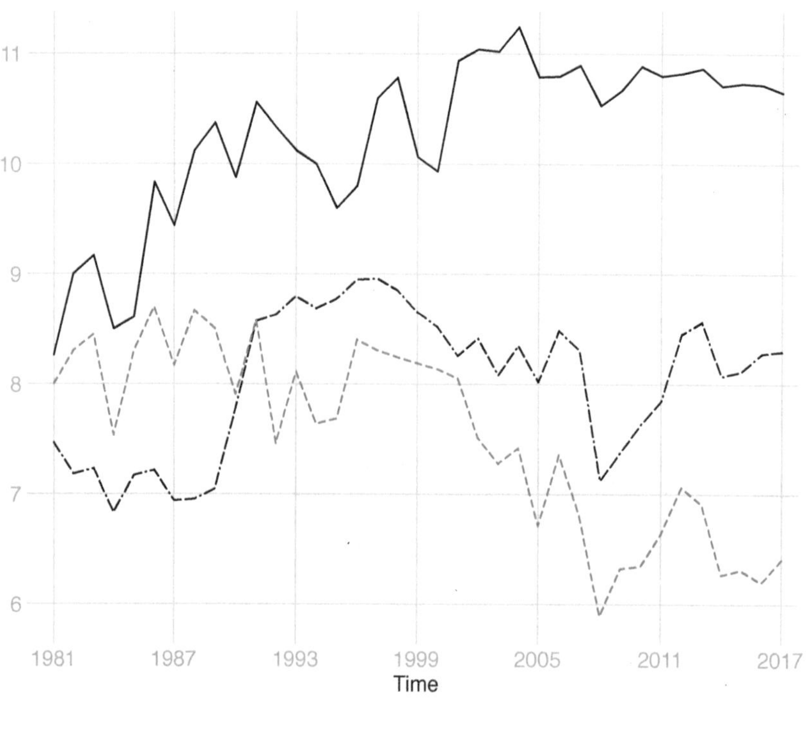

Figure 3.1. Empowerment rights and population size.

For every year on the graph, small population countries have significantly higher human rights scores than medium and large countries. Average global empowerment scores for small countries also improved from 1981–2016. The pattern is almost as clear for medium- and large-sized countries. Between 1981 and 1990, medium- and large-sized countries had similar empowerment scores, though large countries scored a little higher throughout that period. In 1991, the two groups of countries began to diverge and show the expected pattern: medium countries had higher scores than large countries and an improving trend. Empowerment rights actually declined in large countries.

Population size also appears to be a significant predictor of a country's score on respect for physical integrity rights. As population size increases, respect for physical integrity rights decreases. Figure 3.2 below examines physical integrity rights: extra-judicial killing, disappearance, political impris-

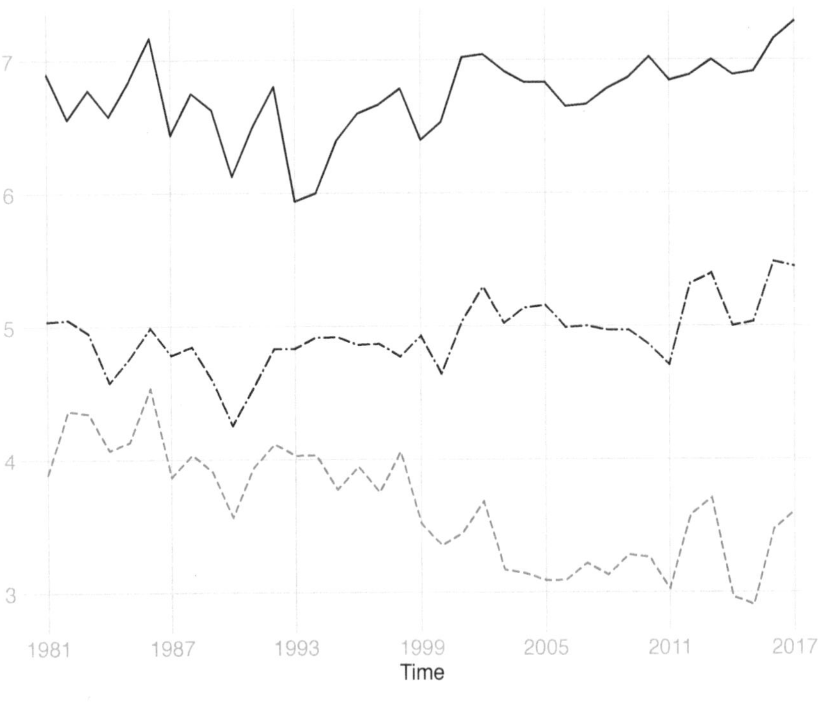

Figure 3.2. Physical integrity rights and population size.

onment, and torture. The vertical (Y) axis indicates the average score on the physical integrity. The horizontal (X) axis indicates the year.

The patterns for physical integrity rights are even clearer than they were for empowerment rights. Small population countries scored significantly better than medium and large countries for every year. Medium-size countries scored significantly better than large countries for every year as well. The gap between scores for medium and large countries has also increased over time. As was the case for empowerment rights, medium-size countries began to separate themselves from large countries at a higher rate beginning in 1991. Throughout the 1981–2016 period, the gap between small countries and medium countries was far greater than the gap between medium and large countries. Small countries maintained a very high level of respect for physical integrity rights for the entire period. Medium countries experienced some improvement over time, but government respect for physical integrity rights declined in large countries over this period.

Figure 3.3 displays scores for the most recent year we have collected data: 2017. For empowerment rights respect, small countries score 2.4 points higher than medium-size countries and 4.3 points higher than large countries. Medium-size countries scored 1.9 points higher on average than large countries. This pattern holds for physical integrity rights as well. The average physical integrity rights score for small countries is 7.3, which is

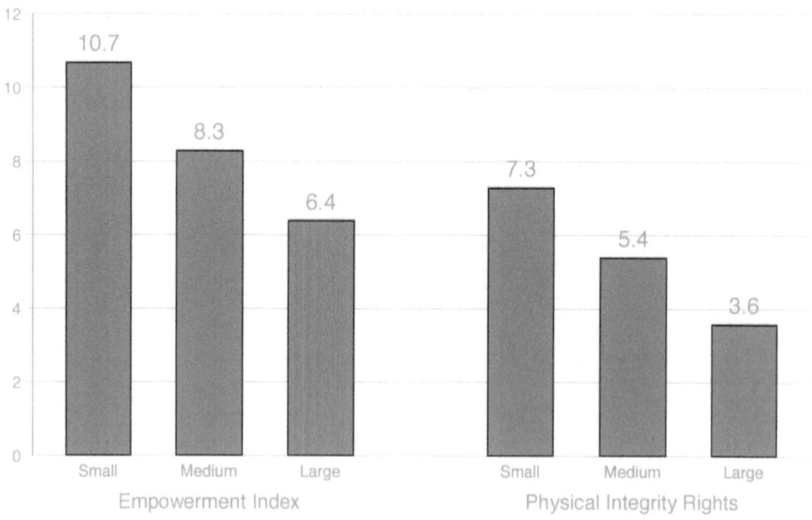

Figure 3.3. Average human rights respect in 2017.

associated with full respect for three out of four physical integrity rights, and moderate to full respect for the final right. This suggests that on average small countries do not see the government using violence against citizens. Medium-size countries score 1.9 points lower on the physical integrity scale than small countries. Large countries score 3.7 points lower on the physical integrity scale than small countries and 1.8 points lower than medium-size countries.

Taken together, these results indicate that population size is a very good predictor of human rights scores. The use of statistical techniques such as multiple regression indicate that these differences are meaningful even when statistically accounting for differences among the groups due to different levels of democracy and economic development (Cingranelli, Fajardo-Heyward, and Filippov 2014).

Why Do Small States Respect Human Rights?

Favorable conditions for human rights protection exist "when countries are at peace and when they already enjoy some institutional, economic, and social facilitating conditions for democracy" (Hopgood et al. 2017, 2). Those favorable conditions tend to prevail in smaller population countries. Smaller states tend to have open economies that are highly dependent on international trade and cooperation (Briguglio 2018). It makes smaller states more vulnerable to external influences than larger states. The international influences might successfully pressure national elites in smaller states to follow the rule of law and their international obligations (Ott 2000; Olsson and Hansson 2011). It might also indirectly explain why smaller countries have better and improving human rights scores.

Overall, smaller states tend to have high-quality democratic institutions and enjoy "good governance," with efficient and accountable bureaucracy (Oostindie and Sutton 2006). Several studies have found that smaller states are more likely to be democratic (Anckar 2008; Diamond and Tsalik 1999; Hadenius 1992; Ott 2000; Srebrnik 2004). A smaller state tends to have a homogenous population that is interconnected and actively engaged in domestic politics. Smaller size directly enhances a spirit of cooperativeness and accommodation, making the country easier to govern (Veenendaal 2020). Political elites of smaller societies are also more interconnected and less likely to view politics as a zero-sum game (Lijphart 1977). Political disputes rarely lead to large-scale conflict (Samy et al. 2008).

Many smaller states are relatively prosperous economically. Armstrong and Read (2006) have demonstrated that smaller states significantly outperform larger states in terms of economic growth, with a disproportionate number of states with populations less than three million occupying the "upper middle" and "high" income World Bank categories. Gaps between formal promises to respect human rights and practices can occur because of a lack of capacity and economic resources to implement human rights rules (Chayes and Chayes 1993; Cingranelli et al. 2014). Smaller states also tend to have a lower level of economic inequality (Oostindie and Sutton 2006). Both wealth and economic equality have been found to be associated with better human rights practices (Landman and Larizza 2009).

Finally, the theoretical argument that international and domestic threats lead to repression is well developed in the literature and is relevant here. When political regimes are threatened internally or externally, their political leaders have to decide how much repression to use for political survival. Leaders become repressive if they believe that the strength of domestic threats or international threats or both combined is equal to or greater than the strength of the regime they wish to protect. If it is, they are likely to use repression of human rights as one of the strategies to redress an undesirable imbalance in the strength/threat ratio (Gartner and Regan 1996; Poe and Tate 1994). Absent threat, such models predict that the state would respect human rights. On the other hand, theoretically even the best democracies could show deterioration of their human right records in times of extraordinary challenges (Rosenau 2002; Conrad et al. 2018).

Small population states may have better human rights practices mainly because they experience relatively low levels of domestic and international political violence. On the other hand, larger population countries might have less perfect records due to their relatively frequent engagement in domestic and international conflicts. For example, an increased use of torture led to lower physical integrity rights scores for many large democracies in the most recent period (Carver and Handley 2017; Conrad et al. 2018).

Discussion

In their classic study *Size and Democracy*, Robert Dahl and Edward Tufte (1973) discuss the disadvantages and benefits of small nations for creating and sustaining democratic regimes. They noted that small population societies can more easily fall prey to a "tyranny of the majority," a lower level of state capacity and suboptimal level of public goods provisions. However, they concluded that these weaknesses are in most cases counterbalanced by the advantages of small states' other typical conditions. We have used the numerical human rights scores produced by the CIRIGHTS Data Project to show that small nations also tend to have advantages leading them to produce superior human rights practices and to improve their human rights performance over time.

This graph of trends in respect for empowerment rights for the three population size categories of countries (figure 3.2) showed strong support for the notion that as population size increases, a government's respect for empowerment human rights decreases. It also raises questions about why the pattern was not fully evident until 1991, which marks the end of the Cold War and the beginning of a period of rapidly increasing economic globalization. These questions should be pursued in future research.

In the previous section, we asked why smaller population states provided greater respect for most human rights. Though we provided some possible answers, future research should further examine those and other reasons why small population countries tend to outperform large population countries in their human rights practices. Population size should be treated as a theoretically important determinant of human rights practices of countries. And future research should give even more attention to human rights policies and practices in large population countries, where human rights practices of all kinds are worse and are declining.

A large country focus for human rights scholars is particularly important, because most of the world's people live in a few large countries. The largest countries in the world in terms of population are China and India. Each has a population of well over a billion, and together they account for approximately 35% of the world's population. The United States comes in as the third most populous country in the world with just under 325 million people. All three countries now have significant human rights problems and have had a long history of government human rights abuses. A large country focus also is necessary because the policies that work well in smaller countries may be ineffective in the largest ones. Therefore, policy implications that emerge from statistical analysis of the effects of policy interventions using all countries of the world as units of analysis may be misleading when applied to the largest countries.

Still another reason to focus on large countries is that they are among the most influential in the world in international fora where human rights norms are developed and enforced. Unless their own human rights practices improve, they are likely to be reluctant to lead the way towards greater international pressure to improve human rights. Brazil, Russia, India, and China, generally regarded as the four major emerging economies that are expected to dominate in the 21st century, are all in the top ten most populous countries, indicating how important population size is to their economic expansion. The leaders of small states have been among the most persistent and energetic voices promoting more and stronger international human rights norms in international fora such as the United Nations, but their voices are much weaker on the world stage. China and Russia, both members of the UN Security Council, often obstruct international interventions to improve human rights. The United States has also reduced its support for human rights initiatives at the United Nations and in other international fora.

One "out-of-the-box" implication of these findings is that, other things being equal, people who live in large population countries with poor human rights practices could be better off if their countries broke into smaller jurisdictions. For example, Russian human rights might be better if Russia broke into smaller jurisdictions. The smaller states that emerged also would probably advocate for better human rights globally. Qualitative scholars should be able to contribute to this discussion. They may be able to derive lessons from the study of particular nations that have broken into smaller parts (such as Czechoslovakia, the USSR, or the Sudan), and cases where two territories or states have been combined (because of colonial conquest or territorial conflicts for example). Qualitative scholars who have conducted in-depth studies of politics of particular small-scale societies may also provide insights we have missed. As with many other research questions, collaboration between quantitative and qualitative scholars will help us to better understand the human rights consequences of population size.

Works Cited

Anckar, Carsten. 2008. "Size, Islandness, and Democracy: A Global Comparison." *International Political Science Review* 29, no. 4: 433–459.

Apodaca, Clair. 2014. "Human Rights Measurement." In *The Sage Handbook of Human Rights: Two Volume Set*, 840–856. New York: Sage.

Armstrong, Harvey W., and R. Read. 2006. "Insularity, Remoteness, Mountains and Archipelagoes: A Combination of Challenges Facing Small States." *Asia Pacific Viewpoint* 47, no. 1: 79–92.

Bagozzi, Benjamin E., and Ore Koren. 2017. Using Machine Learning Methods to Identify Atrocity Perpetrators. Paper read at 2017 IEEE International Conference on Big Data (Big Data).

Bello-Villarino, Jose-Miguel, and Ramona Vijeyarasa. 2017. "The Indicator Fad: How Quantifiable Measurement Can Work Hand-in-Hand with Human Rights-a Response to Sally Engle Merry's the *Seductions of Quantification.*" *New York University Journal of International Law and Politics* 50, no. 3: 985–1020.

Briguglio, Lino. 2018. *Handbook of Small States: Economic, Social and Environmental Issues*. New York: Routledge.

Brysk, Alison. 1994. "The Politics of Measurement: The Contested Count of the Disappeared in Argentina." *Human Rights Quarterly* 16, no. 4: 676–692.

Carver, Richard, and Lisa Handley. 2017. *Does Torture Prevention Work?* New York: Oxford University Press.

Chayes, Abram, and Antonia Handler Chayes. 1993. "On Compliance." *International Organization* 47, no. 2: 175–205.

Cingranelli, David, Mikhail Filippov, and Brendan Skip Mark. 2021. The CIRIGHTS Dataset. Version 2021.01.21. The Binghamton University Human Right Institute, www.binghamton.edu/institutes/hri/.

Cingranelli, David, Paola Fajardo-Heyward, and Mikhail Filippov. 2014. "Principals, Agents and Human Rights." *British Journal of Political Science* 44, no. 3: 605–630.

Cingranelli, David, and Mikhail Filippov. 2018. "Are Human Rights Practices Improving?" *American Political Science Review* 112, no. 4: 1083–1089.

Cingranelli, David L., and David L. Richards. 1999a. "Measuring the Level, Pattern, and Sequence of Government Respect for Physical Integrity Rights." *International Studies Quarterly* 43, no. 2: 407–417.

Cingranelli, David L., and David L. Richards. 1999b. "Respect for Human Rights after the End of the Cold War." *Journal of Peace Research* 36, no. 5: 511–534.

Conrad, Courtenay R., Sarah E. Croco, Brad T. Gomez, and Will H. Moore. 2018. "Threat Perception and American Support for Torture." *Political Behavior* 40, no. 4: 989–1009.

Cordell, Rebecca, et al. 2020. "Changing standards or political whim? Evaluating changes in the content of US State Department Human Rights Reports following presidential transitions." *Journal of Human Rights* 19, no. 1: 3–18.

Dahl, Robert Alan, and Edward R. Tufte. 1973. *Size and Democracy*. Stanford: Stanford University Press.

Davenport, Christian, and David A. Armstrong II. 2004. "Democracy and the Violation of Human Rights: A Statistical Analysis from 1976 to 1996." *American Journal of Political Science* 48, no. 3: 538–554.

Davenport, Christian, and Allan C. Stam. 2009. "What Really Happened in Rwanda?" *Miller-McCune*, October 6.

Davis, Kevin, Angelina Fisher, Benedict Kingsbury, and Sally Engle Merry. 2012. *Governance by Indicators: Global Power through Classification and Rankings.* New York: Oxford University Press.

Diamond, Larry, and Svetlana Tsalik. 1999. "Size and Democracy: The Case for Decentralization." In *Developing Democracy: Toward Consolidation*, edited by Larry Diamond, 117–160. Baltimore, MD: Johns Hopkins University Press.

Donnelly, Jack. 1999. "The Social Construction of International Human Rights." In *Human Rights in Global Politics*, edited by Tim Dunne and Nicholas J. Wheeler. Cambridge: Cambridge University Press.

Foot, Rosemary. 2000. *Rights Beyond Borders: The Global Community and the Struggle over Human Rights in China.* Oxford: Oxford University Press.

Fukuda-Parr, Sakiko, Terra Lawson-Remer, and Susan Randolph. 2011. Serf Index Methodology: Version 2011.1, Technical Note.

Gartner, Scott Sigmund, and Patrick M. Regan. 1996. "Threat and Repression: The Non-Linear Relationship between Government and Opposition Violence." *Journal of Peace Research* 33, no. 3: 273–287.

Hadenius, Axel. 1992. *Democracy and Development.* Cambridge: Cambridge University Press.

Hafner-Burton, Emilie M. 2008. "Sticks and Stones: Naming and Shaming the Human Rights Enforcement Problem." *International Organization* 62, no. 4: 689–716.

Hafner-Burton, Emilie M., and James Ron. 2009. "Seeing Double: Human Rights Impact through Qualitative and Quantitative Eyes." *World Politics* 61, no. 2: 360–401.

Hill Jr., Daniel W., Will H. Moore, and Bumba Mukherjee. 2013. "Information Politics Versus Organizational Incentives: When Are Amnesty International's 'Naming and Shaming' Reports Biased?" *International Studies Quarterly* 57, no. 2: 219–232.

Hopgood, Stephen, Jack Snyder, and Leslie Vinjamuri. 2017. *Human Rights Futures.* Cambridge: Cambridge University Press.

Landman, Todd, and Marco Larizza. 2009. "Inequality and Human Rights: Who Controls What, When, and How." *International Studies Quarterly* 53, no. 3: 715–736.

Lijphart, Arend. 1977. *Democracy in Plural Societies: A Comparative Exploration.* New York: Yale University Press.

Mau, Steffen. 2019. *The Metric Society: On the Quantification of the Social.* New York: John Wiley & Sons.

Merry, Sally Engle. 2016. *The Seductions of Quantification: Measuring Human Rights, Gender Violence, and Sex Trafficking.* Chicago: University of Chicago Press.

Merry, Sally Engle. 2018. "Measuring the World: Indicators, Human Rights, and Global Governance." In *The Palgrave Handbook of Indicators in Global Governance*, 477–501. New York: Springer.

Neuendorf, Kimberly A. 2002. *The Content Analysis Guidebook.* New York: Sage.

Olsson, Ola, and Gustav Hansson. 2011. "Country Size and the Rule of Law: Resuscitating Montesquieu." *European Economic Review* 55, no. 5: 613–629.

Oostindie, Gert, and Paul Sutton. 2006. "Small Scale and Quality of Governance." Leiden: KITLV.

Osterlind, Steven J. 2019. *The Error of Truth: How History and Mathematics Came Together to Form Our Character and Shape Our Worldview*. New York: Oxford University Press.

Ott, Dana. 2018. *Small Is Democratic: An Examination of State Size and Democratic Development*. New York: Routledge.

Payne, Caroline L., and M. Rodwan Abouharb. 2016. "The International Covenant on Civil and Political Rights and the Strategic Shift to Forced Disappearance." *Journal of Human Rights* 15, no. 2: 163–188.

Poe, Steven C., and C. Neal Tate. 1994. "Repression of Human Rights to Personal Integrity in the 1980s: A Global Analysis." *American Political Science Review* 88, no. 4: 853–872.

Poe, Steven C., Sabine C. Carey, and Tanya C. Vazquez. 2001. "How Are These Pictures Different? A Quantitative Comparison of the Us State Department and Amnesty International Human Rights Reports, 1976–1995." *Human Rights Quarterly* 23, no. 3: 650–677.

Rosenau, James N. 2002. "The Drama of Human Rights in a Turbulent, Globalized World." In *Globalization and Human Rights*, edited by Alison Brysk, 148. Los Angeles: University of California Press.

Samy, Yiagadeesen, David Carment, Stewart Prest, and Jean-François Gagné. 2008. "Small States, Resilience and Governance." In *Small States and the Pillars of Economic Resilience*. Malta and London: Islands and Small States Institute/ Commonwealth Secretariat. 217–242.

Sikkink, Kathryn. 1993. "Human Rights, Principled Issue-Networks, and Sovereignty in Latin America." *International Organization* 47, no. 3: 411–441.

Sikkink, Kathryn. 2004. *Mixed Signals: Us Human Rights Policy and Latin America*. Ithaca: Cornell University Press.

Sikkink, Kathryn, and Lisa L. Martin. 1993. "Us Policy and Human Rights in Argentina and Guatemala, 1973–1980." In *Double-Edged Diplomacy: International Bargaining and Domestic Politics*, edited by Peter Evans, Harold Jacobson, and Robert Putnam, 330–362. Berkeley: University of California Press.

Simmons, Beth A. 2009. *Mobilizing for Human Rights: International Law in Domestic Politics*. New York: Cambridge University Press.

Srebrnik, Henry. 2004. "Small Island Nations and Democratic Values." *World Development* 32, no. 2: 329–341.

Steiner, Nils D. 2016. "Comparing Freedom House Democracy Scores to Alternative Indices and Testing for Political Bias: Are Us Allies Rated as More Democratic by Freedom House?" *Journal of Comparative Policy Analysis: Research and Practice* 18, no. 4: 329–349.

Taschereau Mamers, Danielle. 2018. "The Face and the Number: Memorial and Statistical Narratives in Auschwitz-Birkenau's Central Sauna Portrait Exhibit." *Photography and Culture* 11, no. 1: 41–59.

Veenendaal, Wouter. 2020. "Does Smallness Enhance Power-Sharing? Explaining Suriname's Multiethnic Democracy." *Ethnopolitics* 19, no. 1: 64–84.

Verpoorten, Marijke. 2014. "Rwanda: Why Claim That 200,000 Tutsi Died in the Genocide Is Wrong." *African Arguments*.

Wood, Reed M., Mark Gibney, and Peter Haschke. 2016. "Evaluating Global Patterns of Abuse with the Political Terror Scale." *Peace and Conflict*.

Chapter Four

Forensic Science or Junk Science?

How the Justice System Violates Human Rights When Science Is Misused or Misunderstood

ELIZABETH A. DIGANGI

> The law's greatest dilemma in its heavy reliance on forensic evidence . . . concerns the question of whether—and to what extent—there is science in any given forensic science discipline.
>
> —*Strengthening Forensic Science in the United States*

Using science to help solve criminal investigations in the West has a storied history. The narrative arguably showcases Sherlock Holmes at its inception, who has become one of the world's most famous fictional crime solvers; and who more than a century after his creation continues to find his way into anglophone media on the basis of his uncanny abilities to analyze crime scene evidence. Sir Arthur Conan Doyle's creation of this iconic character in the late 19th century coincided with the development of laboratories exclusively for the purpose of supporting investigative efforts via scientific analysis of evidence by law enforcement agencies, first in Europe, then in the United States.[1] In the century plus since, forensic science laboratories have been established in all industrialized countries and many developing ones. Likewise, the public's fascination with crime solving has not abated since Doyle's books began populating the shelves in Victorian England. As a result of fictionalized accounts and infamous cases, forensic science has become enormously popular and accessible to the general public, as evidenced by numerous examples in the entertainment media and the increase in students interested in such a career. Contemporary examples, both fictional and nonfictional, include the decades-long and continuing popularity of the multiple renditions of two American television series: *CSI: Crime Scene Investigation* and *Law & Order*, along with their cousins;[2] in addition to the real-life pop culture phenomena that became the OJ Simpson and Casey Anthony murder trials in the late 20th and early 21st centuries. The public's perception of forensic science is therefore that of a fast-tracked, cutting-edge, and dynamic set of fields.[3]

However, a more troubling reality underlies this perception. In 2005, given concerning reports of substantial case backlogs, the United States Congress directed the National Academy of Sciences (NAS) to form a special committee to investigate the current state of forensic science (Senate Report No. 109-88 [2005]). The resulting landmark report identifies "serious problems" which include, among other things, flawed or nonexistent applications of the scientific method; misinterpretation of scientific evidence and results; inadequate, incorrect, or nonexistent generation of error rates; and ignorance of the possibility of bias and human error (NAS 2009, *xx*). Numerous examples abound; few, if any, forensic science disciplines are immune. This includes those primarily based on objective analyses, such as DNA, and those at least partially based on subjective analyses, such as fingerprints. The basic technology that underlies either type of analysis is that of the scientific method, a series of steps designed to logically structure scientific questions and analyses so that resulting interpretations are sound.

Objective analyses are those where a sample is analyzed by a machine or chemical test; the results generated typically include some threshold that indicates the composition of the sample and/or how frequently a sample with that composition would be found. For example, analysis of an unknown white powder would be done to indicate its composition; if it turns out to be an illegal drug such as cocaine, a further test would be done to ascertain what percentage of the sample is cocaine versus other substances. DNA analysis is also based on objective evaluation, done for positive identification of a deceased victim or to compare samples from the crime scene or victim to a suspect. Biological samples (blood, semen, saliva, etc.) are analyzed by a machine with the results often placed into a database. Note that both the drug and DNA examples are rooted in objective analysis, but the output must be interpreted by a human analyst, and this part of the process is often where problems may ensue. Certainly, analysis equipment can malfunction, and this is always a concern to mitigate, but several examples also exist where analysts behaved unethically and falsified results or misinterpreted evidence.[4]

Subjective analysis, on the other hand, is different because it relies upon an expert analyst's informed opinion about some characteristic of the evidence. Such an opinion is based upon the analyst's education of what particular evidence characteristics mean or indicate and their experience from analyzing a large number of cases or mock cases. Fingerprint analysis is one example: even though digital databases are used to narrow down possibilities, examiners are presented with the computer's choices and make subjective assessments about the strength of discriminating features that lead to their determination of matches (de Jongh et al. 2019).[5]

The NAS report led to the creation of a centralized organizational system for scientific working groups in the different forensic science disciplines, known as the Organization of Scientific Area Committees (OSAC), operated under the auspices of the National Institute of Standards and Technology. The different committees consist of subject matter experts who collaborate on assembling best practice documents for different techniques or theoretical underpinnings of each included forensic science specialty. However, some have argued such attempts at reform have not gone far enough (e.g., Mnookin 2018). This has been made further evident by a follow-up report commissioned by the Obama administration of the President's Council of Advisors on Science and Technology (PCAST), which found that many of the issues raised by the 2009 NAS report persisted, alarmingly to include whether common methods being presented in court are reliable and valid from a scientific standpoint (PCAST 2016). The 2017 disbanding by the Trump administration of the National Commission on Forensic Science (a 30-person advisory panel to the Justice Department consisting of scientists, attorneys, and members of the judiciary, initiated in 2013 as part of reform efforts following the NAS report) (Hsu 2017), compounds concerns that any reforms have been no more than "Band-Aids" (Mnookin 2018, 99).

Such issues are not purely academic and without consequence. A substantial number of people have been convicted in part on the strength of later-discovered erroneous forensic science techniques or interpretations and were later exonerated (Giannelli 1993; 2007; Garrett and Neufeld 2009).[6] The Innocence Project (a nongovernmental organization whose mission is criminal justice reform in part via securing exonerations for wrongfully convicted people) reported that of 360 DNA-based exonerations in the United States as of 2019, nearly half of those wrongful convictions had erroneous forensic science as a contributing factor; a further finding is that misleading or junk forensic science is the second-highest contributing factor to false convictions (Saks and Koehler 2005). Mnookin (2018, 107) properly notes the "human cost" to the use of incorrect science in the courtroom: on an individual level, some innocent people have been falsely imprisoned, in many cases for decades;[7] and on a societal level, some true perpetrators remain uncaught while potentially continuing to commit crimes.

In this chapter, I frame the use of junk science that supports criminal investigations as a human rights issue; with junk science defined as evidence analysis techniques which do not rest on a valid scientific foundation, the misapplication of methods, or the willful or ignorant misinterpretation of results. I begin by discussing how the right to a fair trial is violated by the continued use of junk science in the courts, and discuss how the general problems outlined by the NAS and PCAST reports continue to violate international standards for human rights.

Junk science as presented in the courtroom generally falls into two categories: (1) techniques that are presented as scientific despite the lack of any meaningful scientific foundation; and (2) supported techniques that are misapplied or misinterpreted (Mnookin 2018). I discuss throughout how such misrepresentations are not actually science *per se* from the standpoint of the technology used to produce science, because the scientific method (the foundation for all science) is not being followed. I present two case studies that illustrate each of the above fallacies, respectively: first, the use of bitemark analysis, and second, age determination of unaccompanied migrant teenagers using x-rays of the third molar (i.e., wisdom tooth).

Right to a Fair Trial

The Universal Declaration of Human Rights was adopted by the United Nations General Assembly in December 1948; its impetus was in part the horror of the abuses during the Holocaust and World War II (Ishay 1997). Article 3 deals with the right to life and liberty; and Articles 8 to 11 focus on provisions for a fair trial (Weissbrodt and Hallendorff 1999), and read in part:

> Article 10: *Everyone is entitled in full equality to a fair and public hearing . . . of any criminal charge against him.*
>
> Article 11: *Everyone charged with a penal offense has the right to be presumed innocent until proved guilty according to law in a public trial at which he has had all the guarantees necessary for his defense.*

The use of junk science to support criminal proceedings in court therefore violates the fair hearing section of Article 10, as the use of unvalidated methods or misinterpretations cannot be construed as a fair practice. Further, while those without means in the United States are assigned defense counsel, such public defenders often do not have the resources or time to mount the kind of defense that could include a complete dismantling and interrogation of any faulty forensic science analysis.[8] In addition, such admissions of testimony would also violate the latter portion of Article 11, as mounting a defense against what is essentially junk testimony would present a number of insurmountable challenges. Finally, those individuals falsely convicted in part on the strength of such testimony have had their right to liberty violated.

The Scientific Method as Basic Scientific and Technological Bedrock

The use of unverified techniques or misinterpretation of results is also a technology issue. Forensic science has embraced the benefits that advanced technology can have on evidence analysis, such as those involving microscopy techniques. However, with a few notable exceptions, overall forensic science has suffered from a general disregard of basic scientific tenets—tenets that logically structure any scientific endeavor. This is likely because forensic science in general has not had the same research culture that exists in academic science. It was conceived exclusively for law enforcement, rather than for the pursuit of knowledge that typifies the majority of the sciences (NAS 2009; Saks and Koehler 2005; Saks et al. 2016; Mnookin 2018). The National Research Council notes that there are several examples of ostensibly scientific evidentiary analysis that do not have uses beyond a criminal investigation context (NAS 2009). Further, depending on the specialization, many of its practitioners do not hold advanced degrees in science (NAS 2009; Saks and Koehler 2005; Mnookin 2018),[9] where they would have learned basic scientific principles such as the scientific method and where practice with its application would have been a major part of the curriculum.

The bedrock of all science is the scientific method, which involves a series of steps that are designed to disprove hypotheses (i.e., scientific guesses) based on observations of the natural world. The starting point is construction of a hypothesis indicating some difference or effect occurs upon application of a given test to an item of interest. Examples relevant to forensic science include hypotheses that an unknown powder is a particular controlled substance, that a fiber found on a victim could have come from a carpet in the suspect's home, that a suspect's weapon shot the bullet found at a crime scene, or that an injury to a person's body was caused by a particular type of object. At the same time, we construct an opposite hypothesis, known as the null hypothesis, which indicates that no difference or effect will occur upon application of the test. The results of the test we perform will provide support for this null hypothesis of no difference or effect *or* will allow us to reject it. This point regarding disproval of hypotheses is an important detail, and one that is often misunderstood. Our ultimate aim is to determine whether the null hypothesis can be disproven; if our test does so, this will in essence support the alternative hypothesis as being one *possible* explanation for the questions we have about the evidence.

Critically, we need to take as much care with interpreting the findings as we do with devising the hypotheses and designing the tests. Science rests on the law of parsimony; namely, that the simplest answer is most likely to be the correct one. Interpretations should logically follow from the results (DiGangi and Moore 2013), and conflicting or unclear results should be stated as indeterminate. This is particularly imperative for analyses of evidence where the interpretations are used in prosecutorial decisions and court proceedings.

Importantly, the steps of the scientific method also allow determination of whether a given technique is reliable (i.e., repeatable) and valid (i.e., gives the correct answer). Note that both elements are necessary: a test that cannot be repeated in the same way by multiple practitioners will not have any value; nor will a test that can be repeated in the same way but does not provide a correct answer (Saks et al. 2016). First, a hypothesis as to which sort of test could analyze the evidence in question would be devised. Second, that test would be carried out ideally multiple times on large enough samples to enable a determination as to whether or not it produces reliable and valid results. Third, based on these results the test would be accepted or rejected as a possible analysis technique. While the advent of DNA analysis led to multiple commissions and scientific studies examining the uniqueness of matches, techniques in many of the other forensic disciplines have not been subjected to similar scrutiny (Saks and Koehler, 2005). In several cases, only the first step as above has been carried out (i.e., hypothesizing which sort of test *could* analyze a given piece of evidence), without the subsequent and crucial steps of designing validation tests for the analytical technique and determining its error rates.

A related step that has also been typically neglected is the determination of population characteristics for common types of evidence so that juries can properly evaluate comparisons and conclusions (Mnookin 2018). For instance, in the universe that exists of all brown human hairs, are there unique features to every single one? Is it possible that two brown human hairs could be matched to the exclusion of all others as coming from a single unique source? What are the probabilities (generated from the analysis of a sample size of hundreds to thousands) associated with both of those scenarios?

In many cases, the various forensic science disciplines and scientists involved have not done their due diligence when it comes to ensuring the scientific method is and was followed, a basic technological, scientific, and conceptual failure on our part. Essentially, we must be able to demonstrate that the methods and generated results are valid, replicable, and have known error rates, when applicable. Further, methods must have been evaluated by the relevant scientific community via peer-reviewed publication. Finally, the way we interpret the results and how we communicate this interpretation in our reports and in oral testimony must follow the law of parsimony and be in line with accepted scientific communication practices. We must be able to articulate the strengths and weaknesses of any given method and present the results within that specific context for them to have meaning for judges and juries.[10]

Case Studies

BITEMARKS

Bitemarks are impressions left by teeth on a victim's skin or in some inanimate object, such as food; such impressions have been used by US law enforcement and courts since at least 1975 to match a suspect with a victim (Mnookin 2018) (see figure 4.1). Before the advent of DNA analysis (allowing any remaining saliva to be sequenced), these impressions were seen as a major way to connect a perpetrator with their victim, based on two main assumptions: (1) the dentition of each person is unique and can distinguish them from every other person in the world; and (2) skin could accurately record the impressions of teeth and therefore preserve this individuating quality of dentition (Bush 2011). A third assumption is that dentists could be trained to evaluate such evidence with little resulting error. These assumptions should be regarded as linked: assumption 3 relies on assumption 2 being true, and assumption 2 relies on the foundation set by assumption 1. Therefore, problems with any one of the assumptions would

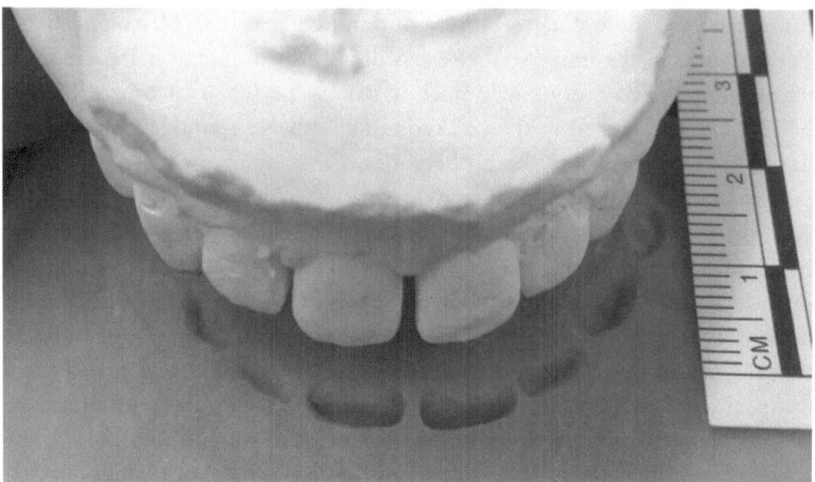

Figure 4.1. Comparison of plaster cast of the upper dentition to bitemark in a malleable substrate for illustrative purposes. Photo credit Elizabeth A. DiGangi.

render bitemark analysis invalid. As we will discover, each assumption has substantial issues, not the least of which includes a general dearth of an established scientific foundation, and existing tests whose results undermine the stated presumptions.

For decades, none of the assumptions was rigorously tested, yet forensic odontologists continued to perform such analyses. In fact, such analyses have been in part responsible for sending several innocent people to prison (Bowers 2014). Further, as of 2015, fifteen people whose convictions were at least in part based on bitemark analysis were on death row in the United States (Balko 2015). Despite warning calls about the unlikelihood of there being any veracity to the assumptions inherent to bitemark analysis (NAS 2009; PCAST 2016), courts around the country continue to accept bitemark evidence (Bowers 2014; Mnookin 2018).[11]

BITEMARKS AS PATTERN EVIDENCE

Pattern and impression evidence is defined as marks left behind by a person or object on some other person or object during the commission of a crime and given the characteristics of the impacting surfaces, some sort of pattern results (Saferstein 2019). Examples include tire or footwear impressions, toolmarks, fingerprints, and bloodstains. Bitemarks are included in this category of pattern evidence since the human mouth has a consistent organization in terms of types of teeth present and anatomical location where they are found.

Unfortunately, pattern and impression evidence is particularly infamous for its general lack of a solid scientific foundation. This is partially because this type of analysis was developed in crime laboratories for the express purpose of criminal investigations and not as a part of normal scientific inquiry typified by rigorous use of the scientific method (Mnookin 2018). In addition, as opposed to objective analyses of evidence such as DNA, the analysis of pattern and impression evidence involves subjective assessments, notorious for being particularly subject to bias, especially when irrelevant contextual information is known to the examiner (Dror and Charlton 2006). As a result, the 2009 NAS report took special umbrage with pattern evidence, as widespread population studies for the uniqueness of patterns caused by common objects have not been generally conducted. Bitemarks are one specific example.

As mentioned, forensic odontologists who analyze bitemarks do so under the assumption that each individual human dentition is unique: that tooth sizes and shapes, jaw shape and size impacting tooth alignment, and whether or not any teeth have been extracted will differ substantially between people. Inextricably linked with this assumption is a second one: that this uniqueness of teeth can be preserved when they impact skin, on parts of the body with inherently different elastic properties and characteristics of underlying structures (e.g., breasts, heels, shoulders, cheeks). A third assumption is that trained individuals can accurately analyze the patterns left behind and come to a conclusion including or excluding a suspect's mouth as having caused the marks—a conclusion that would be shared by other practitioners, if they were to repeat the analysis.

The uniqueness of every set of human dentition is an assumption that has seen little testing (Bowers 2014; NAS 2009; Saks et al., 2016). Studies that evaluated hundreds of dentitions to establish statistical models of uniqueness would have to be conducted. A conclusion based on an assumption underlaid by no existing scientific foundation is meaningless and in essence is no conclusion at all. The second assumption, that skin faithfully records tooth impressions to such a level that impressions can be matched to a suspect, is just as shaky as the first. A bitemark on skin creates a contusion (i.e., bruise). Forensic pathologists well know that contusions are notoriously difficult to interpret due to the number of variables that impact their formation: the amount of force used, the elasticity of the skin and morphology of underlying structures dictated by the location on the body and the victim's age, the victim's skin color and any scars or tattoos in the area of interest, whether or not the victim moved or struggled at the time, and how much time has passed between the creation of the contusion and it being photographed (DiMaio and DiMaio 2001).

Unfortunately, many forensic odontologists have essentially ignored all of this information and have nevertheless maintained that what are essentially patterned bruises can be matched to a suspect dentition (Saks et al. 2016). Recent studies examining the skin elasticity problem have found that depending on the placement of a body part during photography, the resultant skin distortion of a mock bitemark substantially decreased accuracy by examiners (Lewis and Marroquin 2015); that several bites made by a single dentition on different parts of a cadaver model could not be distinguished as having been made by the same dentition (Bush et al., 2009); and that attempts to correct for distortion with a photo editing software program do not solve the problem (Bush et al., 2010). Such evidence led to the PCAST (2016, 83) recommendation that further research on bitemark analysis would not be a sensible use of resources given the "serious doubt" involved.

BITEMARKS, ERROR, AND BIAS

The third assumption involved in bitemark analysis, resting on the supposed veracity of the first two, is that a trained expert in human dentition can determine the evidentiary value of a suspect mark on human skin, and assuming the mark is determined to be analyzable, compare photographs of it to a mold made from a suspect's dentition. Several studies have shown high error rates associated with even experienced observers analyzing bitemark evidence, with Saks and Koehler (2005, 895) citing a 64% false positive error rate. These high error rates hold for interobserver error (when two separate observers analyze the same evidence) and for intraobserver error (when one observer analyzes the same piece of evidence at some later time) (Saks et al. 2016). High error rates in either category are unacceptable from the standpoint of forensic testimony and essentially render any testimony based on bitemark analysis deceptive.

Researchers have generally found weak interobserver and intraobserver agreement (Pretty and Sweet 2001; Miller et al. 2009; Page et al. 2013; Reesu and Brown 2016) unsurprising for an endeavor based on subjective assessment without a foundational underpinning of the uniqueness of dentitions and their ability to be accurately recorded in skin. In part due to such studies as well as the fallout caused by the NAS 2009 report with regard to its findings on bitemark analysis, the American Board of Forensic Odontology (ABFO), the major certifying body for forensic dentists in the United States, sponsored a study presented at the 2015 American Academy of Forensic Sciences annual conference designed to address whether practitioners could reliably assess 100 examples of possible bitemark evidence.[12] While the findings are not available in the published abstract (Freeman and Pretty 2015), the authors distributed the dataset to a few outside people whose independent analysis found unacceptable rates of disagreement, which included determinations such as whether or not a mark in question was even a bitemark at all (Saks et al. 2016; Balko 2015).

Of most concern is the fact that as of the time of this writing, the study has yet to be published, implying an understanding by the ABFO that to do so would sound the death knell of bitemark analysis. In response to the fallout from the 2009 NAS report, forensic odontologists have been attempting to make up for the fallacies in bitemark analysis with one 2010 paper calling for a "paradigm shift," "a new level of caution," and "hypothesis-driven research" in light of research debunking its supposed foundation, several exonerations, and the NAS report findings (Pretty and Sweet 2010, 38). Bowers (2014, 240) notes that of their own admission, forensic odontologists have been "flying blind" when it comes to bitemark analysis.

In court, some forensic odontologists have gone as far as to use terminology indicating absolute certainty as to the matches they have made, such as "positive match" or "medical-dental certainty" (Bowers 2014, 231). Their hubris would be laughable if not for the suffering incurred by more than two dozen exonerated people, their families, and their communities as a result of bitemark analyses and inflated claims (not to mention the suffering of the unknown number of innocents who languish in custody and of those subsequently victimized by unprosecuted perpetrators).[13] All human assessments, especially subjective ones, can be affected by bias (Dror and Charlton 2006). Unfortunately, forensic scientists in particular have erroneously assumed that we are immune from error and bias (Cooper and Meterko 2019).

HOW THE CONTINUED USE OF BITEMARK ANALYSIS VIOLATES HUMAN RIGHTS

A recent review paper written by 38 forensic scientists and academic scientists, medical doctors, dentists and professors of dentistry, lawyers and law professors, and statisticians discusses the multitude of problems with bitemark analysis (Saks et al. 2016). Such a collaboration between experts in disparate fields highlights the serious concerns shared by many in the legal, medical, dental, forensic, and scientific communities about the harms brought by the continued practice and allowance of bitemarks as a legitimate forensic technique. As Bowers (2014) notes, the right to a fair trial is violated when evidence used against a defendant is, in essence, garbage—with a possible consequence being the seizing of an innocent person's liberty.

Third Molar and Age Estimation/Determination

A second case study about junk forensic science highlights a separate issue: sometimes an accepted scientific foundation exists, but the problem lies with the methods that rely on the facts of that foundation and/or the interpretation of the results. Age determination of a living person from analysis of the third molar (i.e., wisdom tooth) to ascertain if they have met a legal age threshold is one example.

Many countries, including the United States, are currently experiencing an influx of migrants seeking asylum due to a variety of complex social, economic, and political issues in the Global South. Occasionally these migrants are unaccompanied children who, in accordance with US federal law,[14] will be placed under the care of the Office of Refugee Resettlement (ORR) rather than in a detention facility run by Immigration and Customs Enforcement (ICE). Unaccompanied migrant children as opposed to adults seeking asylum are afforded distinct benefits under immigration law such as a more direct path to legal residency.[15] Therefore, from a legal standpoint, it is important to establish a migrant's actual age as someone older than 18 would not necessarily be automatically eligible for such benefits. Occasionally when teenagers seek asylum, doubt is cast on their claim that they are under 18. As a result, the onus is on the government to establish the person's age. There are several technologies that can be used: interviews of any available family or acquaintances, review of any available documents, legal or otherwise (e.g., birth certificate, passport, social media posts), and/or requiring a dental or bone x-ray to assess the person's stage of tooth or bone growth and development. Dental x-rays would typically be examined by a forensic odontologist, while bone x-rays would be examined by a forensic anthropologist.[16]

Given the special benefits afforded to unaccompanied minors, the government is concerned about fraud. Therefore, once a suspicion about a claimant's age has been raised, ORR will inform ICE, which will hire a forensic odontologist to examine a dental x-ray for the state of tooth development. The resulting odontology report is then submitted as evidence in court proceedings.

GROWTH AND DEVELOPMENT BASICS

In general, growth and development of bones and teeth are a regular, predictable, and timed process. People move sequentially from infancy to childhood to adolescence to adulthood, and there are certain anatomical markers along the way that we can use as milestones to indicate these different stages. These principles are firmly supported by scientific data. For instance, the completed growth of one of the eight wrist bones is used as a marker to indicate that a person has finished puberty (Shapland and Lewis 2013).

However, the reality of assessing age from bones and teeth is that is an *estimation*, not a *determination*. This distinction may seem semantic, but it is an important one. The reason we do not determine age is because of a fundamental truth about growth and development and aging: a one-to-one correlation between a person's *biological* age and their *chronological* age does not exist. Biological age is simple to assess: for instance, does a person display signs that they are an infant or a teenager? Chronological age, on the other hand, indicates the number of years that have passed since a person's birth—and while there can be rough correlations with stage of development (i.e., biological age) and year count, there are a number of factors that influence *when* a person will pass from one stage to the next.

This inherent variation exists between individuals, populations of people, and boys and girls due to a variety of reasons that include genetics and environmental stressors such as nutrition and disease exposure. Therefore, the challenge that we face when estimating an age from a person still in some stage of growth and development is correlating the markers we see with chronological age. While there is literature on the ages at which different stages occur for different bones and teeth in populations around the world, these data tend to be difficult to come by, and the population most represented tends to be people of European descent.

As indicated, the stages are ordered and predictable. This is true for major stage changes, such as from infancy to childhood, as well as for minor stage changes, such as the particular sequence that any given bone or tooth will pass through on its way to completion. While we can accurately predict that each person will move in order from stage A to B to C, the precise timing of those transitions in terms of a person's exact chronological age is more flexible. To be clear, certainly we can talk about a person being *about* ten years old when their lower permanent canine teeth begin to erupt, or *about* six years old when all their wrist bones have appeared. However, each of these milestones or developmental stages is associated with an age range rather than an exact year.

The younger a person is, the more generally complex the picture is with their bone and tooth development. Paradoxically, this makes it easier to estimate an age: there are several bones and teeth to examine, each of which contributes its own information, and this allows a final estimate to be made from the entirety of all the data. However, as a person reaches late adolescence, bone growth is almost complete (i.e., the bones will be adult size with almost all growth plates fused), and generally all the teeth have completed development as well—with the possible exception of the third molar. As a result, a typical dental x-ray of a person in their late teens may only have this tooth to evaluate for its state of development (figure 4.2). As we shall see, this creates additional problems for age estimation, especially when it is being done to determine if a person has reached or surpassed a chronological age threshold.

As discussed, there are general windows of time when teeth and bones reach different developmental milestones. While variation exists, typically,

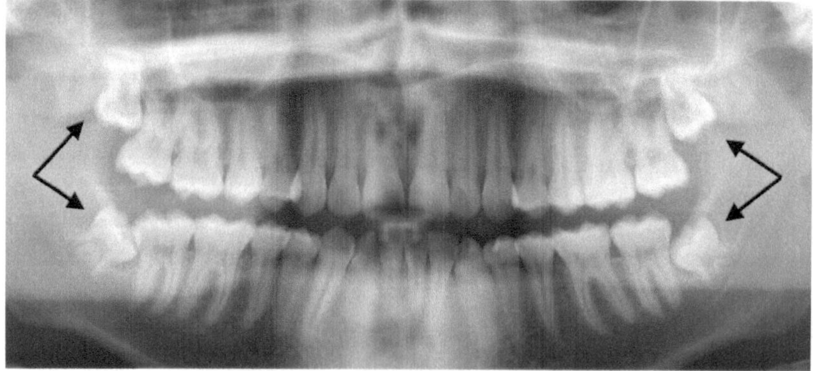

Figure 4.2. Dental x-ray of an adolescent or young adult dentition with developing third molars indicated by the arrows. Image credit: Coronation Dental Specialty Group, CC BY 3.0 <https://creativecommons.org/licenses/by/3.0>, via Wikimedia Commons.

there is a restrained amount of time comprising each window surrounding each milestone. However, of all the teeth in the mouth, the third molar is the most variable: occasionally it doesn't form at all, when it does form its shape may be abnormal, and there is very wide variation in terms of when it hits its different developmental milestones (Liversidge et al. 2017). The reason is evolutionary: humans no longer need this tooth to help us process our food and therefore survive (Carter and Worthington 2015), and as a result, over evolutionary time people with wisdom tooth variations survive to pass those genes on to their children.

Unfortunately, from the standpoint of establishing if a person has reached a legal age threshold, the third molar also happens to be the tooth that is usually the last to form, erupt, and complete development; and this latter stage occurs after the other teeth are fully formed. This means that from a biological standpoint, this tooth is the only one that can potentially give us information about whether a person has reached their late teens. However, its developmental timing is extremely variable. When all molars have reached the final maturity stage, the average chronological age (regardless of population) is 16 years with the 3rd percentile being 13.5 years and the 97th percentile being over 17 years (Liversidge 2012). In other words, some children will have completed third molar development by 13.5 years while most will not complete it until 17 or later.

FORENSIC ODONTOLOGY AND LEGAL AGE THRESHOLD DETERMINATION[17]

In the case of unaccompanied migrants who claim to be minors when seeking asylum, typically the only time a question would be raised would be for those individuals who look or perhaps act like they might be older than 18 (as subjective as both of these assessments are). That leaves the aforementioned third molar as the only dental marker which might help clarify the situation. The forensic odontologist would take a dental x-ray of all the molars, and evaluate their development using the Demirjian and colleagues (1973) method, which places tooth development into eight sequential stages, ordered as A through H. Teeth grow from the top of the crown (part of the tooth that is in the mouth) to the roots, and the final stage (H) consists of the tip of the root being closed, indicating growth completion (Demirjian et al. 1973) (figure 4.3). While each tooth will progress through all stages, the assignment of any given stage is ultimately a subjective one based on education and experience.

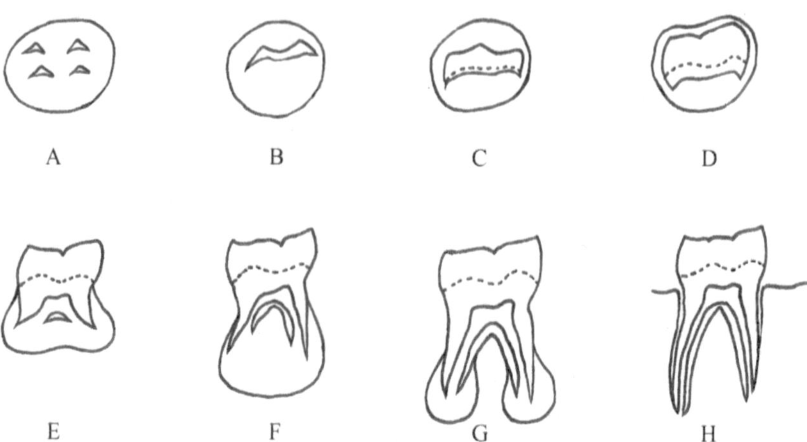

Figure 4.3. Sequential stages of permanent molar development, from A (calcification of initial cusps) to H (root canal is closed). Drawn by Megan K. Moore after Demirjian et al. (1973). Reprinted by permission.

POPULATION COMPARISON AND ENVIRONMENTAL STRESSORS

Following an assignment of development stage for each third molar, the odontologist will apply known information about what age people in a chosen population were when they hit the assigned stage, and this is where most of the problems ensue. The population data they typically use are from European or African Americans[18]—individuals born in one of the most developed countries in the world—while the migrants being evaluated come from developing countries with a number of substantial environmental stressors associated with high levels of poverty. Although data on growth and development simply have not been collected for every place in the world, it is generally not appropriate to compare a person from one population to a disparate one, and certainly not without including a caveat to this use in the report. The major reason is because environmental stressors impact growth and development (Chaillet et al. 2005), although we are still discovering the extent to which this occurs.

Exposure to pathogens can have a major effect on growth, as the body expends its resources on combatting them (Dewey and Mayers 2011). Variables such as waste disposal practices, climate, clean water availability, and vaccination status all play a role in a person's (and community's) overall pathogen load (Lindahl and Grace 2015). Nutrition is also involved, as a well-nourished body has a stronger immune system—although certain pathogens or foods limit the body's ability to absorb some nutrients, even if they are consumed (Scrimshaw 2003). Even something like psychosocial stress has been shown to affect a person's physiology, as prolonged elevated levels of fight or flight hormones negatively affect the body (Cardoso et al. 2019; Yaribeygi et al. 2017). Finally, genetics impact and are impacted by each of these variables (Mandy and Nyirenda 2018). We can certainly make the assumption that by virtue of the fact they are seeking refuge in another country, unaccompanied migrants have been affected by at least one of the aforementioned variables, and perhaps several of them. Research on the role that these variables play in impacting growth continues (e.g., Cardoso 2007; Cardoso et al. 2019).

As a result, the practice of correlating the dental development stage of a given migrant who hails from an impoverished developing country to corresponding chronological ages from individuals born in an advantaged, industrialized one is not scientifically appropriate. While dental development data from a given migrant's country may not exist, at the very least odontologists need to explain these contextual issues in their reports and present the results with caveats. They do not do this; rather, they uncritically state that the person's tooth development has been compared to known ages from either African or European Americans (or some other population).

PROBABILITY THAT A PERSON HAS REACHED LEGAL AGE

The entire point of doing this analysis is to provide the presiding judge with information as to whether or not the migrant has reached the legal age of 18. As a result, odontologists present the results in a statistical framework and report their calculated probability based on the assigned developmental stage that the person is over 18. There are several issues with how they approach this analysis: (1) the scientific articles[19] from which they purport to draw the chronological age information do not list the data in such a way that supports their conclusions (in other words, it is not possible to read the articles and easily determine how the analysis was done or how the raw data were obtained); (2) this at least partially because some odontologists devised a spreadsheet which ostensibly includes data from the articles and allows a statistical analysis to be run (Dwyer et al. 2018); but this spreadsheet is not widely available and its use has not been subjected to the scrutiny of peer review; (3) notwithstanding the issue of inappropriate population comparison as discussed earlier, the statistical analysis that they are doing in and of itself is an incorrect one for the question at hand; and (4) the terminology they use in the report to state the results is at best misleading and at worst inappropriate and scientifically meaningless.

As previously discussed, age estimation in children and teenagers involves attempting to correlate a particular development stage with a chronological age. To do this, most studies rely upon statistical techniques that evaluate the average ages for people in any given maturation stage. However, what these studies fail to consider statistically is that there is an important difference between the age when a person is *in* a given stage (known as age-within-stage) versus the age at which a person *moves from* one stage to the next (known as age-at-attainment) (Konigsberg et al. 2019). It is incorrect to use studies where the sample of individuals was constructed in such a way that the average ages of the people in any given stage is being used for comparison. This is because the group of people *within* a given stage are at slightly different chronological ages: some might be slightly younger, others slightly older. This is different from evaluating the age at which the stage *itself* is obtained. From a legal age threshold perspective, it is this age-at-attainment of a stage that is most appropriate (Konigsberg et al. 2019).

Despite these major issues, forensic odontologists continue[20] to use these incorrect methods and use the phrase, "empirical statistical probability" to refer to a particular migrant having reached the age of 18. This misleading terminology is akin to "reasonable scientific certainty"—another junk phrase, which the National Commission on Forensic Science (2017), in one of its only acts before being disbanded, recommended be prohibited in forensic case reports and testimony.

HUMAN RIGHTS VIOLATED BY CURRENT PRACTICES SURROUNDING AGE DETERMINATION FROM THE THIRD MOLAR

The William Wilberforce Trafficking Victims Protection Reauthorization Act of 2008 (TVPRA) requires that ICE rely on lines of evidence such as interviews and documents to establish legal age and only use analysis of x-rays as supporting information. In several instances, it has been clear that ICE has ignored this stipulation (DiGangi 2018; Armus 2019). However, the true scope of the problem is unknown because according to a 2009 Department of Homeland Security report, ICE does not track how many dental x-rays they order. In the cases we know about, the dental reports have invariably concluded that there was an "empirical statistical probability" of some migrants being over 18, and these reports ultimately led to the children being removed from ORR custody and placed in an adult ICE detention facility while they await adversarial court proceedings.

A series of lawsuits regarding the treatment of minor migrants brought by the Center for Human Rights and Constitutional Law and related organizations against the US Justice Department in the 1980s–1990s resulted in a binding settlement stipulating that minors be kept separate from unrelated adults (Flores Settlement Agreement of 1997). Further, the rights of children are protected under the United Nations' Convention on the Rights of the Child (1990). While the United States is not a party to this convention, from a moral perspective this does not allow disregard for its provisions. These include Article 20, which calls for "special protection and assistance" by the state when children have been "deprived" of their family environment; and Article 22, calling for "appropriate protection and humanitarian assistance" for refugee children.

Conclusion

> He appears to have a passion for definite and exact knowledge . . . He said that he would acquire no knowledge which did not bear upon his object. Therefore all the knowledge which he possessed was such as would be useful to him.
>
> —Sir Arthur Conan Doyle's description of Sherlock Holmes, the intrepid detective and scientist. (Doyle 1887)

Sherlock Holmes got it right in his philosophy regarding knowledge. When it comes to forensic science, the faithful application of the scientific method is what will generate his "definite and exact knowledge," be it knowledge regarding whether a particular pattern analysis has a scientific foundation, whether methods used to estimate some biological characteristic of a person can be used when a particular level of certainty is needed, or knowledge surrounding some other type of evidentiary analysis and result.

Garrett and Neufeld (2009) note that the legal system cannot be held responsible for forensic scientists' negligence regarding proper application of the scientific method, relied upon for centuries as a means to understand the natural world, and concomitant adequate interpretation of results. I echo Mnookin (2018) by urging forensic scientists to re-identify as being on Team Science, rather than on Team Law Enforcement. While the teams can work together, they must remain separate due to their distinct aims. It is only through such an identity shift that we can embrace the scientific method as the main driver of our analyses and interpretations.

Therefore, the onus remains on forensic scientists to advocate for, propose, and initiate reforms. However, because of the unique decentralized nature of the American law enforcement and justice system, reforms at a macro level can only go so far. Individual forensic scientists, whether we work for crime labs, morgues, or as individual consultants, must resolve to embrace the scientific method in every aspect of our work. Inherently this requires flexibility and both a willingness and ability to change course if underlying theories (i.e., accepted explanations) or methods turn out to be unsupported by the scientific evidence. Clement and Blackwell (2010, 33) acknowledge that challenges to bitemark analysis threaten to "disenfranchise" practitioners who exhibit "resistance to change"—but these practitioners as well as others would do well to remember that science at its heart is about construction and change. It is about building theories based on extensive hypothesis testing, and dismantling theories to build new ones when successive data analyses alter an accepted interpretation.

In the meantime, this resistance to change has had a real and substantial impact on individuals and society. Several authors have called for forensic science reform on the basis of preventing "miscarriages of justice" (e.g., Garrett and Neufeld 2009, 97). However, few frame the problem as an ultimate cost to society if such reforms do not take place (viz., Mnookin 2018). Often, those unjustly incarcerated have suffered from the affliction of being in the wrong place at the wrong time—an affliction that may be indiscriminate in whom it plagues. Further, defense counsel cannot adequately guide their clients when inherently flawed evidence is presented willfully or inadvertently as fact or statistical certainty. Perhaps the framework that we need to understand the seriousness of our plight is a human rights one: forensic scientists have an ethical and professional societal obligation to employ the most rigorous methodologies. Therefore, performing and testifying to a faulty forensic science analysis is a human rights violation. A commitment to reforms accordingly deserves the gravitas that comes with such a reproach.

Acknowledgments

I thank the editors for their invitation to contribute to this important and timely volume. I am grateful to Laura Belous, Esq. as well as Drs. Jonathan

Bethard and Michelle Miranda for assistance with references and/or feedback on the content herein and Dr. Megan Moore for useful comments as well as for drawing figure 3.3. Finally, I would like to recognize the people who have been unjustly incarcerated or deported especially on the basis of erroneous forensic interpretations, and call for a commitment to change on the part of my colleagues in forensic science.

Notes

1. The success of Edmond Locard's laboratory in France, established in 1910, led to several other labs being established around Europe; the oldest forensic science laboratory in the United States is the one associated with the Los Angeles Police Department, established in 1923 (Saferstein 2019).

2. *CSI* was the most-watched television show worldwide for five years in the early 2000s (*Huffington Post* 2012); a few examples of other popular shows that involve some aspect of purported scientific evidence analysis as a central theme include several multiseason American or British television series—*Bones*; *Criminal Minds*; *NCIS*; and *Sherlock*—in addition to non-fiction documentary series such as *Forensic Files*.

3. The public is also familiar with the application of forensic science to mass disaster, human rights, and humanitarian contexts; while its use in such contexts is outside of the scope of this chapter, similar issues to those discussed in this essay may exist, although in the author's experience nongovernmental organizations that employ forensic science in such contexts tend to adhere to higher standards.

4. This is manifested in different ways. Annie Dookhan was a rouge analyst who admitted to falsifying hundreds of drug analyses while working for a lab outside of Boston; her misconduct led to the largest single dismissal of convictions in US history, (over 21,000 cases in 2017) (Held, 2017). More systematically, on a laboratory-wide basis, the Houston, TX, crime lab in the early 2000s suffered from (among other things) substantial backlogs and falsified drug testing, leading to its reorganization as an independent agency from the Houston Police Department (Liptak and Blumenthal 2004; Barned-Smith 2019). Incidentally, DNA is one of the few forensic science techniques that has applications outside of law enforcement, and its invention led to a number of commissions to ascertain its validity for criminal investigation purposes (Saks and Koehler 2005); as a result, problems with DNA from a forensic science perspective tend to revolve around faulty interpretation by a human analyst. These issues have the potential to increase as the technology is continually being improved to allow more minute amounts of DNA to be sequenced. Such interpretation issues were made clear in the Amanda Knox case, the American foreign exchange student who was convicted in Italy of murdering her roommate partially on the basis of trace DNA found on an item of clothing belonging to the

victim; she was later exonerated in part because such analyses of trace DNA had not been subjected to full scientific scrutiny (Povoledo 2015). Other complications have arisen with the interpretation of DNA mixtures where the profiles of multiple individuals are present in any given sample.

5. An example of fingerprint analysis gone wrong occurred with the case of Brandon Mayfield, the American lawyer who was arrested in connection with the 2004 Madrid train bombings after his fingerprint was identified on bomb making materials by the FBI. Several days later, Spanish National Police instead identified the fingerprint as belonging to a different person; the similarity of Mayfield's print to this suspect coupled with missteps in the analysis process led to the FBI's misidentification (Office of the Inspector General 2006).

6. Collins and Jarvis (2009) present a different interpretation surrounding the figures about exonerated persons and the forensic evidence used to convict them.

7. Richard Phillips, exonerated in 2018 on a murder conviction based on perjured eyewitness testimony (The National Registry of Exonerations, 2019), holds the distressing title of being the longest innocent person in the United States to serve time (45 years and 2 months); relevant to the discussion here about junk science contributing to erroneous convictions, Steven Chaney served over 25 years for murder largely on the strength of a bitemark analysis (Murphy 2019).

8. An infamous example is that of the O. J. Simpson trial in the mid 1990s: as a person with means, he was able to afford a defense team that was exclusively focused on his case for months, and as a result, that team had the time and resources to construct a defense primarily against the mishandling of forensic evidence from the crime scene; conversely, public defenders often have multiple clients at once and operate on a limited budget.

9. Broad exceptions include many forensic biologists and chemists who hold advanced degrees in the United States; forensic anthropologists who in the United States hold a master's degree or PhD; forensic odontologists who in the United States have a graduate degree in dentistry (although this is not a research degree); and forensic pathologists who in the United States have a graduate degree in medicine (while this is not a research degree, forensic pathology is a specialty of medicine requiring several years of additional training, as opposed to forensic odontology, which is not a named specialty of dental medicine [Bowers 2014]).

10. Outside of the scope of this chapter is a discussion of evidence admissibility in US federal court and how several cases in the late 20th century have shaped the admission of expert testimony; see Dillhoff (2011) for a review.

11. A notable exception has occurred in Texas, whose forensic science commission declared a moratorium on bitemark evidence in 2016 (Mnookin 2018).

12. The study consisted of three questions designed to ascertain the rate of agreement among practitioners regarding their assessment of a bitemark; what the study did not include was whether or not each assessment was a *correct* one—how-

ever, the fact that participants disagreed more often than not indicates that their ability to correctly assess bitemarks is also inadequate (Balko 2015).

13. Mnookin (2018) astutely notes that while data exist on exonerated individuals for whom bitemark or other invalid forensic analysis was partially responsible for their convictions at trial, there is no way to track or know how many people have taken plea deals after being presented with erroneous forensic analyses or conclusions.

14. Flores Settlement Agreement of 1997.

15. William Wilberforce Trafficking Victims Protection Reauthorization Act of 2008 (TVPRA); and Immigration and Nationality Act.

16. In the United States, the relevant immigration law (TVPRA) mentions both dental and bone x-rays as possible lines of evidence, but to my knowledge the government currently only hires forensic odontologists and not forensic anthropologists; however, the situation is different in many European countries where forensic anthropologists routinely analyze bone x-rays to assess age.

17. Note that "determination" is the term used by the government and the odontology reports themselves, but see earlier discussion about why this term is misleading.

18. See Blankenship et al. (2007) for African American data; see Mincer et al. (1993) for European American data.

19. See note 19 (xix).

20. As of this writing in early 2020, I have been privy to over a dozen forensic odontology age determination reports; the most recent one seen was from late 2018, although some of the corresponding cases are still being adjudicated.

Works Cited

Armus, Teo. 2019. "ICE put a 17-year-old asylum seeker in an adult jail. His lawyers blame a 'junk-science' dental exam." *The Washington Post*, 4 October 2019. https://www.washingtonpost.com/nation/2019/10/04/ice-asylum-seeker-dental-exam-adult-jail/.

Balko, Radley. 2015. "A bite mark matching advocacy group just conducted a study that discredits bite mark evidence." *The Washington Post*, 8 April 2015. https://www.washingtonpost.com/news/the-watch/wp/2015/04/08/a-bite-mark-matching-advocacy-group-just-conducted-a-study-that-discredits-bite-mark-evidence/

Barned-Smith, St. John. 2019. "Houston crime lab's move into new space will speed up testing, ensure independence, officials say." *The Houston Chronicle*, 22 October 2019. https://www.houstonchronicle.com/news/houston-texas/houston/article/Houston-crime-lab-s-move-into-new-space-will-14554705.php.

Blankenship, Jane A., Harry H. Mincer, Kenneth M. Anderson, Marjorie A. Woods, and Eddie L. Burton. 2007. "Third Molar Development in the Estimation of Chronologic Age in American Blacks as Compared with Whites." *Journal of Forensic Sciences* 52, no. 2: 428–433.

Bowers, Charles M. 2014. "Bitemark Evidence and Miscarriages of Justice." In *Miscarriages of Justice: Actual Innocence, Forensic Evidence, and the Law*, edited by Brent E. Turvey and Craig M. Cooley, 225–251. San Diego: Academic Press.

Bush, Mary A., Raymond G. Miller, Peter J. Bush, and Robert B. J. Dorion. 2009. "Biomechanical Factors in Human Dermal Bitemarks in a Cadaver Model." *Journal of Forensic Sciences* 54, no. 1: 167–176.

Bush, Mary A., Howard I. Cooper, and Robert B. J. Dorion. 2010. "Inquiry into the scientific basis for bitemark profiling and arbitrary distortion compensation." *Journal of Forensic Sciences* 55, no. 4: 976–983.

Bush, Mary A. 2011. "Forensic Dentistry and Bitemark Analysis: Sound Science or Junk Science?" *Journal of the American Dental Association* 142, no. 9: 997–999.

Cardoso, Hugo F. V. 2007. "Environmental effects on skeletal versus dental development: Using a documented subadult skeletal sample to test a basic assumption in human osteological research." *American Journal of Physical Anthropology* 132, no. 2: 223–233.

Cardoso, Hugo F. V., Laure Spake, Sofia N. Wasterlain, and Maria T. Ferreira. 2019. "The impact of social experiences of physical and structural violence on the growth of African enslaved children recovered from Lagos, Portugal (15th–17th centuries)." *American Journal of Physical Anthropology* 168, no. 1: 209–221.

Carter, Kate, and Steven Worthington. 2015. "Morphologic and demographic predictors of third molar agenesis: A systematic review and meta-analysis." *Journal of Dental Research* 94, no. 7: 886–894.

Chaillet, Nils, Marjatta Nyström, and Arto Demirjian. 2005. "Comparison of Dental Maturity in Children of Different Ethnic Origins: International Maturity Curves for Clinicians." *Journal of Forensic Sciences* 50, no. 5: 1–11.

Clement, John G., and Sherie A. Blackwell. 2010. "Is current bite mark analysis a misnomer?" *Forensic Science International* 201: 33–37.

Collins, John M., and Jay Jarvis. 2009. "The Wrongful Conviction of Forensic Science." *Forensic Science Policy and Management* 1: 17–31.

Cooper, Glinda S., and Vanessa Meterko. 2019. "Cognitive bias research in forensic science: A systematic review." *Forensic Science International* 297: 35–46.

de Jongh, Arent, Anko R. Lubach, Sheryl L. Lie Kwie, and Ivo Alberink. 2019. "Measuring the Rarity of Fingerprint Patterns in the Dutch Population Using an Extended Classification Set." *Journal of Forensic Sciences* 64, no. 1: 108–119.

Demirjian Arto, Harvey Goldstein, and J. M. Tanner. 1973. "A New System of Dental Age Assessment." *Human Biology* 45, no. 2: 211–27.

Department of Homeland Security, Office of the Inspector General. 2009. "Age Determination Practices for Unaccompanied Alien Children in ICE Custody." November 2009. https://www.oig.dhs.gov/assets/Mgmt/OIG_10-12_Nov09.pdf.

Dewey, Kathryn G., and Daniel R. Mayers. 2011. "Early child growth: how do nutrition and infection interact?" *Maternal and Child Nutrition* 7, Suppl. 3: 129–142.

DiGangi, Elizabeth A., and Megan K. Moore. 2013. "Application of the Scientific Method to Skeletal Biology" in *Research Methods in Human Skeletal Biology*, edited by Elizabeth A. DiGangi and Megan K. Moore. San Diego: Academic Press.

DiGangi, Elizabeth A.. 2018. "Immigration agents X-raying migrants to determine age isn't just illegal, it's a misuse of science." *The Conversation*, May 31, 2018. https://theconversation.com/immigration-agents-x-raying-migrants-to-determine-age-isnt-just-illegal-its-a-misuse-of-science-96771.

Dillhoff, Megan. 2011. "Science, Law, and Truth: Defining the Scope of the Daubert Trilogy." *Notre Dame Law Review* 86, no. 3: 1289–1318.

DiMaio, Dominick, and Vincent J. M. DiMaio. 2001. *Forensic Pathology*, 2nd edition. CRC Press.

Doyle, Arthur Conan. 1887. *A Study in Scarlet*. London: Ward Lock & Co.

Dror, Itiel E., and David Charlton. 2006. "Why experts make errors." *Journal of Forensic Identification* 56, no. 4: 600–616.

Dwyer, Mimi, Belle Cushing, and Antonia Hylton. 2018. "The U.S. is checking immigrant kids' teeth to see if they actually belong in adult detention." *Vice News*, 11 October 2018. https://www.vice.com/en_us/article/qv9mbx/the-us-is-checking-immigrant-kids-teeth-to-see-if-they-actually-belong-in-adult-detention.

Flores v. Reno, No. CV 85-4544-RJK(Px) (C.D. Cal. Jan. 17, 1997).

Freeman, Adam J., and Iain A. Pretty. 2015. "Construct Validity of Bitemark Assessments Using the ABFO Bitemark Decision Tree." *Proceedings of the 67th Annual Meeting of the American Academy of Forensic Sciences*, Orlando, FL. 21:744.

Garrett, Brandon L., and Peter J. Neufeld. 2009. "Invalid Forensic Science Testimony and Wrongful Convictions." *Virginia Law Review* 95, no. 1: 1–97.

Giannelli, Paul. 1993. " 'Junk Science': The Criminal Cases." *The Journal of Criminal Law and Criminology* 84, no. 1: 105–128.

Giannelli, Paul. 2007. "Wrongful Convictions and Forensic Science: The Need to Regulate Crime Labs." *North Carolina Law Review* 86, no. 1: 163–235.

Held, Amy. 2017. "Massachusetts Throws Out More Than 21,000 Convictions in Drug Testing Scandal." *NPR.org*, 20 April 2017. https://www.npr.org/sections/thetwo-way/2017/04/20/524894955/massachusetts-throws-out-more-than-21-000-convictions-in-drug-testing-scandal.

Hsu, Spencer S.. 2017. "Sessions Orders Justice Dept. to End Forensic Science Commission, Suspend Review Policy." *The Washington Post*, 10 April 2017. https://www.washingtonpost.com/local/public-safety/sessions-orders-justice-dept-to-end-forensic-science-commission-suspend-review-policy/2017/04/10/2dada0ca-1c96-11e7-9887-1a5314b56a08_story.html.

Huffington Post. 2012. "Most-Watched TV Show in the World is 'CSI: Crime Scene Investigation.'" 14 June 2012. https://www.huffpost.com/entry/most-watched-tv-show-in-the-world-csi_n_1597968.

Immigration and Nationality Act. Pub. L. No. 82-414 (1952).

Innocence Project. n.d. "Forensic Science: Problems and Solutions." https://www.innocenceproject.org/forensic-science-problems-and-solutions/.

Ishay, Michelinw. 1997. "Introduction" in *The Human Rights Reader: Major Political Essays, Speeches, and Documents from the Bible to the Present,* edited by Micheline Ishay. New York: Routledge.

Konigsberg, Lyle W., Susan R. Frankenberg, and Helen M. Liversidge. 2019. "Status of Mandibular Third Molar Development as Evidence in Legal Age Threshold Cases." *Journal of Forensic Sciences* 64, no. 3: 680–697.

Liversidge, Helen M.. 2012. "The Assessment and Interpretation of Demirjian, Goldstein and Tanner's Dental Maturity." *Annals of Human Biology* 39, no. 5: 412–431.

Liversidge, Helen M., Kalaiarasu Peariasamy, Morenike O. Folayan, Abiola A. Adeniyi, Papa I. Ngom, Yuko Mikami, Yukie Shimada, et al. 2017. "A radiographic study of the mandibular third molar root development in different ethnic groups." *Journal of Forensic Odonto-Stomatology* 35, no. 2: 97–108.

Lindahl, Johanna F., and Delia Grace. 2015. "The consequences of human actions on risks for infectious diseases: A review." *Infection Ecology & Epidemiology* 5: 30048. doi:10.3402/iee.v5.30048.

Liptak, Adam, and Ralph Blumenthal. 2004. "New Doubt Cast on Testing in Houston PoliceCrime Lab." *The New York Times,* 5 August 2004. https://www.nytimes.com/2004/08/05/us/new-doubt-cast-on-testing-in-houston-police-crime-lab.html.

Lewis, Cheri, and Leonore A. Marroquin. 2015. "Effects of Skin Elasticity on Bite Mark Distortion." *Forensic Science International* 257: 293–296.

Mandy, Mirembe, and Moffat Nyirenda. 2018. "Developmental Origins of Health and Disease: The Relevance to Developing Nations." *International Health* 10, no. 2: 66–70.

Miller, Raymond G., Peter J. Bush, Robert B. J. Dorion, and Mary A. Bush. 2009. "Uniqueness of the Dentition as Impressed in Human Skin: A Cadaver Model." *Journal of Forensic Sciences* 54, no. 4: 909–914.

Mincer, Harry H., Edward F. Harris, and Hugh E. Berryman. 1993. "The ABFO Study of Third Molar Development and Its Use as an Estimator of Chronological Age." *Journal of Forensic Sciences* 38, no. 2: 379–390.

Mnookin, Jennifer L. 2018. "The Uncertain Future of Forensic Science." *Daedalus, the Journal of the American Academy of Arts & Sciences* 147, no. 4: 99–118.

Murphy Heather. 2019. "When Experts Testifying in Criminal Trials are Guilty of Overstating Forensic Results." *The New York Times,* New York edition. 21 April 2019. Section A, p. 14.

National Commission on Forensic Science. 11 April 2017. "Reflecting Back: Looking Toward the Future." https://www.justice.gov/archives/ncfs/page/file/959356/download.

The National Registry of Exonerations. 9 April 2019. "Exonerations in 2018." Accessed January 9, 2020. https://www.law.umich.edu/special/exoneration/Documents/Exonerations%20in%202018.pdf.

National Research Council of the National Academies. 2009. "Strengthening Forensic Science in the United States: A Path Forward." Washington, DC: The National Academies Press.

Office of the Inspector General, Oversight and Review Division. March 2006. "A Review of the FBI's Handling of the Brandon Mayfield Case. Unclassified and Redacted." https://oig.justice.gov/special/s0601/final.pdf.

Page, Mark, Jane Taylor, and Matt Blenkin. 2013. "Expert Interpretation of Bitemark Injuries—A Contemporary Qualitative Study." *Journal of Forensic Sciences* 58, no. 3: 664–672.

Povoledo, Elisabetta. 2015. "Italy's Highest Court Explains Decision to Clear Amanda Knox." *The New York Times*, 7 September 2015. https://www.nytimes.com/2015/09/08/world/europe/italys-highest-court-explains-decision-to-clear-amanda-knox.html?action=click&module=RelatedCoverage&pgtype=Article®ion=-Footer.

President's Council of Advisors on Science and Technology (PCAST), Executive Office of the President. 2016. "Report to the President: Forensic Science in Criminal Courts: Ensuring Scientific Validity of Feature-Comparison Methods." September. https://obamawhitehouse.archives.gov/sites/default/files/microsites/ostp/PCAST/pcast_forensic_science_report_final.pdf.

Pretty, Iain A., and David Sweet. 2001. "Digital bite mark overlays: An analysis of effectiveness." *Journal of Forensic Sciences* 46, no. 6: 1385–1391.

Reesu, Gowri V., and Nathan L. Brown. 2016. "Inconsistency in opinions of forensic odontologists when considering bite mark evidence." *Forensic Science International* 266: 263–270.

Saferstein, Richard. 2019. *Forensic Science: From the Crime Scene to the Crime Lab*, Fourth Edition. New York: Pearson.

Saks, Michael J., and Jonathan J. Koehler. 2005. "The Coming Paradigm Shift in Forensic Identification Science." *Science* 309: 892–895.

Saks, Michael J., Thomas Albright, Thomas L. Bohan, Barbara E. Bierer, C. Michael Bowers, Mary A. Bush, Peter J. Bush, et al. 2016. "Forensic Bitemark Identification: Weak Foundations, Exaggerated Claims." *Journal of Law and the Biosciences* doi:10.1093/jlb/lsw045.

Scrimshaw, Nevin. 2003. "Historical concepts of interactions, synergism, and antagonism between nutrition and infection." *The Journal of Nutrition* 133: 316S–321S.

Shapland, Fiona, and Mary E. Lewis. 2013. "Brief Communication: A Proposed Osteological Method for the Estimation of Pubertal Stage in Human Skeletal Remains." *American Journal of Physical Anthropology* 151: 302–310.

United Nations. 1948. "Universal Declaration of Human Rights." https://www.un.org/en/universal-declaration-human-rights/.

United Nations. 2009. "Convention on the Rights of the Child." https://www.ohchr.org/en/professionalinterest/pages/crc.aspx.

Weissbrodt, David, and Matthias Hallendorff. 1999. "*Travaux Préparatoires* of the Fair Trial Provisions—Articles 8 to 11—of the Universal Declaration of Human Rights." *Human Rights Quarterly* 21, 1061–1096.

William Wilberforce Trafficking Victims Protection Reauthorization Act of 2008 (TVPRA), Public Law 110-457, 122 Stat 5044.

Yaribeygi, Habib, Yunes Panahi, Hedayat Sahraei, Thomas P. Johnston, and Amirhossein Sahebkar. 2017. "The impact of stress on body function: A review." *Experimental and Clinical Sciences Journal* 16: 1057–1072.

Chapter Five

Hiding in Plain Site

Using Online Open-Source Information to Investigate Sexual Violence and Gender-Based Crimes

ALEXA KOENIG AND ULIC EGAN

Introduction

In 2013, a Guatemalan court convicted former head of state Efraín Ríos Montt of genocide and crimes against humanity for atrocities committed in the early 1980s against the country's indigenous Ixil population. Among those crimes were at least nine instances of rape and other sexual violence that were linked to an intent to destroy the Ixil people (Burt 2013). One woman testified that she was raped by more than 20 soldiers while imprisoned on a military base (Burt 2013). Such horrific testimonies were not confined to a courtroom in Guatemala City. According to a researcher documenting the experiences of the Ixil, a handful of Ixil women turned to Twitter as the case unfolded, finding comradery in sharing their stories of sexual and gender-based violence (SGBV) during the dictator's rule (Olson 2016 and conversation with Olson August 2019).

Social media has also hosted information relevant to cases in other parts of the world. In 2014, a video of a woman—naked and bruised and surrounded by men—appeared on YouTube. The video, taken from Tahrir Square in Egypt, went viral, dominating the headlines despite President Sisi's inauguration, which took place the same day. Nine men were ultimately sentenced to prison for life for their role in the sexual assaults, while another three received sentences of at least twenty years (Barr 2015).

In 2019 in Berkeley, California, a team of student researchers using open-source methods were tasked with investigating atrocities in a country in Africa. One of their many responsibilities was to collect and preserve information on sexual and gender-based violence, among other crimes. What they found far exceeded what they had anticipated: hashtags signaling support for women who had allegedly been raped, videos that depicted a woman screaming off camera, and other circumstantial evidence of sexual violence (Chang and Nambiar 2020).

These experiences directly contravene the assumption made by many individuals—whether specialists in sexual and gender-based violence or in open-source investigation methodologies—that the internet has relatively little to offer in terms of strengthening accountability for SGBV crimes (see, e.g., Hamilton 2019; Banchik 2019).[1]

Since 2010, the use of online open-source information—information that is publicly accessible on the internet (Berkeley Protocol 2020)—for media exposé and legal accountability purposes has skyrocketed (see generally, Dubberley, Koenig, and Murray 2020). Yet even as some investigators are increasingly using social media and other online open sources to strengthen the evidentiary foundations of legal cases, investigators, academics, and others have remained skeptical about such information's utility for investigating and prosecuting cases involving sexual and gender-based violence. As noted by Libby McAvoy and Kelly Matheson (2020) of WITNESS, "video as evidence in the investigation and documentation of SGBV has not yet reached its full potential." Neither have other forms of open-source content.

This article is based on both desk research and a series of interviews that we conducted from July 2019 through February 2020 to probe the assumption that online open-source information has limited utility for strengthening the evidentiary foundation of cases involving sexual and gender-based violence. Interviewees ranged from international investigators and prosecutors to researchers and NGO representatives who specialize in SGBV investigations and/or the use of video and other digital information for case building. Such investigators work for a range of organizations, including ad hoc and international tribunals, international and regional nongovernmental organizations, and academic institutions that focus on open-source fact-finding and verification. We also benefited from parallel research being conducted by Libby McAvoy and Kelly Matheson (2020) of WITNESS into the utility of video content to prosecute SGBV cases, and deeply appreciated the opportunity to brainstorm with them about how to best tackle this research.

As explained below, we found that there are numerous ways that online open-source information can be used to strengthen the evidentiary basis of SGBV crimes, from providing lead and linkage evidence to crime base evidence. And as with the examples above, we found that survivors—as well as perpetrators and bystanders—*are* sharing information related to sexual and gender-based violence online, but that investigators aren't always realizing what to look for, or even how to look.

Ultimately, the assumptions that are being made about where and when and with whom survivors speak may be problematically biasing investigators into overlooking what's hiding in plain sight online. Below we outline some of the most dominant concerns about open-source information's utility to support SGBV cases, and then offer insights as to how such information may nevertheless prove helpful in securing legal accountability for these especially sensitive and difficult to prosecute crimes.

The Relative Invisibility of SGBV Online

One of the biggest challenges with finding and using online open-source information for accountability is the assumption that such information doesn't exist—that survivors will not share the nightmare of their experience with billions of strangers on the Internet. We found that to some extent, this seems to be true, for reasons we explain below. However, in other cases, evidence of sexual violence *is* available online, but isn't recognized for what it is. In a third category of cases, evidence of sexual violence is found online, but it is used against the survivor. We discuss each of these phenomena below.

ONLINE OPEN-SOURCE EVIDENCE OF SGBV DOESN'T EXIST

According to many of the investigators and researchers with whom we spoke, cultural and social norms that result in gendered patterns of access to and use of cell phones, social media, and other digital technologies *do* limit what is available online. As one interviewee explained, "If you have a gender dynamic where women are not necessarily supposed to have a public life, or an online profile or anything like that, they are missing from the ocean of information that comes out of open-source, online intelligence. . . . If there's a massive gender imbalance in your users, there would be a massive gender imbalance in the data they produce."[2]

As another interviewee explained:

> [J]ust because we are not seeing a recording of crimes doesn't mean it's not happening. [O]nce again, you are looking at "where are witnesses?" They are often either in rural areas or refugee camps outside the country. Many of them have lost everything, so they might not have any of the equipment, the access. Many of our victims especially for sexual violence are women who haven't been exposed to the internet or the computers or even cameras or cell phones. I spoke to one victim who had never even seen a video on a cell phone before. If they are not recording, you are missing a huge portion of your victims and witnesses.[3]

She went on to note that when relying on digital technologies to investigate atrocities, "you are [going] to see much more male witnesses, male victims, male-centered crimes and miss out on the females or children or whoever might be an outlier of that group. . . . I think it's one of the major biases we have to be aware of."[4] That investigator went on to further explain that the gender issues compound with other "intersectional factors," including "class, wealth, ethnicity, religion, everything else" to affect not only one's potential vulnerability to and likelihood of being targeted for sexual and gender-based violence, but also access to and representation in digital technologies (see also, Egan 2019).[5]

A related issue is the assumed or actual reluctance of perpetrators to post evidence of sexual or gender-based violence online. As noted by one experienced practitioner who specializes in SGBV cases: "It's very, very rare to have a scenario where somebody is boasting about committing or witnessing or being involved in sexual violence in comparison to other crimes such as attacks on the civilian population or killings."[6]

Yet despite these issues, it is increasingly likely that photos or videos of SGBV *may* exist, given the relative ubiquity of cell phones. For example, as noted by one interviewee, "There is a fact pattern emerging in some of the cases, where the victims of sexual violence in detention are convinced that it's been filmed. . . . [If accessible] that would be very, very incriminating."[7] Such fact patterns mirror earlier situations where filming sexual violence was used to heighten the sense of degradation that victims experience, for example in places like Abu Ghraib and Guantánamo where guards photographed the sexual degradation of detainees (Koenig 2013, 178). As explained by Lara Stemple, "the use of a camera to record the abuse at Abu Ghraib has been described as a 'shame multiplier,' extending the humiliation beyond the time and place in which it occurred" (Stemple 2009, 625; see also Danner 2004, 18–19). Of course, this raises the issue of whether investigators can get hold of such videos. As an investigator we interviewed pointed out, it is less likely such photos would be shared in public online spaces, such as open Facebook pages, than across closed networks on platforms like WhatsApp.[8]

Bias also distorts what information makes its way into online open sources in the first place and how that information is framed. One SGBV expert pointed to the ways reporters and intermediaries who publish user-generated content use photographs and videos to represent communities stricken by conflict:

> There are certain tropes that people want to reproduce. Look at the Rohingya situation and the fact that you had photographers from [major media] going up to fixers and saying "Hey, I want a really good photo of a teenage girl who got pregnant as a result of rape and has since had the baby, that would really make this story pop." Then they use the photograph, and it's a front on photo of someone who cannot give informed consent to the use of their image or the use of their name that you put [on the front page of a major newspaper] with no thought of the ethical ramifications. Because the pictures you see of armed conflict, this is not just a question of evidence, but it's a question of representation. It's battle-weary hero shots of male soldiers, or it's terrified headscarf-wearing huddled female refugees with children hiding behind their skirts. Or it's male prisoners being emasculated by being marched along so that everyone can see that they've been dominated, and they've been broken. Every single one of them is a gender trope.[9]

Referencing a different type of bias, the same SGBV expert, when asked about whether she was seeing a distinction in the type of crimes investigated given the increasing use of online open sources, noted the tendency towards certain kinds of crimes being filmed, as compared with others. She explained: "Yeah, I think it's an issue for sure. It's one issue if it diverts the focus of the investigation towards public crimes, attacks on marches like mass killings, and that kind of stuff."[10]

Given the expanded ubiquity of cameras today—especially in the form of smartphones—the volume of video and photographic material potentially available to investigators has expanded significantly. And yet several interviewees underscored a concern about highly visible crimes drowning out SGBV-related crises. One interviewee explained:

> [There are] two risks. One is that it pulls focus towards [crimes] that are better documented, more notorious, easier to prove, more open source information, more potential sources of evidence other than testimonial evidence. The other problem, though, is that I think it has the risk of reinforcing [a] double standard when it comes to what evidence is sufficient to prove different crimes. If you have a case that includes both categories, SGBV and more public [crimes], the public one has corroborating evidence. It has video shot from multiple different angles. It can corroborate call data records. It places a particular perpetrator there at the time or has them having four different phone calls with people in the perpetrator's network immediately before, during and after [the crime] happened. You don't have any of that for SGBV. You have a victim statement and [a] general perpetrator group identification. Then the judges are going potentially to see one as having been proved, and the other one not, even though there are evidential rules removing the requirement for corroborating evidence of sexual crimes.[11]

Ultimately, she and several other interviewees were concerned that the ubiquity of open-source information, and especially photographs and videos, would not only be an issue for individual cases, but that the increasing use of online open-source information was shifting judges' and others' expectations around what constitutes "proof," essentially increasing the burden with regards to what kinds of content would be needed to meet evidentiary thresholds in SGBV cases.

ONLINE OPEN-SOURCE EVIDENCE OF SGBV EXISTS BUT IS "INVISIBLE"

Ultimately, many of our interviewees concluded that information related to SGBV *can* be found online; it just may be "invisible" to the investigator, for a few reasons. First, sexual violence does not lend itself particularly well to visual imagery. SGBV injuries may be internal to peoples' bodies, as compared with other crimes that may have more external indicia, such as mutilation or murder. Thus, common open-source investigation methodologies may not lend themselves well to exposing relevant information. However, cues may be found in the words captured in or around the video, or in visual content, when someone is specifically scanning for signs of SGBV. One interviewee, who was originally skeptical that open-source information related to SGBV exists online, later agreed that information about sexual violence "is definitely on phones." While sexual violence may be committed out of sight of others (although not always), there could still be indicators of such violence. As she explained, "Even if somebody doesn't visually witness it—which they're more likely to do for SGBV as an international crime than they would be [for SGBV crimes] domestically—they can hear it. It's not necessarily being done in conditions of total privacy. Even in a detention scenario [there may be a] pattern [where] a male guard comes along and removes [a detainee], and then they come back and they're very visibly distressed or they're bleeding. It's actually rare that you would expect sexual violence to be committed in complete secret."[12] A related concern was not whether such content exists, but instead "whether it's shared, or transmitted, or published."[13]

Second, because SGBV tends to be stigmatized—and can be stigmatizing of the survivors—what information *is* shared online is often coded. Investigators need to understand the coded language that sexual violence survivors use to communicate about their suffering, and that perpetrators use to communicate about their crimes, in order to translate what is right in front of them. Whereas search terms for murder might include commonly used terms like "killed" or "massacred," survivors of stigmatized crimes don't tend to talk about the crime itself. As noted by one longstanding investigator of SGBV crimes:

> We tend to censor in terms of our language of sexuality. I think that's why . . . online that you'll have to look at physical gestures [such as] when people lower their eyes and say the phrase you hear a lot, he treats me like a husband, or. . . . Every language has its euphemism for a sexual relationship. That's why it's so important to talk to your interpreter, and you can write down at least 20 euphemisms for sexual violence in at least every language. If you're just beginning to learn a foreign language you learn the word to eat, to walk, to sleep, to drink. No one tells you, well, "to eat" is one of the big sexual euphemisms.[14]

As another interviewee underscored, "the language [of sexual violence, including sex trafficking] changes very, very, very quickly. One week, it may be called 'get a key.' The next week, it may be called 'capturing coffee.' The language that investigators need to learn is very unique [and] changes very quickly."[15]

A similar gap can emerge when open-source investigators don't know how to "read" photos or videos or text posted online for what they actually communicate about sexual violence. One longstanding investigator and SGBV expert explained: "Some of the things that are hiding in plain sight are on open sources, but they're just as hidden on open sources as they are anywhere else. Because I think people come with their own perspective of looking at information."[16] That investigator underscores how gender stereotypes and bias may distort what we see and understand, especially with sexual violence. "You can't get a more obvious criteria," she said, "than to have [photos and videos of] dead male bodies that have been brutalized, and not pose the question about what possibly could be missing. If there had been female bodies there I bet [investigators] would ask the question, 'Do you think that the women were raped?' "[17] This quote suggests that investigators might be less likely to look for signs of sexual violence in cases where men were the victims and therefore might not pick up on signals that the men depicted in a photo or video may have experienced sexual or gender-based violence.

Another challenge comes with using digital technologies to do the "viewing." Open-source investigators are increasingly using machine learning technologies to review digital content given the size and scope of online information: with 6,000 tweets produced every second,[18] 500 hours of video uploaded to YouTube every minute,[19] and Facebook boasting 2.50 billion monthly active users,[20] it is impossible for humans to adequately search such mammoth datasets for relevant information without electronic help. However, many of the machine learning technologies that are currently being developed to support open-source investigators are focused on object detection (for example, identifying military vehicles or weapons). That increases the tendency towards certain crimes becoming hypervisible, such as chemical weapons attacks or the bombing of hospitals, potentially drawing attention to those crimes while detracting from other online information, such as that related to sexual violence, which may not as easily be captured by machines.

Yet another technical capacity issue is *where* the investigators are looking, with much attention paid to the surface web, as opposed to the deep web and dark web, and the different, gendered ways in which these domains may be used. As noted by one of our interviewees: "I'm sure ISIS is using the dark web as much, [even] much more than they're using the above web. . . . [I]t's interesting to contrast what they choose to put on the open-source web. [Ignoring that is] like thinking that the world economy is really the GDP, and not understanding that there's a huge percentage of the world economy that's drug running, gun running, and trafficking in people."[21]

What *is* recognized can also be influenced by the gender and geographic sensitivities of the investigator. More than one interviewee underscored the prevalence of male investigators in the open-source investigations space as potentially affecting both what is looked for and what is seen: "The military analysts and the data analysts that are working for, let's say, Bellingcat, [are] there a lot of women there? Think of those two specialties. They are not traditionally overrepresented by female staff."[22]

Another experienced investigator similarly noted the intersection of gender and power and the roles they play in terms of what's seen—and what's not seen—online: "There's a lot of power to make certain things visible and other things less visible. That power is entrusted to the investigator, the lawyer, and particularly in a male-dominated space, they may not have the same awareness of the power that they're having in terms of that space."[23] This may compound what the investigator refers to as an already "uneven digital topography. From the outset, you're going into Google or social media and [investigating the US or Cameroon and] that topography is not equal, particularly in terms of gender divide."[24]

ONLINE OPEN-SOURCE EVIDENCE OF SGBV EXISTS BUT IS USED AGAINST OR OTHERWISE HARMS SURVIVORS

While open-source content has immense potential as a resource for investigators, such content can also be used as a tool to discredit or endanger survivors. A human rights advocate and investigator highlighted the difficulty of documenting SGBV in the context of Yemen due to cultural and political realities. She described a rape case that was published online without the survivor's permission or consideration of the survivor's security or well-being. That posting resulted in the case she was working on becoming "very political and a very bad experience" for the survivor. She explained that they ultimately "lost" the victim as a witness because of information about the situation being posted on social media.[25] She also noted other consequences that could result from even well-meaning bystanders putting information related to sexual violence online: "It is a stigma, yes. The victims cannot talk about it, and if the victim talks about it, he or she might be victimized more. Like the case I told you [about]. It was published [on] social media and the victim was not protected, so she had to change what she said."[26] Thus, the victim essentially recanted her story for her own safety. This raises the risk of a defense team, or political group, using such a retraction to strengthen their argument that a very real assault never occurred.

ISIS's persecution of LGBTQ+ communities further highlights the "double-edged" nature of social media as a tool for securing justice. As part of ISIS propaganda efforts, ISIS supporters have posted photos and videos of ISIS members throwing individuals accused of engaging in homosexual acts from buildings.[27] Such visual content can provide investigators with important evidence, including clear pictures of the faces of perpetrators, uniforms, locations, weapons, and even of the commission of the crimes. However, ISIS has also mined social media to identify and target their victims by, for example, using current detainees' Facebook contact lists to identify and round up other individuals from LGBTQ+ communities.[28] Social media platforms therefore face a dilemma when endeavoring to identify what should be removed and what should be left on their sites in order to minimize violence and maximize justice (Ali 2015).

Social media platforms can also act as a medium for the nonconsensual dissemination of sexually explicit photos and videos (Bahar 2019). Sextortion, the exploitation or sexual blackmail of a victim, is easily facilitated through the use of social media platforms and closed-messaging apps, from which the content may eventually migrate ("Sextortion: A new name, an age-old crime" 2019). For example, one investigator explained that in the Sri Lankan conflict, there were recordings of "perpetrators raping or sexually violating individuals" that the perpetrators then used to "blackmail the victims to submit to further acts of sexual violence on the threat the videos would be disseminated if they [didn't]."[29]

While those videos were initially closed source, the universality of social media has major implications for the potential widespread reach of such videos, and resulting shame and stigma of the survivor. Sextortion has similarly been employed against migrants traveling through conflict-stricken countries such as Libya and has been "confirmed throughout at all stages of migration, from the country of origin to the destination country" (Bruni and Merkle 2018). The criminal connections among sextortion, sexual and gender-based violence, migration, human trafficking, conflict, and armed groups are fairly easy to imagine and beginning to be well documented (see, e.g., 'More Than One Million Pains" 2019).

Finally, human rights advocates and investigators may themselves be placed at risk by using social media for documentation, investigation, or advocacy. Female and LGTBQ+ advocates are especially targeted for violence and abuse, both online and offline (Bahar 2019). In 2018, the UN High Commissioner for Human Rights Zeid Ra'ad Al Hussein noted, "These new forms of harassment, intimidation and defamation are shockingly frequent, frequently terrifying, and often spill over into the real world. Death threats, threats of sexual and gender-based violence, and online defamation and disinformation campaigns—often of a sexualized nature, and often including the victim's real-life addresses—are used to torment and terrorize women who speak out" (OHCHR 2018).

Other challenges arise when a political situation suddenly changes. An investigator we spoke to who works within the Syrian context explained:

> A lot of people documenting human rights violations since the early days—right now some of them are living under Syrian controlled areas but their footage [remains] online. So, this could be really handy for [an] investigator but at the same time it could put the same people who documented these violations at risk. For example, we have many request[s] where people will tell us, can you take this video down or can you talk to Google or Facebook or Twitter and, you know, make sure they remove this video because we are living in Syrian government-controlled areas and we are in danger.[30]

Ultimately, as noted above, the assumption of many investigators has been that SGBV-related crimes do not benefit from online open-source investigations—and may even become disadvantaged by online open-source information being heavily relied on during an investigation. Such assumptions are usually based on the sensitive nature of the crimes, past use by defense counsel, and the presumed reluctance of survivors to speak about such sensitive experiences online. However, as noted below, there are ways that many of those challenges can be minimized.

Overcoming the Invisibility Challenges

In this section, we focus on potential strategies for finding and recognizing the open-source information that *does* exist online. One of the most effective ways to overcome the relative invisibility of digital information related to SGBV crimes is to analyze how language is used in online open spaces.

With online open sources, investigators need to think about language in two ways; first, by focusing on the language that people use in particular geographic territories (like English, Kiswahili, Mandarin), and then—within that language—the phrases and slang used by survivors and perpetrators.

For example, the researcher mentioned in the introduction pointed out that while the Ixil women were talking about their rapes on Twitter, most Twitter users are not fluent in Ixil. While this provided the women with a degree of privacy and community in such a public online space, it also meant that anyone who is not adequately fluent in Ixil would overlook information relevant to these cases. An effective response to this is, of course, to map the local languages of an affected population and have someone fluent in those languages partner in the investigation. Alternately, the investigator can place key words and phrases into Google translate or a similar language processor to come up with search terms. While this risks overlooking critical contextual information that can influence meaning, such techniques can help provide a crude overview of what is available online. Open-source investigators can also develop a "cheat sheet" at the outset of an investigation that captures relevant phrasing or names and have a fluent or native speaker provide the relevant translation in an accompanying field.

Of course, as explained above, one must know which terms are relevant. Tom Trewinnard, an experienced open-source trainer, regularly reveals how language differs on social media from other contexts. Trewinnard explains that people who have experienced or witnessed an atrocity don't use "objective language":

> They've just gone through a traumatic experience—they're going to use human language—'what the hell? What have I just seen? I'm so scared!' Often times, they're going to be talking about their emotions [and thus] it helps if you don't use the cold, journalist search string, it's not going to return the kind of stuff you're going to be looking for. So, it's really useful to come up with [search phrases from the perspective of the people living the event]. (qtd in Banchik 2019, 48)

Given this, it is especially critical when investigating stigmatized crimes to create a lexicon of the both the emotive and coded language that survivors use to discuss what they've suffered. This is no different than creating code books to investigate neo-Nazi groups, who are unlikely to declare themselves as such but—as pointed out by Paul Myers, who trains open-source investigators—are likely to use codes like 1488 to signal their identity to each other without drawing obvious attention from outsiders (Myers 2020).[31]

As mentioned above, international criminal investigators also need to assess where such language is being shared online and learn how to access digital spaces with which they may not already be familiar. For example, much crucial information may only be available on the deep or dark web, as opposed to the surface web. Thus, investigators should include a review of such spaces in any online investigation plan, if it is likely that helpful information may reside there. Machine learning processes are often needed to comb the extraordinarily large quantities of content available online, but they are often optimized to detect objects as opposed to language. In the case of sexual violence, natural language detection tools may be much more helpful for identifying SGBV than object detection tools—although of course the language and phrases used would have to be culturally adjusted to capture the coded signals used by perpetrators and survivors.

Finally, it is important that governments, corporations, nongovernmental organizations, and other members of civil society continue to provide and advocate for increased access to technology and technological literacy for underserved communities, with particular attention paid to empowering women and vulnerable minorities to access and use such technologies. Such efforts should be supported by philanthropists, governments, and corporations as part of an overarching effort to further close the digital divide. Given the 2020 COVID-19 pandemic and the increased potential that communities will be ordered to shelter in place, access to digital technologies is needed more than ever to connect with needed resources and to share information about human rights violations and international crimes with those in a position to help.

Diversify Potential Uses of Open-Source Information

Even if crime-base evidence is not available, there may still be contextual information about the circumstances that proves crucial to a successful prosecution. Online open sources can provide rich data around key dates, geographies, and incidents (see, e.g., Integrating a Gender Perspective into Human Rights Investigations: Guidance and Practice 2018). Such sources can provide critical lead information or linkage evidence, for example, by revealing which military units were in a region at the time of an alleged attack, the timing of the attack, who else may have been in the area, etc.

This is where videos or photographs of tanks, military personnel, weapons, and other objects can be especially helpful, for example by pointing to who may have been perpetrators. Such videos and photographs may also capture images of possible survivors, who may be shown in the background or even as the focus of the imagery. Given the ubiquity of sexual violence in conflict, such troop movements and identity can be especially helpful as background to inform on the ground investigators (including those gathering testimonial and physical evidence) to know who to speak with and where to look. Too often, these issues are not explored to the extent that they should be and are overlooked for their connection to more blatantly obvious crimes, like a massacre or a chemical weapons attack.

One of our interviewees, who started her interview expressing deep skepticism about the potential role that online open-source information can play in SGBV cases, later retracted that skepticism, providing several examples of cases in which open-source information had proven helpful to prosecutions. She described how in some of the early cases at the International Criminal Court, the judges had warned prosecutors not to rely too much on open-source content, such as NGO reports. However, she said:

> You can still use it for lead evidence, you can use it to prove the contextual elements, because you have to show a pattern of a widespread or systematic attack. That's where [open-source information is] a lot more useful, because you don't have time to go and interview every rape victim in the whole country to try to establish that SGBV was part of the attack. That's where you can buttress the testimonial evidence you have by saying, look, here's a report [that documents] 393 [incidents of sexual violence]. It was used in [the *Bemba* case[32]] and it was really, really important. [The prosecutors introduced] an FIDH report [which documented] murder and rape by the MLC in the Central African Republic. [FIDH] did something amazing the day they released [their] report, they faxed a copy to Bemba to ask him, did he have any comment on it? To give him a right of reply. Bemba was being charged [with command responsibility] under Article 28, [so] you've got to show notice. You've got to show that he knew, or he should have known, that the crimes were happening. [The prosecution also used] media statements from Bemba for the same purpose. In that sense, they established a direct link between the open source information, and the

defendant, and his level of knowledge and contribution. That was very clever.[33]

Several of our interviewees, especially experienced investigators, underscored the deep importance, when wanting to be sensitive to SGBV crimes, of knowing that SGBV often happens in tandem with more visible crimes[34] and that those visible crimes can be the alert to look and listen even more carefully than the investigator would otherwise. For example, one noted that "if sexual violence goes with the burning of a village, [the burning] can be used, then, as a proxy to start to investigate other crimes that may also be taking place."[35] Investigators "need to act more proactively" in order to see if there's evidence of SGBV that may be overlooked when investigating more obvious crimes.[36]

Notably, satellite imagery is increasingly being used by open-source investigators to detect violence and may be helpful for identifying where SGBV may have occurred. For example, in 2016 Micah Farfour of Amnesty International detected the burning of villages in Myanmar through her careful review of satellite images. As a first glimpse into the destruction of villages, such materials could also provide the first indication of where to look for evidence of SGBV crimes such as rape and other sexual violence, as those violations frequently accompany the destruction of villages. Finally, satellite imagery may reflect troop movement, illuminate the location of detention facilities (locations particularly known for sexual and gender-based violence), or demonstrate areas rife with destruction. Where that destruction was perpetrated by ground troops, rape and sexual violence may have been—and unfortunately likely were—contiguous.

Ultimately, though, one of the most powerful ways to bring in videos and other open-source user-generated content is to have witnesses in the courtroom who can corroborate the open-source information. As one experienced investigator explained, "any video evidence that you have is only as good as the witnesses who you have corroborate [it]."[37]

Sophie Dyer and Gabi Ivens have posed the question: "What can feminist thought bring to open source investigations?" In the case of investigations of SGBV, this question seems particularly urgent. Open-source investigations are manifestations of—and constitutive of—power relations, much like sexual and gender-based violence itself. As they explain in making the case for bringing a feminist lens to the conduct of open-source investigations: "For decades feminist scholars and activists have been working to problematize unequal power relations and to find ways to resist and transform them" (Dyer and Ivens 2020). It's incumbent on open-source investigators to similarly problematize the practice of open-source investigations and do the hard work of understanding how a powerful set of methods can be used to even more effectively right classic imbalances of power, through everything from what is looked for to who does the looking, and how.

Conclusion

In 2012, a teenager in Ohio "woke up naked on a couch in a basement, surrounded by three teen boys. . . . In the days that followed, the girl began to discover Tweets and videos that suggested something awful may have taken place. Without social media, she may never have known she was raped" (Dissell 2013). While not charged as an international crime, this open-source content triggered a case "that, from end to end, illustrated the influence, and perils of social media on justice, on victims, and on journalism. Text messages, Tweets, and videos were the primary forms of evidence used by investigators to identify witnesses and even the accused. . . . And they were the key pieces of evidence that led to the guilty verdicts seven months after the incident took place" (Dissell 2013).

From Kenya (e.g., Hatcher 2014) to Nigeria (e.g., Fisher 2011) to Egypt (e.g., Barr 2015) to the United States (e.g., Dissell 2013), evidence of rape and other forms of sexual violence are circulated online, in places as commonly perused as Twitter, Facebook, and YouTube. There is more information online related to SGBV than many people assume. As one of the investigators interviewed for this chapter concluded with regards to combing online open sources to strengthen SGBV cases: "there's absolutely utility in it, from looking at potential victims and alleged perpetrators [to] patterns of communication or underlying linkage information [especially] in terms of understanding patterns . . . that take place when there's clustering of sexual violence"[38] with other conflict-related crimes.

As McAvoy and Matheson (2020) have pointed out, there are good reasons why video content and other forms of open-source information have not been used more broadly in SGBV cases. These include "ethical considerations and personal security, both of which . . . are especially complex and nuanced challenges when working to address SGBV crimes." Nevertheless, as they also emphasize, "considering the widespread impunity of perpetrators of SGBV, there is a real, urgent need for better, more reliable accountability and justice for survivors." Similarly, while raising serious questions about the ethics of using open-source methods to investigate SGBV, both Catherine

Chang and Kavya Nambiar (2020) of the Human Rights Center Investigations Lab at UC Berkeley concluded that they should use the information they found online related to SGBV, feeling a "responsibility, indeed, an imperative to act" given the utility of "open source methods [to] provide a new and critical avenue for justice for sexual violence crimes."

In addition to investigators, researchers may also play an important role in advancing the use of open-source information to prosecute gendered crimes. First, more careful study is needed to identify patterns underlying sexual violence and gender-based violence: what *are* the correlations between sexual violence and other types of crimes? Identifying the relationship between SGBV and other, more visible, atrocities could help investigators know when deeper digging into open sources for evidence of SGBV may be helpful—especially if victims, perpetrators, and/or bystanders in the affected communities are known to use social media and other online, public sites. Another role for researchers would be to conduct ethnographic research in communities in conflict to identify how women, men, and children who are at greatest risk of SGBV communicate in digital spaces (if at all), and how they want to—and do—share their stories, ranging from what technologies they use, to the phrasing and coded signals they may be sending.

In the meantime, women's access to technologies and education around how to use those technologies can and should be strengthened, giving women a broader array of tools for communication. Empowering women and LGBTQ+ activists to investigate and document sexual and gender-based crimes may also help counter any Western or gendered biases embedded in those investigations, fostering a more culturally appropriate and welcoming model for people who may not have traditionally felt or been welcome in online digital spaces.

But ultimately, and perhaps most urgently, we strongly recommend that SGBV experts work closely with digital open-source investigators—and vice versa—to improve open-source investigators' ability to see the evidence that may be hiding in plain sight online. This could go a long way towards strengthening both fields of practice, and even more importantly, helping to secure justice for survivors.

Notes

The authors thank the following for so generously sharing their time and insights to inform this article: Catherine Chang, Stephanie Croft, Lindsay Freeman, Andrea Lampros, Kelly Matheson, Libby McAvoy, Kavya Nambiar, Krisjon Olson, Francesca

Stepanov, Eric Stover, and students in Professor Jennifer Urban's Law and Technology Scholarship Seminar at UC Berkeley School of Law. Thank you as well to our interviewees, represented throughout this article pseudonymously as Elizabeth Kirk, Lisa McCabe, Alisha Patel, Beatrix Romanoff, Amy Wilson, Suzanna Smith, Adara Saeed, Farid Ahmed, Karam Khaled and Maya Hansberry. This chapter is based on findings from a multi-year study that the authors are conducting into the use of online open-source methods to investigate SGBV. It is further informed by research undertaken as part of Ulic's PhD dissertation, "A Sociolegal Intersectional Analysis of the Role of Technology in the Investigation of Conflict-Related Sexual and Gender-Based Violence," and has been conducted in compliance with the ethical policy of Swansea University and the College of Law and Criminology.

1. See also interview by the author(s) with Adara Saeed [21st August 2019]; interview by the author(s) with Farid Ahmed [23rd September 2019]; interview by the author(s) with Karam Khaled [23rd August 2019].

2. Interview by the author(s) with Beatrix Romanoff [4th November 2019].

3. Interview by the author(s) with Lisa McCabe [11th December 2019].

4. Ibid.

5. Interview by the author(s) with Beatrix Romanoff [4th November 2019].

6. Ibid.

7. Ibid.

8. Interview by the author(s) with Amy Wilson [20th December 2019].

9. Interview by the author(s) with Beatrix Romanoff [4th November 2019]; see also, Minwalla et al. 2020. The authors provide an analysis of "widespread breaches of United Nations Global Protection Cluster Guidelines (UN) for ethical reporting on gender violence that potentially compromise the safety and well-being of survivors and increase the risk of re-victimization and collective stigmatization of Yazidi women."

10. Ibid.

11. Ibid.

12. Ibid.

13. Ibid.

14. Interview by the author(s) with Maya Hansberry [15th January 2020]. Understanding coded SGBV language has been critical for SGBV investigations for decades. See, e.g., *Prosecutor v. Jean-Paul Akayesu*, Judgment, Case No. ICTR-96-4-T, 2 Sept. 1998, paras. 152–154.

15. Interview by the author(s) with Elizabeth Kirk [25th October 2019]; see also, e.g., Basil, 2018 (noting how children who use internet-based sites create keywords and hashtags to evade platform censors and effectively communicate in code, as well as how quickly that code can change: "Some kids hashtag their videos with words like *thot*—shorthand for *That Ho Over There*—or *fgirl, hottie, sxy, whooty,* or *sin*. But good luck keeping up, the code changes week-to-week").

16. Interview by the author(s) with Maya Hansberry [15th January 2020].

17. Ibid.

18. Twitter Usage Statistics, at https://www.internetlivestats.com/twitter-statistics/ (last visited 20 Feb. 2020).

19. Hours of Video Uploaded to YouTube Every Minute as of May 2019, at https://www.statista.com/statistics/259477/hours-of-video-uploaded-to-youtube-every-minute/ (last visited 20. Feb. 2020).

20. Facebook Q4 2019 Results (December 2019), available at https://s21.q4cdn.com/399680738/files/doc_financials/2019/q4/Q4-2019-Earnings-Presentation-_final.pdf

21. Interview by the author(s) with Maya Hansberry [15th January 2020]. Open-source data may provide especially useful lead information for the investigation of sexual slavery and human trafficking as traffickers use online platforms to both recruit and sell victims. As noted by one expert on the subject, "Social media platforms are being used to facilitate trade and trafficking—women and children are offered in the same online forums as rifles and rocket-propelled grenades." See also Bangura 2016 and Warrick 2016.

22. Interview by the author(s) with Beatrix Romanoff [4th November 2019].

23. Interview by the author(s) with Elizabeth Kirk [25th October 2019].

24. Ibid.

25. Interview by the author(s) with Adara Saeed [21st August 2019].

26. Ibid.

27. Nineteen public executions were documented by OutRight Action International between December 2014 and August 2015. "ISIS's media center corroborated these events with photo reports and videos, which have also been shared over social media by ISIS supporters." See Counter Extremism Project, 'ISIS's Persecution of Gay People,' available at https://www.counterextremism.com/content/isis-persecution-gay-people.

28. Ibid.

29. Interview by the author(s) with Suzanna Smith [4 February 2020].

30. Interview by the author(s) with Farid Ahmed [23rd September 2019].

31. This code references a famous slogan allegedly uttered by Hitler that's comprised of 14 words and the phrase "Heil Hitler," with 8 representing H as the 8th letter of the alphabet.

32. Prosecutor v. Jean-Pierre Bemba Gombo, Aimé Kilolo Musamba, Jean-Jacques Mangenda Kabongo, Fidèle Babala Wandu and Narcisse Arido, ICC-01/05-01/13.

33. Interview by the author(s) with Beatrix Romanoff [4th November 2019]. However it should be noted that, on appeal, the Appeals Chamber "did not question the evidence demonstrating that Bemba had been alerted to the FIDH report" and therefore did not recognize the significance of his action with regard to his knowledge of the report. See SáCouto and Sellers 2019.

34. Interview by the author(s) with Elizabeth Kirk [25th October 2019].

35. Such as, for example, rape. Ibid.
36. Ibid.
37. Interview by the author(s) with Lisa McCabe [11th December 2019].
38. Interview by the author(s) with Elizabeth Kirk [25th October 2019].

Works Cited

Ali, Mah-Rukh. 2015. "ISIS and Propaganda: How ISIS Exploits Women." Reuters Institute Fellowship Paper. University of Oxford. https://reutersinstitute.politics.ox.ac.uk/sites/default/files/research/files/Isis%2520and%2520Propaganda-%2520How%2520Isis%2520Exploits%2520Women.pdf.

Bahar, Meghana, 2019. "Cyber-Violence against the Marginalised in Sri Lanka: New Report by WITNESS ally Groundviews." WITNESS. https://blog.witness.org/2019/09/cyber-violence-groundviews-sri-lanka/.

Banchik, Anna Veronica. 2019. *Throwing Keywords at the Internet: Emerging Practices and Challenges in Human Rights Open Source Investigations.* https://repositories.lib.utexas.edu/bitstream/handle/2152/76187/BANCHIK-DISSERTATION-2019.pdf?sequence=1&isAllowed=y.

Bangura, Zainab Hawa, Special Representative of the Secretary-General on Sexual Violence in Conflict, Security Council. 2016. Open Debate on Sexual Violence in Conflict, 2 June 2016 at 2. https://www.peacewomen.org/sites/default/files/20160602%20SRSG%20Statement%20to%20SC%20Open%20Debate%20June%202016%20FINAL.pdf.

Barr, Madeleine. 2015. "Navigating the Ethics of Citizen Video: The Case of a Sexual Assault in Egypt." *Arab Media & Society*, September 23, 2015. https://www.arabmediasociety.com/navigating-the-ethics-of-citizen-v-case-of-a-sexual-assault-in-egypt/.

Basil, Anastasia. 2018. "Porn is not the worst thing on Music.ly." *Medium*, 5 March 2018.

Berkeley Protocol on Digital Open Source Investigations. 2020. UN Human Rights Office and Human Rights Center.

Bruni, Vittorio and Ortrun Merkle. 2018. "Gendered effects of corruption on the Central Mediterranean route." *Great Insights Magazine* 7, no. 1. https://ecdpm.org/great-insights/migration-moving-backward-moving-forward/gendered-corruption-central-mediterranean/.

Burt, Jo-Marie. 2013. "Rios Montt Convicted of Genocide and Crimes against Humanity: The Sentence and its Aftermath." *International Justice Monitor*, 13 May 2013. https://www.ijmonitor.org/2013/05/rios-montt-convicted-of-genocide-and-crimes-against-humanity-the-sentence-and-its-aftermath/.

Chang, Catherine, and Kavya Nambiar. 2020. "Survivors, Hashtags, and Justice: The Ethics of Investigating Sexual Violence Online." *Medium*, 17 March 2020.

Counter Extremism Project. "ISIS's Persecution of Gay People." https://www.counterextremism.com/content/isis-persecution-gay-people.

Danner, Mark. 2004. *Torture and Truth: America, Abu Ghraib, and the War on Terror*. New York Review of Books.

Dissell, Rachel. 2013. "The Steubenville Rape Case: Social Media on Trial." Dart Center for Journalism and Trauma, March 18, 2013. https://dartcenter.org/content/social-media-trial.

Dubberley, Sam, Alexa Koenig, and Daragh Murray, eds. 2020. *Digital Witness: Using Open Source Information for Human Rights Documentation, Advocacy and Accountability*. Oxford University Press 2020.

Dyer, Sophie and Gabi Ivens. 2020. "What would a feminist open source investigation look like?" *Digital War*, April 14, 2020.

Egan, Ulic. 2019. "Digital Accountability Symposium: Intersectionality and International Criminal Investigations in a Digital Age." *Opinio Juris*, 19 December 2019. http://opiniojuris.org/2019/12/19/digital-accountability-symposium-intersectionality-and-international-criminal-investigations-in-a-digital-age/.

Fisher, Jonah. 2011. "Cyber Anger at Nigeria Gang Rape Footage." *BBC News*, 23 Sept. 2011.

Hamilton, Rebecca. 2019. "The Hidden Danger of User-Generated Evidence for International Criminal Justice." *Just Security*. 23 Jan. 2019.

Hatcher, Jessica. 2014. "Nairobi's miniskirt march exposes sexual violence in Kenya." *The Guardian*, 18 Nov. 2014. https://www.theguardian.com/global-development/2014/nov/18/nairobis-miniskirt-march-exposes-sexual-violence-in-kenya.

Integrating a Gender Perspective into Human Rights Investigations: Guidance and Practice. 2018. UNOHCHR. https://www.ohchr.org/Documents/Publications/IntegratingGenderPerspective_EN.pdf.

Koenig, K. Alexa. 2013. "Indefinite Detention / Enduring Freedom: What Former Detainees' Experiences Can Teach Us About Institutional Violence, Resistance and the Law" (July 2013), unpublished dissertation. https://digitalassets.lib.berkeley.edu/etd/ucb/text/Koenig_berkeley_0028E_13595.pdf.

McAvoy, Libby, and Kelly Matheson. 2020. "Using Video to Support Accountability for Sexual and Gender-Based Violence Crimes." *WITNESS*.

Minwalla, Sherizaan, Johanna E. Foster, and Sarah McGrail. 2020. "Genocide, rape, and careless disregard: media ethics and the problematic reporting on Yazidi survivors of ISIS captivity." *Feminist Media Studies*. https://www.tandfonline.com/doi/full/10.1080/14680777.2020.1731699.

" 'More Than One Million Pains': Sexual Violence against Men and Boys on the Central Mediterranean Route to Italy." 2019. Women's Refugee Commission, March 2019. https://www.researchgate.net/publication/332082680_More_Than_One_Million_Pains_Sexual_Violence_Against_Men_and_Boys_on_the_Central_Mediterranean_Route_to_Italy/link/5c9e767c299bf111695010c3/download.

Myers, Paul. 2020. "How to Conduct Discovery Using Open Source Methods." *Digital Witness: Using Open Source Information for Human Rights Investigation, Documentation, and Accountability*, edited by Sam Dubberly, Alexa Koenig, and Daragh Murray, 107–142. Oxford University Press.

OHCHR. 2018. "The impact of online violence on women human rights defenders and women's organisations." *Statement by UN High Commissioner for Human Rights Zeid Ra'ad Al Hussein, 38th session of the Human Rights Council, 21 June 2018.* https://www.ohchr.org/EN/NewsEvents/Pages/DisplayNews.aspx?NewsID=23238&LangID=E.

Olson, Krisjon. 2016. "Waging Peace: A new generation of Ixiles confronts the debts of war in Guatemala." *Journal of Genocide Research*, 18, nos. 2–3: 343–359. DOI: 10.1080/14623528.2016.1186959.

Prosecutor v. Jean-Paul Akayesu. 1998. Judgment, Case No. ICTR-96-4-T, 2 Sept. 1998.

Prosecutor v. Jean-Pierre Bemba Gombo, Aimé Kilolo Musamba, Jean-Jacques Mangenda Kabongo, Fidèle Babala Wandu and Narcisse Arido. ICC-01/05-01/13.

SáCouto, Susana, and Patricia Viseur Sellers. 2019. "The *Bemba* Appeals Chamber Judgment: Impunity for Sexual an Gender-Based Crimes?" *William & Mary Bill of Rights Journal* 27. https://poseidon01.ssrn.com/delivery.php?ID409502908508911200900412508910312402702102104803305506806900002911900606612507203002002006004812306303808506600500710502511710507004000004007802002812407900706909501705000809508512700707109109212310309400111900112410408202912208203108006512302511 9&EXT=pdf.

"Sextortion: A new name, an age-old crime." 2019. *The Daily FT*, 23 December 2019. http://www.ft.lk/columns/Sextortion-A-new-name-an-age-old-crime/4-692197.

Stemple, Lara. 2009. "Male Rape and Human Rights." 60 *Hastings Law Journal* (February): 605–647.

Warrick, Joby. 2016. "Isis fighters seem to be trying to sell sex slaves online." *The Washington Post*, May 28 2016. https://www.washingtonpost.com/world/national-security/isis-fighters-appear-to-be-trying-to-sell-their-sex-slaves-on-the-internet/2016/05/28/b3d1edea-24fe-11e6-9e7f-57890b612299_story.html.

Chapter Six

Legal Tragedies

Accounting for Civilian Casualties of Airstrikes in US Military Investigation Reports

CHRISTIANE WILKE

On November 26, 2015, General John F. Campbell, commander of the US forces in Afghanistan, stepped into the Pentagon briefing room and stated:

> I received a report of the U.S. national investigation into the strike on Doctors Without Borders, MSF Trauma Center in Kunduz City, Afghanistan on October 3, 2015. Let me start by offering my sincere condolences to the victims of this devastating event. No nation does more to prevent civilian casualties than the United States, but we failed to meet our own high expectations on October 3. (DoD 2015)

This presentation of the US military's internal investigation raises questions about how military investigations represent and respond to civilian deaths from airstrikes. The attack under investigation killed 42 civilians and injured 37 civilians. While General Campbell reiterated the report's conclusion that the attack "was a tragic, but avoidable accident caused primarily by human error," he also sidestepped questions why the US was not consenting to an independent international investigation as requested by MSF. The report presented at this press conference is one of ten US military investigation reports into airstrikes that killed civilians in Afghanistan, Iraq, and Syria that have been made publicly available in redacted form. These reports make claims about the numbers of civilians killed, the causes of the strikes, and the appropriate legal evaluation of the attacks, which, in turn, are frequently contested by other organizations such as MSF (2015), the Afghanistan Independent Human Rights Commission (2008), the United Nations Mission to Afghanistan (2009; 2016), Human Rights Watch (2008), and Amnesty International (2014).

The US military's interest in investigating, counting, and accounting for civilian deaths was part of a broader shift in understanding the military's relationship with Afghan civilians. Starting in 2008, counterinsurgency (COIN) doctrine increasingly guided military operations in Afghanistan. In this framework, the support of the local population is "critical to defeating the insurgency" (ISAF 2008, 1). The July 2009 Tactical Directive implores soldiers: "We must avoid the trap of winning tactical victories—but suffering strategic defeats—by causing civilian casualties or excessive damage and thus alienating the people" (ISAF 2009, 1). International Security and Assistance Force (ISAF) commanders tried to effect a "cultural shift" within their troops (ISAF 2009, 2) that entailed restraints on the use of force and being "first with the truth" about their conduct (ISAF 2010a, 3). Civilians started to matter because they are the "human terrain" on which the war is fought (ISAF 2010a, 1).

This chapter reads US military investigation reports on civilian casualties as technologies of representing human deaths and lives, seeing and knowing, violence and law, tragedy and redress. It traces the shift from aggressive denials of civilian casualties to a framework in which the military still minimizes civilian casualty numbers and distrusts the testimony of Afghan witnesses, but treats civilian deaths as "strategically damaging" (ISAF 2011) incidents that call for "civilian casualty mitigation strategies" and "consequence management" (CALL 2012), including the performance of standardized expressions of regret.

The military investigation reports are informed by techniques of counting and identifying civilians. Visual technologies, a widely shared "professional vision" (Goodwin 1994), and specific vocabularies that enable soldiers to see people *as* civilians or noncivilians can lead to targeting decisions that lead to the deaths of civilians. Yet these same visual technologies and professional visions guide the investigation of civilian casualties. The institutionally trained and sanctioned visual and classificatory practices that led to airstrikes with civilian casualties are often repeated in the reports.

While reports draw on specific technologies of visual representation, I also propose to see the reports in their entirety as technologies of representing law and violence. The investigation reports offer judgments on the airstrikes, recommend changes in policy, and suggest measures to mitigate the impact of the violence on affected communities. In establishing (contested) facts and narratives of the violence, the military reports become mechanisms of both completing and containing the violence of the airstrike.

After providing context about airstrikes, US military reports, and the concept of the civilian, I will first analyze how the reports dealt with unseen and misidentified civilians. I then suggest that in their judgments on the legality of airstrikes and performances of regret, the reports aim to recognize civilian deaths without taking responsibility for them.

Situating Airstrikes, Reports, and Civilian Casualties

US and coalition forces in Afghanistan and Iraq have access to sophisticated technologies of aerial vision and violence, while other parties to these conflicts rely on inexpensive, intimate, and low-tech forms of violence such as "improvised explosive devices," suicide attacks, and urban warfare. The focus of this chapter on airstrikes as a specific modality of violence therefore implies a focus on the well-resourced militaries of the Global North and West that have a long history of using aerial warfare in the Middle East and Afghanistan and making arguments for its legality. The (British) Royal Air Force (RAF) bombed Jalalabad and Kabul in the 1919 Afghan War of Independence. In 1925, the French military shelled Damascus, an undefended city. The RAF also used "air control" as a tool of imperial policing in Iraq during the 1920s and 1930s, excusing their frequent mistakes as products of the inscrutable geography of the country (Satia 2014; Satia 2006). While some contemporary observers and diplomats have expressed concerns about the bombardment of Damascus, the Western use of air power in the Middle East between 1919 and 1945 was generally not considered in violation of international law (Wright 1926; Pedersen 2015). Not only were Middle Eastern nations long not recognized as states capable of lodging complaints to the League of Nations (Wright 1926), but Western international lawyers did not regard Middle Eastern and Afghan noncombatants as civilians protected by the emerging norms on aerial warfare.

The term "civilian" denoting a noncombatant was developed during World War I (Alexander 2007). Yet during the 1920s and 1930s, international lawyers recognized only European populations under foreign occupation as well as white colonial administrators as civilians (Wilke 2018). Non-European populations under European colonial rule or imperial control were invariably referred to as "natives," not "civilians" (Wilke 2018). The 1923 *Draft Rules on Aerial Warfare* prohibited aerial bombardment "for the purpose of terrorizing the civilian population, of destroying or damaging private property not of military character, or of injuring non-combatants" (Art. 22). In 1938, the League of Nations called for a prohibition on bombing civilian populations (Gregory 2006, 633). These declarations were not adopted as treaties. They also need to be read alongside professional practices that reserved the status of the "civilian" for white nonmilitary colonial administrators and European populations under foreign occupation.

Has the concept of the civilian been successfully universalized? In the wake of the 2001 NATO war in Afghanistan, the 2003 US invasion of Iraq, and the 2006 Israeli offensive in Lebanon, Derek Gregory (2006, 633) asked: "are we witnessing not only the deaths of hundreds of civilians but also the death of the idea of the civilian?" "According to our new masters of war," he added, "*they* don't have any" civilians (2006: 637). The concept of the civilian is fragile and fraught; it is not at home or at ease in the Middle East under Western imperial control. Yet organizations including the US military and the UN count "civilian casualties" with a confidence that belies the conceptual fragility and historical exclusions of the concept of the civilian.

Investigating Civilian Deaths

In 2008, the UN Mission to Afghanistan set up a network of regional offices with the mission to keep track of civilian deaths and injuries. Meanwhile, the US military established the Civilian Casualty Tracking Cell (CCTC), a unit dedicated to counting, mitigating, and investigating civilian casualties in Afghanistan (Center for Civilians in Conflict 2013). According to the reports released by the United Nations Mission to Afghanistan (UNAMA) since 2008, at least 35,755 civilians were killed by the parties to the conflict between 2007 and 2020. This number includes at least 3,997 Afghan civilians who were killed in airstrikes (Wilke 2019a).

The US military, which was involved in the overwhelming majority of NATO airstrikes in Afghanistan and Iraq, has investigated a number of airstrikes in Afghanistan, Iraq, and Syria. At the time that research for this chapter was conducted, the redacted reports of ten investigations into aerial violence in these three countries between July 2007 and October 2015 had been made available on the US Central Command's website in response to Freedom of Information Act (FOIA) requests. These include the following: reports on two separate investigations into the killing of two Reuters employees in Baghdad on 12 July 2007; the airstrikes in Azizabad (Afghanistan) on 21–22 August 2008; the 4 May 2009 attack on Garani, Bala Balouk District, Farah Province (Afghanistan); the 21 February strikes on a convoy near Shahidi Hassas, Uruzgan (Afghanistan); a 26 May 2012 strike in Paktiya Province (Afghanistan); an 28 November 2013 attack in Helmand Province (Afghanistan); a 14 November strike near Harim (Syria); a 13 March 2015 strike on a checkpoint near Al Hatra (Iraq); and the 3 October 2015 airstrike on the MSF Trauma Centre in Kunduz (Afghanistan). It is not known how many internal investigations into airstrikes exist; further FOIA requests by Amnesty International and other researchers have been unsuccessful (AI 2014). While the report on an airstrike in Helmand Province is redacted, except for the paragraph which informs the reader that the weather that morning was "good" with "light and variable" winds but some "haze" (US CENTCOM 2014, 3), the other nine reports on strikes between 2007 and 2015 offer sufficient detail to merit an analysis.

With one exception, all available investigations were conducted as "administrative fact-finding procedure[s]" (Art. 1–5) under Army Rule (AR) 15–16. The "AR 15-6 Investigating Officer's Guide" states that the investigators' primary duties are to "ascertain and consider evidence of all sides of an issue," to be "thorough and impartial," to "make findings and recommendations warranted by the facts," "comply with the instructions of the appointing authority," and "report the findings and recommendations to the appointing authority." Findings have to be "deduced from the evidence in the record" and supported by evidence that makes a specific fact or finding "more credible and probable than any other conclusion" (AR 15-6 Guide, D.1; C.8). The instructions list "issues" that could have contributed to the event being investigated, using terms borrowed from business management, not domestic or international law: "systemic breakdowns; failures in supervision, oversight, or leadership; program weaknesses; accountability for errors" (AR 15-6 Guide, D.4). These investigations are designed as administrative procedures fixing errant behavior or faulty policies; they are not designed to offer legal analyses of the conduct investigated or to make legal judgments on the (mis)conduct of soldiers.

The reports differ in format and detail. In the early AR 15-6 reports, investigators filled out the forms by hand, checked the appropriate boxes, and attached short descriptions of the incident (US CENTCOM 2007a, 2007b). The form used in 2007 was developed in 1983 and contained a half-page box for findings and a similar sized box for recommendations (see US CENTCOM 2007b), suggesting that it was intended for minor incidents rather than for exhaustive investigations of airstrikes with dozens of casualties. Later AR 15-6 reports visible exceeded the scope and format of the standard-issue AR 15-6 form: the report on the October 2015 strike on the MSF clinic in Kunduz was 95 pages long, with appendices offering 3000 pages of evidence.

All of these reports are partially redacted. Each redaction is accompanied by a superscript code that explains the rationale for the redaction. Yet the extent of the redactions varies. The Helmand report (US CENTCOM 2014) is almost completely redacted, other reports have significant portions of the analysis and recommendations redacted, and some reports have only light redactions, mainly involving the names of personnel and places as well as the types and call codes of aircraft involved. In working with the reports, I am cognizant that each word accessible to me is connected to portions of the text that are inaccessible to me. The hidden text not only includes the redactions in the reports, but also the Rules of Engagement (ROE), the military's internal norms governing the use of force. While awareness of the limitations of the texts is important, it is still possible to read this archive of state violence and knowledge creation "along the archival grain" (Stoler 2009), to ask how the reports construct facts, evaluate them according to different sets of rules, and understand the violence they seek to assess.

Scholars have used these reports as primary sources in order to reconstruct the event and causes of an airstrike (Gregory 2011). In this essay, I ask not what the reports reveal about the airstrikes, but what they reveal about the ways the US military makes sense of the aerial violence it authorizes. Investigations conducted by the same institution that caused the harm benefit from complete and fast access to records. Yet the interpretation of these records and the search for physical and testimonial evidence will be shaped by the institutional cultures and assumptions that are—to some degree—shared by the purveyors and the investigators of the violence. How can investigators see and know differently than the authors of the airstrike? The next section shows that while the reports do not simply ratify the airstrikes, their use of language and practices of assessing evidence and credibility perpetuate the conceptual frames that guided the airstrikes.

For communities affected by airstrikes, the US military's reports matter precisely because they are the official statements by the purveyors of the violence that killed families, destroyed homes, and displaced survivors. As reports by human rights organizations stress, the survivors are seeking explanations and acknowledgment from the armed forces that perpetrated the attacks (AIHRC 2008; AI 2014). Yet because many reports are not released and other reports vindicate the violence they report on, the US military reports have not been able to provide the acknowledgment that survivors have sought.

Finding Facts

How many civilians died in each airstrike that was investigated? The numbers offered by the US military are substantially lower than the numbers arrived at through investigations by the United Nations Assistance Mission to Afghanistan (UNAMA) or NGOs such as AIHRC, HRW, and AI. For example, the Afghan Independent Human Rights Commission lists 86 civilian victims of the May 2009 Garani attack; the UN Mission to Afghanistan (UNAMA) lists 64 (UNAMA 2010, 17); and the US military public summary of the US military investigation report claims that 78 Taliban and 26 civilians were killed that night. According to UNAMA, the February 2010 strikes on a civilian convoy in Uruzgan killed 32 civilians and injured 26 (UNAMA 2011, 50). The US military counted 15–16 civilians killed and three civilians injured but later paid compensation to the families of 23 victims identified by elders (US CENTCOM 2010, 43). Casualty numbers are not cold and hard: they are subject to pressures, interpretation, revisions, and uncertainties. The disagreement about the numbers of civilian deaths has two dimensions: the reports differ on the number of persons killed in the attacks, and they disagree how many of these victims should be considered civilians.

There are three different types of scenarios in which airstrikes kill civilians. In each scenario, the degrees of visibility and recognizability of civilians before the airstrike have implications for the investigation of casualties after the strike. First, *incidental deaths* are caused by airstrikes that hit a legitimate military target but kill civilians in the vicinity due to excessive force (Crawford 2013). Second, civilian casualties occur due to *civilian misidentification*: the people being targeted are "misidentified as hostile" (CALL 2012, 33) or combatants but should have been recognized as civilians. Third, civilian casualties can result from airstrikes in which the civilians were not seen: "unknown civilians in the target area" (CALL 2012, 33), for example persons who were passengers in cars or sleeping in buildings. These three scenarios can occur in different combinations. The literature on civilian deaths largely focuses on incidental deaths, arguing that they are largely the result of systematic risk taking rather than genuine "accidents" (Owen 2003; Crawford 2013; Cronin 2018). The US military's own analysis unit suggests that although "misidentification" was the cause of most civilian casualties from air strikes, this "challenge" has "received less attention" than other causes of civilian deaths that are amenable to technological fixes (JCOA 2013, 10).

The airstrikes investigated in the nine available US military reports on nine separate attacks suggest the importance of moving beyond the focus on incidental deaths. Only one of the strikes (Harim, Syria, 28 November 2013) is predominantly a case of "incidental deaths." Six of the eight attacks that were investigated included civilian misidentification: New Baghdad (12 July 2007), Azizabad (21–22 August 2008), Farah Province (4 May 2009), Uruzgan (21 February 2010), Al Hatra (13 March 2015), and Kunduz (4 October 2015) attacks. In seven of the eight attacks, some of the civilian victims who were in buildings or vehicles were not seen by those who authorized the violence. The following section focuses on the two main causes of civilian deaths in the incidents examined: unseen civilians and misidentified civilians, omitting "incidental deaths" that have been aptly analyzed in the literature (Crawford 2013; Cronin 2018; Halpern 2018).

UNSEEN CIVILIANS

Civilians who were not seen by the aircrews before the strike were frequently not counted as victims by the investigators. For example, on 13 March 2015, two civilian cars carrying families from a part of Iraq that had been occupied by the Islamic State stopped at a checkpoint. The drivers left the cars to talk to the soldiers. Unbeknownst to them, the checkpoint had been approved as a target for a US military aircraft circling overhead. The officers had designated the cars and drivers as noncivilian on the grounds that the drivers spent about 40 minutes talking to the checkpoint personnel while other cars stopped only briefly. This conjecture was used to designate the cars as legitimate targets. The US military investigation of the strike reviewed the video footage and found some visual evidence of civilian presences:

> At 6 seconds prior to rounds impact, 4 PAX [persons, C.W.] are seen emerging from both vehicles. One of the persons exiting the SUV presents a signature smaller than the other persons. This signature was assessed . . . as a possible child. The small signa-

> ture is only visible for approximately one second before rounds impact—meaning the [redacted] pilot had completed firing before the small signature became visible. (US CENTCOM 2015b, 3)

Four passengers had become visible after the bomb had been released but before it killed them. The report recognizes these four passengers as civilian casualties, but it makes no inquiries about other passengers who might have remained in the cars. The owner of the cars had testified to the US forces that initiated the investigation that her car alone had carried five civilian passengers (US CENTCOM 2015b); other sources mention eleven civilian victims from the two cars combined (Jaffe 2016). The military's report only recognizes the people who were visible before their deaths as victims. The testimony of Iraqis is not accepted as evidence of additional and unseen civilian lives and deaths.

A similar focus on individual visibility underlies the contestation about the number of civilians killed between 2 am and 8 am of 21–22 August 2008 in Azizabad. The UN Mission to Afghanistan had found evidence for 92 civilian casualties, and the Afghan Independent Human Rights Commission offers testimony from multiple survivors who were woken up by bombs, fled their houses, and later pulled families killed in their sleep from the rubble (AIHRC 2008, 16–17). The US military report, in contrast, insisted on 55 casualties, including 33 civilians and 22 "Anti-Coalition Militants" (US CENTCOM 200, 1). The publicly available summary of the report supports this claim by counting the number of fresh graves in the vicinity: "Since 24 June 08, 48 graves in a 20km radius from Azizabad" (US CENTCOM 2008, 4). This method of counting graves by aerial surveillance is validated in reference to local practices: "According to the General Director of the Haj, in the GIRoA [Government of the Islamic Republic of Afghanistan], all casualties in this incident would have been buried one body per grave" (US CENTCOM 2008, 4). Bombs, however, do not just cause death. The force of the blast rips bodies apart, and the heat burns them beyond recognition. In the aftermath of airstrikes, relatives often find only fragments of bodies to mourn and to bury. Investigators from the UN and NGOs interviewed witnesses and family members to compile lists of victims. Only the US military, the purveyor of the violence under investigation, insists on seeing burial evidence of the bodies that their bombs obliterated. The US military reports' insistence on visual evidence of civilian presences before and after the strike is part of a larger turn from relying on testimonial evidence to forensic evidence (Weizman 2012, 103). The voices of survivors and witnesses, deemed unreliable, are replaced with allegedly objective physical and visual evidence. While the US investigation into the Azizabad airstrike confidently deduced the number of deaths from the number of fresh graves counted by means of aerial surveillance, the report chides the UN and the AIHRC for relying on "inconsistent villager statements," "limited forensics," and not having "access to a multi-disciplined intelligence architecture" (US CENTCOM 2008, 2). As a result, "their reports lack independent evidence to support the allegations of higher numbers of civilian casualties" (US CENTCOM 2008, 2). In these allegations, the US report privileges an epistemology based on the use of high-end visual technologies and disparages careful research with survivors and communities. Yet physical and visual evidence cannot speak for itself; it needs to be presented, contextualized, and interpreted (Weizman 2012, 105). In Azizabad and elsewhere, unseen civilians were killed because the aircrews did not see them, and they were not counted because the investigators relied on visual technologies that could not render the full impact of the bombs sufficiently visible.

CIVILIAN MISIDENTIFICATION

While "unseen civilians" account for the gaps between *overall casualty numbers* reported by US military and other investigations, "civilian misidentification" accounts for the gaps between *civilian casualties* recognized by US military investigations and independent reports. Misidentified civilians were seen, but not *seen as civilians*: the people being targeted had been "misidentified as hostile" (CALL 2012, 33). Research into specific airstrikes has raised the issue of civilian misidentification (Gregory 2011; Kolanoski 2017; Wilke 2017; Wilke 2019b), but the literature on civilian deaths largely locates civilian deaths in the sphere of "incidental" or "collateral" damage (Crawford 2013; Cronin 2018; Halpern 2018). Yet the US military acknowledges that civilian casualties from air strikes are frequently the result of civilian misidentification (CALL 2012, 33). In order for investigations into airstrikes to recognize civilian misidentifications, they need to see differently than the aircrews did. Yet the same visual and perceptual practices that led to the misidentification of people as noncivilians can thwart their recognition as civilians in military reports.

Civilian misidentification involves the visual identification of people on the ground as noncivilians. In aerial warfare, seeing is a networked and technologically aided activity that relies on a common conceptual vocabulary and agreed-upon proxies for civilian status such as gender, age, and patterns of mobility. Women and children are often imagined as the perfect or quintessential civilians (Kinsella 2011; Garbett 2015). Afghan and Iraqi men, in contrast, were described as "military-aged male" (MAM). The 2012 *Civilian Casualty Prevention Handbook* acknowledges that this term wrongly "implies that the individuals are armed forces and therefore legitimate targets" (CALL 2012, 5). This institutionally sanctioned language that treats Afghan and Iraqi men as probable combatants is rooted in the history of aerial warfare in the region. The repeated bombardments of Syria, Iraq, and Afghanistan from 1919 to the 1930s were enabled by the refusal of Western powers to recognize the victims of aerial warfare as civilians. While the civilian status has technically been universalized, US and coalition forces in Iraq and Afghanistan have tended to imagine local men as potential or likely noncivilians.

The investigation into the 2010 Uruzgan attack shows that soldiers assumed persons on the ground to be male unless they saw evidence of clothing typical for women and children. After the vehicles were hit, the passengers who were not immobilized by the blast fled the convoy. At this moment, the re-assessment of the status of the passengers in the convoy began:

> As they were coming around to re-engage, the pilots observed the "squirters" had brightly colored clothing and looked like females [. . .]. The females appeared to be waving a scarf or a part of the burqas [. . .]. The OH-58Ds immediately ceased engagement, and reported the possible presence of females to the JTAC. (US CENTCOM 2010, 24)

The attack was stopped once women were spotted because gender was accepted as a proxy for civilian status. The men were classified as "military aged males" and, upon their deaths, initially as "enemies killed in action." The investigation report recognizes that the institutional vocabulary and individual language choices framed the passengers as likely noncivilians. For example, soldiers had described the movement of civilian vehicles as "flanking" (US CENTCOM 2010, 22) or "tactical maneuvering" (US CENTCOM 2010, 21) and the drone operators had pressured the screeners to reclassify children as "adolescents" and thereby possible combatants (US CENTCOM 2010, 33). Overall, crew members "emphasized information suggesting the vehicles were hostile, while downplaying or ignoring information to the contrary" (US CENTCOM 2010, 61).

The 2015 Kunduz report also criticizes the language used by individual soldiers as "non-standard, leading communication" that "prevented the mutual understanding of targeting data and commander's intent" (US

CENTCOM 2015b: 74). However, reports frequently adopt the language used by the officers they investigate. For example, one investigation describes the villagers fleeing an airstrike as "a group of similarly-sized adults moving in a tactical manner—definitely and rapidly in evenly spaced intervals across difficult terrain in the dark—behind the enemy's front line" (US CENTCOM 2009, 7).

Civilian misidentification resulted from assumptions about the status of persons on the basis of their inferred demographics and from the "desire" of the drone pilots, as one report puts it (US CENTCOM 2010, 33), to use force. The recognizability of civilians in Afghanistan is shaped by a history of imperial warfare that is hesitant to recognize Afghan men as civilians and by a collective imagination that sees civilian convoys as "flanking" armed groups and villagers fleeing a firefight as "similarly-sized adults moving in a tactical manner." While the reports problematize and reject some terminological choices, they consistently back the institutionally sanctioned terminology that makes it easier for US soldiers to imagine the people on the ground as noncivilians engaging in hostile activities. The use of visual technologies does not displace, but rather aids such imagination of bodies as suspicious and dangerous.

Judging Violence

The US military reports not only reconstruct the facts of the airstrikes, but they also assess whether the strikes have violated any applicable norms. Five reports on four separate incidents vindicated the actions of the soldiers involved. Three reports (on Uruzgan, Suri Kheyl, and Garani) found violation of some internal rules. Only the report on the October 2015 airstrike on the MSF hospital in Kunduz found violations of the "Law of Armed Conflict," though not a war crime. These assessments are partially echoed by other institutions: the prosecutor of the International Criminal Court concluded that none of the US and Coalition airstrikes in Afghanistan merits further investigation as a possible war crime because there was no indication that the aircrews deliberately targeted civilians (ICC 2017, para. 259). In a 2014 report, Amnesty International flagged several instances of US military conduct in Afghanistan as possible war crimes, but it did not include any airstrikes (AI 2014). Since the end of the Cold War in 1990, no NATO soldier has been indicted for authorizing or carrying out an airstrike. The absence of war crimes under international criminal law does not, however, imply the compliance of airstrikes with international humanitarian law (IHL), also called the Law of Armed Conflict (LOAC). While IHL permits the killing of civilians "so long as their deaths are either unforeseen or considered 'proportional' to the 'military advantage' gained" (Jones 2015, 690), it requires assessments of proportionality as well as the taking of adequate and feasible precautions to protect civilians from the violence of the conflict (Dinstein 2010, 138). These criteria and requirements are vague enough that they can be used to legitimize many forms of aerial violence, leading international lawyers to warn that "the laws of war have facilitated rather than restrained wartime violence" (Jochnick and Normand 1994, 50).

In the US military reports, international law plays a complex role. On the one hand, the reports acknowledge international law as a basic set of norms governing armed conflict and affirm the importance of complying with international law. On the other hand, the reports consistently evaluate the airstrikes for compliance with the institutionally specific and allegedly more demanding Rules of Engagement instead of international law. The presence of international law in these reports, I argue, is not (only) "facilitative" (Lieblich 2019), but *decorative*: IHL is used to legitimize the actors that commit violence without being invoked as a relevant restraint on US conduct. For example, the *Civilian Casualty Prevention Handbook* states: "The U.S. military has long been committed to upholding the law of armed conflict and minimizing collateral damage" (CALL 2012, 1). Some enemies of the United States, in contrast, are allegedly using "dirty tactics in violation of international law, such as refusing to identify its fighters and using human shields" (CALL 2012, 3). Here, international law is not invoked to impose any specific obligations, but to establish the relative moral standing of the parties to the conflict. This echoes arguments from the 1920s, when US military lawyers had advocated using the "overwhelming, strange, and devastating force" of aerial warfare against "elusive savage or semisavage people" because "when natives go to war, they don't observe the decencies of civilized regular soldiers" (Colby 1927, 284).

Within the US military reports on airstrikes, international law does not appear as a relevant restraint on aerial violence. The reports as well as related publications by the US military identify three sets of norms relevant for judging airstrikes: international law, US military rules encapsulated in the "rules of engagement" (ROE), and ISAF/NATO Tactical Guidances and Tactical Directives. Following Craig Jones, this amalgam of norms can be treated as "operational law" that "concentrates and directs military power through a language of law" (2015, 691). The *Handbook* relegates international law to an undemanding minimum standard: "The LOAC is an essential 'floor,' or minimum baseline, of legal behavior for armed forces" (CALL 2012, 3). The Rules of Engagement (ROE) and "other theater guidance" such as Tactical Directives are presented as the more relevant and demanding set of norms: "ROE are a more detailed set of rules consistent with LOAC that direct and guide the use of force and address self-defense, protection of civilians, detention, and restraint," (CALL 2012, 4) and "the ISAF tactical directive exceeds the legal requirements of the LOAC" (CALL 2012, 4). As a result of this specific blend of operational law, the analyses contained in the reports and related policy documents consistently refer to Rules of Engagement and Tactical Guidances, which are only partially available to the public. Yet these documents seem to ignore the actual IHL/LOAC requirements. For example, the *Handbook* explains: "While the use of force may be legally justified, not all permissible force is necessary in every case, and forces must also consider second-order effects" (CALL 2012, 3). However, any use of force that causes disproportionate harm to civilians is in violation of international humanitarian law and not just strategically inadvisable (Dinstein 2010, 128–134). In short, international law is invoked and used to bolster the institution's "law-abiding" status. Yet the rules of international law appear merely decorative: they are not used to analyze and constrain conduct.

In most of the cases analyzed, the US military reports largely found the strikes to be lawful but raised questions about compliance with directives. For example, the report on the Garani strikes found that the "totality of the circumstances" in each case "validated the lawful nature of the strike" (US CENTCOM 2009, 10), but "the inability to discern the presence of civilians and assess the potential collateral damage of those strikes is inconsistent with the U.S. Government's objective of providing security and safety for the Afghan people" (US CENTCOM 2009, 10). The "collateral damage" is weighed on the US military's own scales: the US report recognizes 26 civilian casualties (and 78 Taliban fighters killed), while the UN claims that 64 civilians were killed (UNAMA 2010, 17). In addition, this "collateral damage" is not assessed in relationship to the norms of IHL but found to be "inconsistent" with a stated institutional "objective." The deaths appear not in violation of shared norms but as failures to live up to self-imposed goals.

Causes and Recommendations

Investigations by the institutions that authorized the violence under scrutiny have the potential of directly prompting changes in policies and practices.

For example, in response to the communication problems leading up to the October 2015 attack on the MSF clinic in Kunduz, the US military report recommended operational changes, which were implemented (US CENTCOM 2015c). However, not all causes of civilian deaths from airstrikes are susceptible to easy technological fixes. The misidentification of civilians as persons who may be targeted, for example, is a product of networked vision, institutionally sanctioned vocabularies, and the "imagination" that identifies ordinary Afghans as threatening and "hostile."

One possible response to civilian misidentification is to blame the civilians for not being more visible or recognizable. The first set of norms developed to govern airstrikes, the 1923 *Draft Rules on Aerial Warfare*, made civilians responsible for their visibility and recognizability by asking that hospitals and other civilian buildings be "indicated by marks visible to aircraft" (Art. 25). In 2007, two different US military investigations into the killing of two Reuters employees in Baghdad similarly suggested regulating the appearance and conduct of the potential victims of aerial violence. The inquiry by the 1st Air Cavalry Brigade recommended to "enforce prohibitions on photographing aircraft" (US CENTCOM 2007a, 4) and that "reporters undergo 'hazardous duty training' " (US CENTCOM 2007a, 4). The latter recommendation was rejected by the commander. The inquiry by the 2nd Brigade Combat Team into the same incident recommended that "members of the press be encouraged or required to wear identifying vests or distinctive body armor" (US CENTCOM 2007b, 10) and that "Coalition Forces be notified when members of the press are operating" within their sector (CENTCOM 2007b, 10). By focusing the recommendations on modifying the behavior and clothing of the journalists, the reports locate the blame for the deaths partially with the victims. In addition, the reports focus on the killing of the journalists and not the men they had been talking to. The recommendations would have done nothing to prevent the killing of ordinary civilians. Any set of recommendations that is directed at potential victims instead of purveyors of violence implicates the victims in their own deaths and bolsters a violent status quo.

Starting in 2009, reports regularly recommended more training and fine-grained regulations on the use of language that might lead to misidentifying civilians. Acknowledging that concepts drive visual identification, the investigation into the Suri Kheyl airstrike stresses the need to debrief on "what language a ground force commander should and should not use to designate, name, or identify a target" (US CENTCOM 2012, 15) because a shared and precise use of language would help to "achieve greater overall situational awareness and understanding in difficult situations" (US

CENTCOM 2012, 15). Similarly, the Uruzgan inquiry recommended to "review war-fighting terminology for use in a COIN development" (US CENTCOM 2010, 1). More precisely, the report observed: "The use of the term military age males or 'MAMs' for adult males implies that all adult males are combatants and leads to a lack of discernment in target identification" (US CENTCOM 2010, 49). While the term "military aged males" was indeed used less in subsequent reports, it still appears in the transcripts of the communications that led to the 2015 Kunduz airstrike (US CENTCOM 2015c, 64).

Most recommendations contained in the reports focused on training and small operational changes rather than on deeper structural changes to policies. For example, the 2009 Garani investigation report recommended that coalition forces "should refine the existing guidance that explains both the operational objective and tactical procedures for employment of kinetic weapons" for "situations involving the potential for civilian casualties" (US CENTCOM 2009, 11), coupled with the suggestion to "conduct immediate training/re-training of all personnel already in theater" (US CENTCOM 2009, 11). If the recommendation is "training," the cause of the airstrikes is located not in the doctrines and policies, but in the individual soldier's deficient understanding and application of procedures.

The reports not only recommend more training, but they also become lesson material for future training. The summary of the Garani investigation confidently recommends that the report itself should "become available for the Joint Command's Joint Center for Operational Analysis (JCOA), . . . for them to capture, articulate, and publish lessons learned" (US CENTCOM 2009, 12). Calls for a better training of all units in the understanding and application of the Tactical Directive were renewed in the report on the February 2010 Uruzgan airstrike: "Train all U.S. units and Leaders to apply the Tactical Directive (TD) in the manner it was intended" (US CENTCOM 2010, 47). Five years later, the emphasis on training instead of rethinking remains constant. The summary of the Kunduz investigation reports that in response to the attack, "supplementary training on the applicable authorities' framework, rules of engagement, and the Commander's tactical guidance" was already delivered to 9,000 soldiers within weeks (US CENTCOM 2015c, n.p). The call for more training is a constant throughout the reports, culminating in the 2012 *Civilian Casualty Prevention Handbook* that incorporates AR 15-6 investigations, including a reproduction of the 2009 Garani report. Yet the handbook shows the limits of training more without changing the framework. It frames civilian casualties as a reputational and strategic problem and does not consider international law as a meaningful constraint on conduct in war.

Containing and Mitigating Violence

The shift to counterinsurgency thinking entailed a "move from viewing civilian casualties as a form of collateral damage to seeing civilian casualties as a strategic setback" (Gregory 2020, 169). NATO internal documents and requirements highlight the need to properly investigate civilian casualties: "Accuracy and timeliness of reporting are equally important: we should aim to be 'first with the truth' " (ISAF 2011, 1). After the 2008 Azizabad airstrike, the investigation recommended the taking of poststrike actions that have since become standard (see CALL 2012): "In order to preserve evidence following a military operation, U.S. Forces will attempt to comprehensively document casualties, communicate the facts, and evidence to GIRoA, IGOs, and NGOs; conduct Key Leader Engagements / Shuras, make solatia payments as appropriate, and coordinate immediate humanitarian assistance support" (US CENTCOM 2008, 6). However, none of these recommended actions was taken in the immediate aftermath of the Azizabad attack. The 2010 Uruzgan report, in turn, reiterated these recommendations but also reported on such mitigation measures taken in the aftermath of the attack. The report specifically recommended conducting "Key Leader Engagement (KLE) with village elders including a cultural dinner" as well as "Humanitarian Assistance by distributing food, medical supplies, and assisting in quick projects" (US CENTCOM 2010, 59). This poststrike mitigation work is understood to be part of "psychological operations" (PSYOPS).

Starting in 2009, AR 15-6 reports either report on expressions of regret by US military or political leaders or include such affective language. The range of terms is limited to "regret," "tragedy," and "condolences." The report on the May 2009 strikes near Garani states: "U.S. Leaders at all levels have expressed their deep regret over this incident, noting that the unnecessary loss of even one innocent life is too many" (US CENTCOM 2009, 13). Yet the statement refuses to take responsibility by blaming the Taliban for fighting in the vicinity of civilians, saying that "the Afghans and their Coalition partners continue to engage an enemy force that deliberately chooses—time and time again—to fight from within inhabited areas, placing innocent civilians at risk" (US CENTCOM 2009, 13). This evasion of responsibility and attempt to blame the Taliban for an airstrike conducted by international forces is especially poignant against the backdrop of the United Nations' repeated complaints that international forces have chosen to locate their "military facilities within or near areas where civilians are concentrated" in possible violation of international law (UNAMA 2010, 19). In the battle for the hearts and minds of civilians, both warring parties want to work with and among civilians even though this jeopardizes the safety of civilians whose deaths later appear as "collateral damage."

Where responsibility for the strike is not deflected by blaming the other party, the US military characterizes the strike as a "tragic mistake" (US CENTCOM 2010, 54) or "tragic incident" (US CENTCOM 2015c, n.p.). The public summary of the report on the 2015 airstrike on the MSF clinic in Kunduz assures the reader: "Senior U.S. representatives have spoken with MSF officials, including the MSF Executive Director, over two dozen times to express condolences, explain how the tragic incident occurred, and outline future steps" (US CENTCOM 2015c, n.p.).The report concludes: "The comprehensive investigation concluded that this tragic incident was caused by a combination of human errors, compounded by process and equipment failures" (US CENTCOM 2015c, n.p.). The language of "tragedy" is consistent across several investigations ranging from Garani 2009 to Kunduz 2015. While this language concedes the wrongfulness of the deaths, it disavows responsibility and replaces it with a performance of mourning as well as a lament for "errors." Such "errors," as Patricia Owens (2003) and Neta Crawford (2013) have shown drawing on Charles Perrow's concept of "normal accidents" (1999), are predictable: systematically risky behavior will lead to situations in which the risks taken materialize. Richard Halpern has argued that the use of "tragedy" removes these deaths "from human hands and places them in a timeless realm of inevitable suffering devoid of human agency" (Halpern 2018, 49). Designating airstrikes on civilians misidentified as noncivilians as "tragic" suggests that both the victims and the purveyors of the aerial violence are pained and troubled by it. The talk of "tragedy" sounds like a "lament" (Halpern 2018, 51) but treats civilian deaths as the materialization of risks inherent in the US military's policies on identifying and pursuing targets for airstrikes without taking moral responsibility for the deaths or contemplating systemic changes that would reduce these risks.

The rehearsed expressions of regret and tragedy are accompanied by an increasing willingness to issue "solatia" or "condolence payments" to injured survivors and relatives of civilians killed in the attacks—without any acknowledgment of legal liability. After the 2008 Azizabad strike, US forces issued no condolence payments but noted that the government of

Afghanistan made payments "to each family of the alleged 90 civilians" (US CENTCOM 2008, 5). Two years later, in contrast, the US military officially recognized "there were 15–16 Afghan Nationals killed" in the Uruzgan strike, but "claims were paid to the families of all 23 identified by the elders as killed" (US CENTCOM 2010, 43). As Thomas Gregory points out, condolence payments are conceptualized as "a weapon of war" that can "be used to mitigate or manage the strategic costs of civilian casualties" (2020, 173). The larger apparatus of "civilian casualty mitigation" is designed to follow up on and contain the physical violence of the airstrike through verbal communication and monetary repair to families and communities.

Conclusion

Since 2008, civilian casualties in Afghanistan and Iraq have been counted, tracked, and disputed. To the US and coalition forces, civilians have become the "human terrain" on which the war is fought. The strategic importance of civilian lives shapes how civilian deaths are counted and accounted for. The US military investigations into airstrikes with civilian casualties work as technologies of both representing human suffering and responding to it: they count overall and civilian casualties, identify manageable causes of civilian deaths, assert conformity with international law, and offer standardized expressions of regret.

The US military investigation reports rely on similar epistemic and conceptual assumptions as the aircrews that conducted the strikes. When read against independent reports that incorporate interviews with survivors and community members, the US military reports' reliance on distanced and distancing visual technologies is especially striking. Civilians who were in buildings and cars at the time of the airstrike were not "seen" by the aircrews and not recognized as victims by the investigators. The misidentification of civilians as targetable persons, in turn, is based on visual practices augmented by institutionally shared vocabularies. While some reports criticize the use of "nonstandard" and "leading" language as a contributor to the misidentification of civilians, the institutionally sanctioned and standardized terms such as "hostiles" and "local nationals" still foster an imagination that allows aircrews to see people on the ground as noncivilians. Civilians who were not seen by the aircrews were frequently not counted by the investigators because they had not been visually identified. The reports reflect and partially question the technologies of (un)seeing civilians in Afghanistan, Iraq, and Syria.

By asserting the conformity of US conduct with international law, the reports become part of "legal armature" of the conflicts in Afghanistan, Iraq, and Syria (Gregory 2015, 198). The reports contain sprinkles of international law insofar as they accuse other parties of the conflict of violating it, but the reports do not seriously contemplate international law as a restraint on US military action. The reports assess the conformity of the airstrikes not with international law but with the allegedly more demanding rules of engagement. This decorative use of international law paves the way for a standardized language of "regret" and "tragedy" that refuses responsibility. Starting in 2010, the reports aim to perform what they recommend: the calculated and rehearsed communication of regret coupled with material compensation designed to maintain the goodwill of the local population. US military investigation reports perform closure after violence; they are the bureaucratic end points of the airstrikes they investigate.

Note

The chapter was researched and written before the withdrawal of US and international troops from Afghanistan in 2021. The chaotic formal end of this phase of the war reinforces the urgency of thinking about how knowledge about armed conflict is produced, represented, and shared. I would like to thank Alexandra Moore, James Dawes, and Thomas Gregory for their insightful comments and queries. An early version of this essay was presented in the Law & Legal Studies research colloquium at Carleton University; I'm grateful to participants for challenging me to clarify key points.

Works Cited

Afghan Independent Human Rights Commission. 2008. *From Hope to Fear: An Afghan Perspective on Operations of Pro-Government Forces in Afghanistan.*

Alexander, Amanda. 2007. "The Genesis of the Civilian." *Leiden Journal of International Law* 20, no. 2: 359–376. https://doi.org/10.1017/S0922156506003347.

Amnesty International (AI) 2014. *Left in the Dark: Failures of Accountability for Civilian Casualties Caused by International Military Operations in Afghanistan.* August 2014, Index number: ASA 11/006/2014.

Butler, Judith. 2010. *Frames of War: When Is Life Grievable?* London: Verso.

Center for Army Lessons Learned (CALL). 2012. *Afghanistan Civilian Casualty Prevention Handbook.* June 2012.

Colby, Elbridge. 1927. "How to Fight Savage Tribes." *American Journal of International Law* 21: 279–288.

Crawford, Neta. 2013. *Accountability for Killing: Moral Responsibility for Collateral Damage in America's Post-9/11 Wars*. Oxford: Oxford University Press.

Cronin, Bruce. 2018. *Bugsplat: The Politics of Collateral Damage in Western Armed Conflicts*. Oxford: Oxford University Press.

Department of Defense (DoD). 2015. Transcript: *Department of Defense Press Briefing by General Campbell via teleconference from Afghanistan*, 25 November 2015. https://www.defense.gov/Newsroom/Transcripts/Transcript/Article/631359/department-of-defense-press-briefing-by-general-campbell-via-teleconference-fro/.

Dinstein, Yoram. *The Conduct of Hostilities under the Law of International Armed Conflict*, 2nd ed. Cambridge: Cambridge University Press.

Garbett, Claire. 2015. *The Concept of the Civilian: Legal Recognition, Adjudication and the Trials of International Criminal Justice*. Abingdon: Routledge.

Goodwin, Charles. 1994. "Professional Vision," *American Anthropologist* 96 (1994): 606–33.

Gregory, Derek. 2006. "The Death of the Civilian?" *Environment and Planning D: Society and Space* 24: 633–638. DOI: https://journals.sagepub.com/doi/10.1068/d2405ed.

Gregory, Derek. 2011. "From a View to a Kill: Drones and Late Modern War." *Theory, Culture & Society* 28, nos. 7–8: 188–215. https://doi.org/10.1177/0263276411423027.

Gregory, Thomas. 2012. "Potential Lives, Impossible Deaths." *International Feminist Journal of Politics* 14, no. 3: 327–347. https://doi.org/10.1080/14616742.2012.659851.

Gregory, Thomas. 2015. "Drones, Targeted Killing, and the Limitations of International Law." *International Political Sociology* 9: 198—212.

Gregory, Thomas. 2019. "Dangerous Feelings: Checkpoints and the Perception of Hostile Intent." *Security Dialogue* 50, no. 2: 131–147. https://doi.org/10.1177/0967010618820450.

Gregory, Thomas. 2020. "The costs of war: Condolence payments and the politics of killing civilians." *Review of International Studies* 46, no. 1: 156–176.

Halpern, Richard. 2018. "Collateral Damage and Tragic Form." *Critical Inquiry* 45 (Autumn): 47–75.

Human Rights Watch (HRW). 2008. "Troops in Contact': Airstrikes and Civilian Deaths in Afghanistan." https://www.hrw.org/sites/default/files/reports/afghanistan0908web_0.pdf.

International Criminal Court (ICC). 2017. Public redacted version of "Request for authorisation of an investigation pursuant to article 15," 20 November 2017, ICC-02/17-7-Conf-Exp.

International Security Assistance Force (ISAF). 2008. Tactical Directive (public version), 30 December 2008.

International Security Assistance Force (ISAF). 2009. Tactical Directive (public version), 6 July 2009.
International Security Assistance Force (ISAF). 2010a. Memorandum: COMISAF's Counterinsurgency Guidance. 1 August 2010.
International Security Assistance Force (ISAF). 2010b. Memorandum: Updated Tactical Directive (public version). 1 August 2010.
International Security Assistance Force (ISAF). 2010c. ISAF Commander's Counterinsurgency Guidance.
Jaffe, Greg. 2016. "U.S. reopens investigation into bombing that killed at least 11 Iraqi civilians." *Washington Post*, 27 June 2016. http://wapo.st/28Zx0lS.
Jochnick, Chris, and Roger Normand. 1994. "The Legitimation of Violence: A Critical History of the Laws of War." *Harvard International Law Journal* 35, no. 1 (Winter): 49–95.
Jones, Craig A. 2015. "Frames of law: targeting advice and operational law in the Israeli military." *Environment and Planning D: Society and Space* 33: 676–696.
Lieblich, Eliav. 2019. "The Facilitative Function of Jus in Bello." *European Journal of International Law* 30, no. 1: 321–340.
Kinsella, Helen M. 2011. *The Image Before the Weapon: A Critical History of the Distinction between Combatant and Civilian.* Ithaca and London: Cornell University Press.
Kolanoski, Martina. 2017. "Undoing the Legal Capacities of a Military Object: A Case Study on the (In)Visibility of Civilians." *Law & Social Inquiry* 42, no. 2: 377–397.
MacKenzie, Adrian, and Anna Munster. 2019. "Platform Seeing: Image Ensembles and Their Invisualities." *Theory, Culture & Society* 36, no. 5: 3–22.
Owens, Patricia. 2003. "Accidents Don't Just Happen: The Liberal Politics of High-Technology 'Humanitarian' War." *Millennium—Journal of International Studies* 32, no. 3: 595–616.
Pedersen, Susan. 2015. *The Guardians: The League of Nations and the Crisis of Empire.* Oxford: Oxford University Press.
Perrow, Charles. 1999. *Normal Accidents: Living with High-Risk Technologies*. Princeton: Princeton University Press.
Satia, Priya. 2006. "The Defense of Inhumanity: Air Control and the British Idea of Arabia." *American Historical Review* 111: 16–51.
Satia, Priya. 2014. "Drones: A History from the British Middle East." *Humanity* 5, no. 1: 1–31.
Stoler, Ann Laura. 2009. *Along the Archival Grain: Epistemic Anxieties and Colonial Common Sense*. Princeton: Princeton University Press.
United Nations Assistance Mission to Afghanistan (UNAMA). 2009. *Afghanistan: Annual Report on the Protection of Civilians in Conflict, 2008*. January, 2009.
United Nations Mission in Afghanistan (UNAMA) 2019. *Afghanistan: Annual Report on the Protection of Civilians in Conflict, 2018*. February, 2019.

United States Central Command (US CENTCOM). 2007a. *Report of the AR 15-6 Investigation into Conditions Surrounding the Possible Death of Two Reuters Reporters during an Engagement on 12 July 2007 by Crazyhorse 18 and 19 in the New Baghdad District of Baghdad (1st Cavalry Air Brigade, 1st Cavalry Division).* 20 July 2007.

United States Central Command (USCENTCOM). 2007b. *Investigation into Casualties from an Engagement on 12 July 2007 in the New Baghdad District of Baghdad, Iraq (2nd Brigade Combat Team, 2nd Infantry Division).* 17 July 2007.

United States Central Command (USCENTCOM). 2008. *Report on the AR 15-6 Investigation into new information relative to civilian casualties from engagement by U.S. and Afghan Forces on 21–22 AUG 2008 in Azizabad, Shindand District, Herat Province, Afghanistan.* October 1, 2008.

United States Central Command (USCENTCOM). 2009. *Unclassified Executive Summary of the U.S. Central Command Investigation into Civilian Casualties in Farah Province, Afghanistan on 4 May 2009.*

United States Central Command (USCENTCOM). 2010. *Report on the AR-15-6 Investigation, 21 February 2010 Air-to-Ground Engagement in the Vicinity of Shahidi Hassas, Uruzgan District, Afghanistan.* May 21, 2010.

United States Central Command (USCENTCOM). 2012. *AR 15-6 Investigation, Alleged CIVCAS Incident, Paktiya Province, Afghanistan, 26 May 2012.* 5 June 2012.

United States Central Command (USCENTCOM). 2014. *AR 15-6 Report of Investigation for 28 Nov 2013 Helmand Province CIVCAS.* 14 February 2014.

United States Central Command (US CENTCOM). 2015a. *AR 15-6 Report of Investigation into the Civilian Casualty near Harim, Syria, 5 November 2014.* 13 February 2015.

United States Central Command (USCENTCOM). 2015b. *Report on the Commander-Directed Investigation into Possible CIVCAS IVO Al-Hatra Checkpoint, Iraq, 13 Mar 15.* June 1, 2015.

United States Central Command (USCENTCOM). 2015c. *Report on the AR 15-6 Investigation into the Airstrike on the MSF Trauma Center in Kunduz, Afghanistan on October 3, 2015.* November 21, 2015.

United States Joint and Coalition Operational Analysis (JCOA). 2013. "Reducing and Mitigating Civilian Casualties: Enduring Lessons."

Weizman, Eyal. 2012. *The Least of all Possible Evils: Humanitarian Violence from Arendt to Gaza.* Brooklyn: Verso.

Wilke, Christiane. 2017. "Seeing and Unmaking Civilians in Afghanistan: Visual Technologies and Contested Professional Visions." *Science, Technology & Human Values* 42, no. 6: 1031–1060.

Wilke, Christiane. 2018. "How International Law Learned to Love the Bomb: Civilians and the Regulation of Aerial Warfare in the 1920s." *Australian Feminist Law Journal* 44, no. 1: 29–47.

Wilke, Christiane. 2019a. "Asymmetric Legality: The Invisibility of High-Tech Violence in Afghanistan." *Public Seminar.* May 2, 2019. http://www.publicseminar.org/2019/05/asymmetric-legality/.

Wilke, Christiane. 2019b. "High-Altitude Legality: Visuality and Jurisdiction in the Adjudication of NATO Air Strikes." *Canadian Journal of Law and Society* 34, no. 3: 261–280.

Wright, Quincy. 1926. The Bombardment of Damascus. *The American Journal of International Law* 20, no. 2 (Apr., 1926): 263–280.

Zehfuss, Maja. 2018. *War & the Politics of Ethics.* Oxford: Oxford University Press.

Chapter Seven

Contested Memories

The Intimate Public and Technologies of Affect in Memorializing Holocaust Trauma

BARBARA LESAVOY AND DONNA M. KOWAL

Public memorials are interactive, polysemic spaces where remembrance is shaped by technologies of visual culture, historical preservation, and individual memory practices, such as using mobile devices to document and share our encounters with landmark sites and representations of important events. No matter the form—an official or institution-sponsored, permanent monument or a spontaneously created, temporary commemoration—public memorials are critical to a community's need to remember, to heal, and to glean lessons from life-changing events and influential people. Memorials dedicated to remembering the Holocaust, the focus of this study, articulate a global culture of trauma and reify the extent of institutionalized crimes against humanity. Whether we enter the Auschwitz-Birkenau Memorial and Museum in Oświęcim, Poland, passing beneath the "Arbeit macht frei" iron gate, or walk through the Memorial to the Persecuted Jews of Europe in Berlin, Germany, we step into an environment where we interact with the unfathomable: the systematic annihilation of six million European Jews amongst tens of thousands of persecuted others and millions of additional civilian deaths. It is difficult to confront this reality, to come face to face with technologies of mass murder that white supremacist nationalist ideals calculated. But Holocaust memorials serve this intent: to (re)present mass collective trauma as undeniable historical fact.

This chapter is a rhetorical analysis of memorials associated with the Holocaust and is aimed at understanding how social media and related technologies transform how we archive emotional affect and represent competing narratives of human rights atrocities. We seek to call attention to the role of technology in negotiating the public/private tension inherent in the public memory of collective trauma and the rhetorical potential that emerging technologies offer for human rights activism aimed at challenging the erasure of memory. Upon analyzing several Holocaust memorials located in Germany, we argue that technology intervenes, disrupts, and alters the public memory of trauma.

As a map to the chapter, we open with a theoretical framing of the performative intersection of personal and public in how we archive trauma. We then analyze three Holocaust memorials in the city of Berlin, Germany, where we draw upon the theme of witnessing with a focus on ways the affective dimension to memorializing Holocaust trauma intersects with technologies of human rights: Track 17 at Grunewald Station, Memorial to the Murdered Jews of Europe, and Memorial to Homosexuals Persecuted under Nazism. We close with a discussion of how emerging technologies transform how we discover and represent human rights as a dimension of visual culture and collective memory as well as the rhetoric of trauma memory.

Technologies and the Intimate Public of Holocaust Memory

To encounter a Holocaust memorial is to enter an intimate public space where we "bear witness" to suffering, affirm collective identity, and engage in spiritual contemplation. In the process of consuming sites of trauma memory, which are often tied to commercial tourist activity, we perform identities, participate in collective meaning making, and document our personal impressions of the pursuit of human rights. Equipped with mobile devices, we record and share static and moving images to archive memories and affect and, in turn, re/constitute a self-narrative. Some memory practices are driven by the tourist sensibility of taking photos and posting selfies, thereby disrupting the solemnity involved in remembering tragedy and denying a potentially transformative emotional experience in favor of a souvenir. Put differently, digital technologies can act as "cognitive prostheses" by extending, enhancing, and even replacing memories (Lupton 2014, 33). To confront this cognitive prosthesis, artist Shahak Shapira created Yolocaust, a now terminated website, where he overlaid graphic archival images of actual death camp scenes onto transgressive social media posts of visitors documenting Holocaust tourism. We discuss Shapira's Yolocaust website and other social media imprints later in the chapter as we consider ways different technologies can interface and clash with Holocaust tourist and memory practices. Included in this digital analysis are individuals and groups who assert oppositional narratives and who have defaced Holocaust memorial sites with graffiti and acts of protest and violence. This sociocultural phenomenon, which Richard Sharpley theorizes as dark tourism, involves the confluence of "a tourist site, attraction or experience, and death, disaster, or suffering" (Sharpley 2009, 10). While the contexts for dark destinations vary widely—for example, public memory of wars, natural disasters, nuclear accidents, and terrorist attacks—the tourist interest in tragedy and morbidity raises important challenges that center on ethical considerations related to voyeurism; marketing and commercial gain implications; impacts of conflicting interpretations of reconciliation processes; and complexities associated with site curation and preservation (Sharpley 2009, 8–9). Articulating the incongruous and paradoxical discourse of dark tourism, where we empathize with while at the same time disassociate ourselves from state and nation-orchestrated tyranny and reconciliation, is central to our inquiry.

Our research is contextualized by the currents of heightened nationalism across the Global North, which is fueling resurgences of antisemitic, racist, and sexist violence. Technology has widened this footprint exponentially—for example, a quick Google search of "#whitenation" produces Twitter and Instagram accounts linked to Neo-Nazi platforms. The work of Anne Cvetkovich and Lauren Berlant, taken together, provide a cogent theoretical framework to consider this violent rhetoric, particularly, ways we negotiate affect, embodiment, and contested nationalities in the context of memorializing collective trauma (Cvetkovich 2003, Berlant 2011). Cvetkovich, writing on depression and private and public dimensions of lesbian marginality, categorizes trauma across a range of private and public affect that includes feelings of harm, sadness, and loss juxtaposed alongside sentiments of joy, worry, and confusion (Cvetkovich 2003, 48). In casting this wide emotive net, Cvetkovich deploys affect to depict and describe ways subordinated social identities experience and often clash with historical and social atrocities (48). This links to Berlant's concept of "cruel optimism," theorized as a relational dynamic between person and public, where living a good life is intricately entangled within capitalist power systems rooted in national dominance (Berlant 2011, 1–5). In the context of Holocaust horror, we see ways state-orchestrated violence can become normative, placing social pressure on individuals who do not adhere to nationalist identity conventions. For Berlant, and certainly those persecuted under Nazi tyranny, the presumption of equality accessible to all creates a false "optimism" that is, in reality, "cruel" (Berlant 2011, 1–5). The writings of Berlant and Cvetkovich push us to confront these traumatic cruelties, to become intimate with a counterpublic under which marginalized identities become the lifeblood of despotic regimes. We recognize that there is strategic utility here, as Berlant argues, insofar as the culture of "trauma can be a foundation for creating counterpublic spheres rather than evacuating them," and, as applied to geopolitical national traumas, the "intimate public sphere" is a discursive space where trauma defines identity (Berlant 2011, 15).

As a means to excavate an intimate counterpublic that shapes the experience of Holocaust trauma, we examine sites where human rights atrocities unfolded in Germany and Poland. With the discursive boundaries of personal and public trauma memory becoming more fluid through mobile technology, we employ an intertextual lens. Cvetkovich's analysis of trauma discourse shows the connections between Holocaust memorials and personal trauma—specifically, ways that public feelings as a dimension of trauma bleed into interactions with trauma victims and survivors, which informs personal and public displays of activism as part of a larger human rights agenda (Cvetkovich 2003, 3). This bleeding of personal into public and public into personal shapes the affective qualities of the intimate public that Berlant describes, where our personal resilience requires us to navigate treacherous impasses that public atrocities impose. As Berlant argues, "public spheres are always affect worlds, worlds to which people are bound, where they are, by affective projections" (2011, 226).

Theorizing this intimate public further involves naming and placing Holocaust trauma in social and political arenas that link emotion with the politics of state and nation. As Cvetkovich explains, this allows us to make connections between personal trauma and world historical events, which in turn forges an axis to what and how we remember trauma (3). Indeed, Holocaust trauma is not only experienced by survivors, but also by those who circulate in and around memory sites, and who, in encountering unforeseen and vulnerable spaces, are marked by trauma (3). Put differently, Holocaust trauma constitutes " 'spreadable media' or media produced digitally that circulate or 'spread' across multiple sites, platforms, and cultures in messy and difficult to govern ways" (Lupton 2014, 29). This digital unruliness is salient to how tourists use social media to reconstitute and archive interaction with

Holocaust memory, and this complicates the legibility of the human rights purpose of Holocaust remembrance. At the close of the chapter, we detail the case of an American teen who tweeted a smiley selfie while standing at the Auschwitz-Birkenau concentration and death camp. The controversial tweet and its ripple effect capture Lupton's notion of ethical self-formation, where social media posts and "like" and "share" buttons constitute identity while also extending and replacing traditional, embodied forms of memory practices (Lupton 2014, 28). The cognitive prostheses to these digital assemblages engender visual and cultural consumption of Holocaust memory that potentially supplant the personal corporeality inherent to witnessing and absorbing trauma. This circles back to the intimate public and affect world tensions that Berlant and Cvetkovich describe, where, in visiting sites that memorialize Holocaust death, we travel across national cultures of harm and indifference, mediated further by technologies that ostensibly disrupt the tenors of collective trauma that Holocaust memorials seek to preserve. These competing memories of Holocaust trauma, generated through survivor accounts as well as firsthand interactions with and digital representations of Holocaust memorials, juxtaposed against Holocaust memorials as state and nation reconciliation projects, demonstrate the complex nature of human rights work intended to memorialize genocides.

Trauma and Memory: A Public Feeling

Holocaust memorials contribute to our ability to reconcile state-sponsored human rights atrocities as we come to terms with ways personal identities clash with national ideals and origins. Cvetkovich maintains that the "presence and promise of cultural formations . . . bring traumatic histories into the public sphere" and that describing and accounting for affective experience with trauma "transform our sense of what constitutes a public sphere" (16). Memorials that recognize Holocaust trauma constitute these public and intimate public spheres where visitors bear witness to tragedies that bridge history with memory and culture. This gives rise to what Maria Sturken qualifies as cultural memory, where we link historiography to new and often embodied forms of memory as we bear witness to atrocities reconstituted in public sphere configurations (Sturken 1997; Cvetkovich 2003). With respect to the performative nature of cultural memory, we seek to reify the intimate public that Berlant theorizes while "not being defeated by what is overwhelming" (227). For Berlant, hope resides in resistance, a phenomenon that has jettisoned her 2011 cultural criticism from academic circles into the currency of 2019 sociopolitical analysis of Donald Trump's presidency. Writing on Berlant in a recent essay for *The New Yorker,* Hua Hsu (2019) notes, "The political backdrop that inspired *Cruel Optimism* seems quaint compared with the divisiveness of the present." Hsu goes on to reflect on ways Berlant's work helps fortify our day-to-day resilience against state and nation catastrophes and ways that her once complex literary framing of how we can flourish in the context of capitalist and global trauma now has pragmatic reach across wide audiences and histories.

World War II's mass genocide, measured against this larger geopolitical scope, constitutes a catastrophic event that differs from everyday trauma (Cvetkovich 2003, 19). This is not to say that everyday trauma is not part of catastrophic events, but rather, the emotive qualities that impact and create trauma are scaled differently in the landscape of public life as opposed to living day to day in a traumatic context. The seeping of personal into public and public into personal then "places moments of extreme trauma alongside moments of everyday distress" (Cvetkovich 2003, 20). This parallel is not without conflict, as Berlant and Cvetkovich explain, both in the need to remember national trauma, and in the emotive pain and subsequent tendency to distance ourselves from the anguish traumatic memories evoke. Rises in antisemitism and skepticism about the Holocaust as fact smack up against multiple human rights projects where public remembrance operates. Public practices such as the installation of monuments and preservation of historic sites and artifacts juxtaposed against private practices such as commercial tourism and social media posts of memorial imagery can each operate on contrasting planes. Berlant's construct of the intimate public makes clear that what we attune to politically can diverge from what we must contend with as public beings (228).

As we archive these sometimes-competing modes of Holocaust affect, we must traverse through complex terrain in the rhetoric of cultural memory. On this point, Cvetkovich turns to Lisa Kron's *2.5 Minute Ride,* a performance pieces that considers a range of affect associated with Holocaust trauma and memory (Cvetkovich 2003, 20–21). Part of Kron's performance wrestles with she and her father visiting Auschwitz as tourists and her father returning as a Holocaust survivor. The Nazi murder of Kron's grandparents and her father's survival loom over the script in ways that capture the paradox of tourism intersecting horror. Cvetkovich explains that, in *2.5 Minute Ride,* Kron fears that she will be numb to the atrocities of her grandparents' murder, that the prescribed, automated structure to the Auschwitz-Birkenau Memorial and Museum will distance her from its real and gruesome realities 21). Cvetkovich then asks if Auschwitz as a tourist site can divorce itself from the tourist attraction quality that comes with visiting an amusement park, suggesting that, even with the historic materiality of mass extermination, it compartmentalizes lessons of terror into safely consumable bites. This contrast is paramount to Kron's *2.5 Minute Ride*, where she scripts the devastation of her grandparent's death alongside the mundanities of tourism, such as revisiting Auschwitz so her father can retrieve his forgotten sunglasses, or she and her father fumbling with German language barriers as they navigate restaurant menus or street signs. This juxtaposition of the everyday situated in the context of genocide resonates with the private-public tensions that Berlant and Cvetkovich theorize, particularly ways we catalogue multiple iterations of national trauma as we simultaneously grasp for what is routine and secure in everyday life, so we are not defeated by larger geopolitical oppressions. In what follows, we explore the rhetoric of trauma memory manifested in the discourse of three particular Holocaust memorials.

Archiving Human Rights Abuse

The Track 17 (Gleis 17) Holocaust memorial at the Berlin Grunewald S-Bahn station provides a fitting point of departure for contemplating the intersection of memory, human rights, trauma, technology, and visual culture. Beginning on October 18, 1941, Track 17 was the primary depot used to deport Jews living in Berlin to ghettos, concentration camps, and death camps. The design contest that resulted in this memorial installation was led by Deutsche Bahn, the national railway company of Germany—the direct predecessor and beneficiary of the German National Railway (Deutsche Reichsbahn), the very freight and passenger car network that made the "Final Solution" possible. The meticulously coordinated and devious "resettlement" system included routine procedures such as publishing train timetables and collecting fares from those destined for concentration and extermination camps. Figure 7.1 shows the memorial installed in 1991, designed by Polish artist Karol Bronaitowski. The wall depicts a series of recessed, hollow figures of various sizes, representing men, women, and children who had walked this very path to board a train for deportation. The emotional affect of the concrete design is raw; the figures appear as mere shadows, lives that have been erased. Passersby may pause and reflect upon the traumatic import that the hollowed-out silhouettes project, or they

Figure 7.1. *Monument to the Deported Jews of Berlin* at the Grunewald S-Bahn Station in Berlin, Germany. Photograph by Donna M. Kowal.

may overlook the magnitude of horror altogether as the shadowy figures blend into the streetscape.

There is a second piece to this memorial that is somewhat hidden, even though Track 17 is an active train station that is used daily by commuters. The accompanying memorial is accessed from a narrow, shaded, and wooded path next to the station entrance. The path leads to a preserved railway track with inscriptions on the platform (figure 7.2). These inscriptions detail individual dates in which trains left from Grunewald station, the number of deportees on board that day, and where they were transported. Most were sent directly to Auschwitz, and, in total, there were approximately 50,000 individuals who were deported from the station ("Gleis 17 Memorial, Berlin-Grunewald"). Walking along the secluded railway, one can hear the unsettling sound of passing trains on the adjacent commuter track. Track 17 thus viscerally informs our understanding of the connections between technologies, human rights, and trauma memory; technologies of rail transit are a practical means of traveling across time and space, and, as

Figure 7.2. *Track 17 Memorial* at the Gruenwald S-Bahn station in Berlin, Germany. Photograph by Donna M. Kowal.

memorialized in this installation, they can be appropriated by despotic state and non-state actors to engineer and orchestrate genocide.

Etched into concrete and preserved in steel, Track 17 invites introspection as we consider memory of the trauma of human extermination under the Nazi regime, made possible by the combined conditions of modern technology, industrial progress, and capitalist enterprise. Engineers, doctors, and scientists were employed by the Nazi regime to orchestrate mass murder with the utmost efficiency. This included the creation of a rail system for the purpose of deportation, as discussed above; tracking the Jewish population through a calculating machine (known as the Hollerith, it preceded the invention of the computer); spreading propaganda by radio and film; manufacturing nerve gas and gas chambers; and repurposing human hair collected from corpses to make ignition mechanisms for bombs, ropes and cords for ships, and stuffing for mattresses (Leventhal 1995). Thus, technology consists not only of tools—that is, machinery and media—but it constitutes a belief and value system that prioritizes efficiency and systematization. French sociologist Jacques Ellul coined the term "technique" to capture "the *totality of methods rationally arrived at* and having absolute efficiency . . . in *every* field of human activity" (Ellul 1964, xxv). Ellul's view of technology highlights its ideological implications and contrasts with the commonplace notion that technology is morally neutral, as demonstrated by the assertion "guns don't kill people, people do." As Eric Katz submits, this assertion fails to recognize how technology *a priori* transforms human identity and decision making to "reflect the *requirements of the technologies* that we use" (Katz 2005, 420).

Even with the corporeal imagery and railway remains that the Track 17 memorial presents, memory can fade when historical events connected to public trauma become distant in time, supplanted by newer and more recent oppressions. Consider the implications for contemporary state-engineered violence. Migrant families, children and parents separated and imprisoned at the U.S. Mexico border, reify current politically engineered trauma. New York Rep. Alexandria Ocasio-Cortez recently likened the US southern border detention crisis to the Holocaust, while the Holocaust Museum in Washington DC cautioned against such analogy, fearing that one trauma would dilute the other (Cronin-Furman 2019). Despite parallels and differences between the Holocaust and violations unraveling at the US southern border, as public misconduct spills into private spaces, we must be careful not to eschew liability as a means of coping with abusive leaders exerting systemic oppression. In other words, we can't retreat as we witness governments violating human rights; rather, we must reach for government accountability in the face of such violations. Cvetkovich uses the phrase "amnesiac power" to explain the way national culture makes us "adept at using one trauma story to suppress another" and that we can become numb under the echo of repeating national traumas (16). The Holocaust. The AIDS crisis. Gender-based violence. These recurring crimes against humanity, performed across a local and global stage, are hard to endure. As Cvetkovich argues, we can see how a blunted affect to public atrocities can increase when iterations of national trauma multiply (16). Tragically, recent surges in ethnic and antisemitic hate affirm that old does supplant new.

A clashing of ideological interests is further illustrated by the intertextual discourse of two other memorials situated in the city of Berlin: Memorial to the Homosexuals Persecuted Under Nazism (figure 7.3) and Memorial to the Murdered Jews of Europe (figure 7.4). Both are located near Brandenburg Gate in the so-called memory district, an area of high tourist activity that is also part of the normative, everyday urban landscape

Figure 7.3. *Memorial to Homosexuals Persecuted under Nazism* in Berlin, Germany. Photograph by Donna M. Kowal.

Figure 7.4. *Memorial to the Murdered Jews of Europe* in Berlin, Germany. Photograph by Donna M. Kowal.

common to the city's inhabitants. In other words, it is a public space that has been distinguished for official memory that blends reflexive and unreflexive performativity (Edensor 2001, 61–62)—notably more so than Track 17, which is nestled in a quiet neighborhood. Encounters at or in close proximity to these two memorials positioned in the heart of Berlin include religious pilgrimages, guided tours, mourning the dead, employee lunch breaks, children playing, vandalism, and more. Although designed by different artists and installed several years apart, these memorials share some recurring postmodern architectural features. Both are abstract in design; they are constructed of dark concrete, tilted or uneven slabs. Not to be solely looked upon from a distance, they are highly interactive; they invite us to peer through and walk in and around, invoking our senses of touch, sight, and sound. The rhetorical impact of these memorials centers on their emotional affect; they invite us to feel anxiety, fear, despair, loneliness, isolation, and even terror. Yet, consistent with their postmodern design, these two memorials also invite multiple, competing readings. According to Carole Blair, Martha S. Jeppeson, and Enrico Pucci Jr., "Postmodern architecture symbolically undercuts modernism's progressivist faith in the new and its valorization of rationality, technology, and corporatism, all of which objectify and dehumanize the social sphere and the individuals who inhabit it. Moreover, postmodern architecture formally and symbolically questions the value of metanarrativity at large" (Blair et al. 1991, 226). Indeed, rather than convey a unified narrative of Holocaust trauma or sacralize its memory, the indeterminate and participatory qualities of the memorials raise crucial questions about who is being memorialized and how, as well as call attention to the appropriation and erasure of trauma memory.

The Memorial to Homosexuals Persecuted under Nazism was dedicated in 2008, designed by Michael Elmgreen and Ingar Dragset with the intention of recognizing the LGBTQ+ victims of the Holocaust who had long been excluded from or marginalized by official narratives. From a distance the cuboid appears strange, as it is tilted and lacks conspicuous signage (figure 7.3). The only signage is a small, discrete metal plaque positioned close to the ground at the main path leading to the memorial. Consequently, there is a potential for some visitors to approach the memorial without any foreknowledge of its commemorative purpose. On the front side of the cuboid is a window through which visitors can peer into and view a short film loop that depicts intimate moments and traumatic experiences in the lives of nonhetero people. The use of video in this memorial design is powerful in invoking life inside the closet and the complexity of the oppressive force of the heteronormative gaze. The video is disquieting not only in exposing private, intimate moments but also in placing the viewer in the position of oppressor by reinforcing the gaze. Moreover, taking a photo of the video loop, as some tourists inevitably do, reveals the reflection of one's own face in the photograph. Ultimately, the use of digital technology in this memorial to archive memory and affect of "the persecution of homosexuals" calls to question who holds the gaze and who is its object.

It is also important to recognize that the content of the video loop, which has changed over the years, has been a point of contention. The original video featuring two white men kissing in a long embrace was met with both praise and opposition. Critics argued that this video, in the process of creating a discursive space for normalizing nonhetero intimacy, served to reinforce norms of exclusion by representing men's experiences of desire and oppression at the expense of women's. As a consequence of that critique, the ensuing debate called attention to the complexity of memory as past interwoven into present and gender identity as intersectional (Wilke 2013). The resolution arrived at was to change the video loop periodically to reflect differing experiences ("Film inside the Memorial"). Accordingly, as Jennifer E. Evans observes, "the memorial changed from being a marker of historical persecution to a place of mobilization around contemporary concerns" that center upon differing experiences of victimization (Evans 2014, 76). For example, the second film, *Neverending Kiss*, by the artists Gerald Backhaus, Bernd Fischer, and Ibrahim Gülnar, captures diverse representations of same-sex desire with multiple layers of gazing at play in the performance. Viewers peering into the cuboid watch a series of same-sex couples kiss while also watching a diverse range of people within the film gaze at the kissers. We see a lesbian couple kissing on a train and then pan to a woman stepping onto the train who quickly averts her gaze as she spots this lesbian affection. A small child looks on in curiosity at two men kissing as a disapproving adult grabs his arm and jolts him away. And an elderly male couple eye two young men kiss as the camera then turns to reveal these watchers kissing. The interchangeable subject to *Neverending Kiss*—gazers gazing upon the gazed and the gazers—resonates with the panoptic surveillance that Lupton describes as we peer at homosexual love thematic to Nazi Germany persecution (Lupton 2014, 25). At the same time, the film's oppositional narrative reifies Evan's mobilization argument, as viewers looking into the cuboid witness performative resistance to same-sex oppression, a theme central to remembering the Holocaust and its recurring human rights abuse (Evans 2014, 76).

The Memorial to the Murdered Jews of Europe, designed by Peter Eisenman and Buro Happold, was commemorated in 2005. It spans 200,000 square feet of individual slabs—memorial "stelae" representing victims of the Holocaust—that are installed on a sloping terrain. The stelae vary in height, towering as high as over 15 feet. Walking among the stelae, it is possible to get completely lost and feel overwhelmed, consumed by the enormity of trauma that the memorials invoke. Critics of this memorial have argued that the stelae are too vague—in fact, it has been argued that the structure, without any plainly visible interpretive signage, constitutes a kind of trauma of its own. This lack of understanding of the memorial is demonstrated by the way some visitors interact at the site, which has led to its nickname "the Holocaust beach." In contrast with the memorial's somber purpose, on any given day, depending on the weather and season, one can find people enjoying a picnic lunch, basking in the sun, hopping on top of the stelae, playing hide-and-go-seek from below, and, of course, taking photographs and selfies. The irony of these behaviors led artist Shahak Shapira to launch "Yolocaust," a now defunct website that provocatively challenged the above habitual behaviors at the memorial. The project involved superimposing graphic archival images of actual death camp scenes onto what he perceived to be shameful social media posts—along with the likes, hashtags, and comments that reinforce the practice. For example, one such image featured a woman doing a yoga pose on top of a stela with the message, "Yoga is the connection with everything around us" and two emojis: a relieved face and hands raised palm-to-palm. Shapira replaced the stelae background with an image of a pile of corpses. Another example featured a photograph of a couple holding up a selfie of themselves amidst the stelae—a double image. Shapira replaced the stelae background with an image of famished prisoners crowded into barracks.

Shapira ended his Yolocaust project over two years ago, prompted by an email response from the subject of his very first picture, where a young man tweeted a selfie jumping on the concrete slabs with the caption, "Jumping on dead Jews @ Holocaust Memorial." As closure, Shapira posted the young man's email to his site:

> The photo was meant for my friends as a joke. I am known to make out of line . . . stupid . . . sarcastic jokes. And they get it. If you knew me you would too. But when it gets shared, and comes to strangers who have no idea who I am, they just see someone disrespecting something important to someone else

> or them. That was not my intention. And I am sorry. I truly am. . . . P.S. Oh, and if you could explain to BBC, Haaretz and aaaaallll the other blogs, news stations etc. etc. that I fucked up, that'd be great.

That Shapira rested his project on this first image and the subject's subsequent request for redemption speaks volumes to technologies' tactical utility in human rights work. Despite the indiscretions that prompted Shapira's Yolocaust intervention, its landing point tells us that there is, in part, potential remedy in personal and public transgression as we understand and make meaning out of Holocaust trauma. Shapira affirms this, concluding that most of his Yolocaust subjects understood their offenses and removed their selfies from their social media sites. The reflexivity demonstrated by perceived offenders of Holocaust memory protocol, along with Yolocaust's research and educational reach, illuminate the restorative promise technology offers as an interactive learning platform. This does not supplant the textbook history lesson as we seek to record and remember Nazi genocide; rather, it widens ways we access and deploy that lesson, introducing a range of variables that build upon and reconstitute a dynamic human rights agenda in the arena of trauma and memory work.

Negotiating Corporeality, Memory, and Affect

As we contemplate the multiplicity of meanings that circulate in and around sites that memorialize Holocaust trauma, we recognize that memory is in part regulated by materiality and visual culture. For example, the entrance sign to Auschwitz that declares "work sets you free" (translated) is an important historical artifact and piece of evidence. It has endured as an iconic symbol of genocide even as it has been vandalized, stolen, repaired, and replicated. Such visual artifacts, along with the corporeal nature of public memorials, are essential to the preservation of memory of both collective and individual trauma. Tourist activity itself is a corporeal performance that shapes meaning making at memory sites. As Tim Edensor argues, tourism sites are "distinguished by boundedness, whether physical or symbolic, and are often organized—or stage managed—to provide and sustain common-sense understandings about what activities should take place" (63). We argue that the digital footprint created by archiving memory expands that "boundedness" exponentially, such that meaning totally lacks reference to materiality, as illustrated by Holocaust denier narratives, and if memories lack materiality or are rendered as "fake," they are at greater risk of being erased. Therefore, the public and personal use of technology to document and share static and moving images—even of representations of trauma that are far removed from the present moment—serve an important purpose in archiving and sharing moments, experiences, and feelings that support human rights work. Still, the use of such memory practices at sites of so-called dark tourism present a notable moral and ontological challenge.

Put simply, the sociocultural phenomenon of dark tourism can conflate holiday sightseeing with sacred pilgrimages to sites that memorialize torture and death (Sharpley 2009, 10). We see this tourist paradox play out in Kron's *2.5 Minute Ride* in the same way that we see Cvetkovich argue that the prescribed regimen of a concentration camp visit can get trapped in an amusement park context. Similarly, because tourist destinations and travel purposes vary widely among individuals and memorial sites, so too do forms of witnessing that reconstitute and archive histories of genocide and trauma. This subjective range results in conflicting interpretations on reconciliation processes, and it also impacts ways memorial sites curate and preserve traumatic histories (Sharpley 2009, 8–9). In his reflective essay about the experience of visiting Auschwitz-Birkenau, William F. S. Miles recounts in vivid detail the massive crowds of tourists walking through barracks and gas chambers, as well as the gruesome exhibits of human hair and personal belongings in the otherwise small, quiet Polish town of Oświęcim (Miles 2001, 11–12). Moreover, factoring in the touristic, normative behavior of documenting and sharing images of "being there," dark tourist sites are arguably *a priori* incongruous with the human need to mourn and contemplate tragedy. This is the case in part because dark tourist sites are perceived by many as sacred spaces—for example, imagine someone taking a photo of a sand pit where bodies were disposed at Birkenau. In addition to the obvious moral affront of this scene, the use of technology encourages an emotional detachment from the human tragedy that is being witnessed.

The practice of taking photos and videos in the context of memory preservation is thus complex because it simultaneously affirms and denies lived experience and emotional affect. In her forward-thinking work *On Photography* (1973), Susan Sontag writes, "A way of certifying experience, taking photographs is also a way of refusing it—by limiting experience to a search for the photogenic, by converting experience into an image, a souvenir. . . . Most tourists put the camera between themselves and whatever is remarkable that they encounter" (5). Put differently, the use of mobile technology can turn us into "roving eyes looking for potential memories"—that is, looking for opportunities to say "I was here" instead of simply being present and directly experiencing and feeling our emotions and bodies in space (Keep 2009, 65). And, even if we seek to experience a dark tourist site without the filter of technology, we are likely to confront the distractions posed by others' digital memory practices. In this sense, as a popular if not obligatory tourist activity, taking photos and videos can discourage us from contemplating the trauma that defines sites of dark tourism.

This filtering of digital technologies in regulating Holocaust memory complicates its human rights dimension. Social media platforms such as Twitter, Facebook, and Instagram have radically shifted ways information is produced and circulated (Lupton 2014, 21). Technology is now an extension of identity, which Donna Haraway theorizes as the cyborg, the blending of human and machine (Haraway 1991), and which Lupton defines as assemblages, "hybrid phenomena that form when human and non-human actors interact" (Lupton 2014, 23). Assemblages help us "understand our relationships to and use of digital technologies" across networks that are not fixed, stable, or natural (24). We watch and are watched over, enabling a power exchange where private and public surveillance and countersurveillances loom. These semiotic and entangled digital configurations carry sociomaterial and subjective inscriptions with wide emotional range. Given this panoptic and its emotive breadth, tweeting or posting imagery or affect as we interact with Holocaust memorials can authenticate Holocaust tragedy while also transgress lived atrocities that constitute that traumatic history. We land in a digital minefield of sorts as we archive multiple layers of Holocaust memory across a human rights landscape that is shifting in its social and political ideals. Safeguarding universal freedoms that state regimes blatantly oppress means that we must be astute to ways digital technologies can facilitate while also violate social histories of what public memory becomes. Thus, in preserving Holocaust memory as part of human rights work, we must be mindful of the nation-orchestrated technologies of mass murder that became the Holocaust, as well as of individual cyborg technologies that bear witness to how we understand and make meaning out of these Holocaust atrocities today. The tourist selfie performed at a Holocaust death camp offers a contemporary yardstick for analysis.

In June 2014, a newly minted high school graduate from Alabama, Breanna Mitchell, gained notoriety after posting on social media a smiling selfie in the Auschwitz-Birkenau death camp. In the Instagram/Twitter sphere, the image went viral and the young teen found herself under a sea of fire for what the public read as insensitivity to the Holocaust and its memory. Breanna countered this criticism with her own explanation: Her dad had died one year to the day of the selfie. The Holocaust was a history topic that they had studied together, so the photo, according to Breanna, was, "Look Dad I made it here," verus, "Haha, me at a concentration camp" (Durando 2014). While smartphones have made selfies and other souvenir photos like it more commonplace, this particular image at a site of dark tourism hit a paradoxical chord. Does a smiley selfie taken at a sacred site transgress the purpose and intent that the site memorializes or are there more nuanced meanings woven into the "I was here" photo captured in spaces of tragedy? The paradox here and in its larger overlay raises the specter of how and in what ways we deploy new technologies as we visit and consume public sites of human rights violations.

Jennifer Ouellette (2014), writing on the "science of self," argues that selfies as posted on social media may not be simple attention grabbers, but rather they represent an attempt to place oneself in a context and make meaning of how we fit in. Breanna's argument, that the happy image of herself at the Auschwitz death camp was a travel tribute to her deceased father, suggests that what might appear disrespectful can have alternate explanations. Despite this ground, Breanna's justification on ways she fits into and makes personal meaning out of Auschwitz does not erase the requisite need for digital decorum as we understand and remember public trauma such as the Holocaust and as we interact with sites that memorialize these human rights abuses. The adage "we will never forget" is grounded in trauma we must remember so we do not let the same atrocities repeat. The need to remember, then, to prevent recurrence and comprehend fully the torture and abuse World War II genocide produced, leaves little room for missed meaning even if, as Ouellette explains, that meaning introduces revisionist narratives with personal footing. Rises in antisemitism and ongoing claims that the Holocaust is fabricated make Holocaust memory paramount. Circling back to Breanna, her initial reaction to the Twitter storm that her selfie generated—"I'm famous y'all"—and the following day, in a video interview posted to YouTube—"Honestly, I don't think I would do anything differently because I didn't mean any harm"—raises a disconcerting note on ways personal rhetoric can inadvertently dislocate collective memory salient to public trauma (Durando 2014). Not intending harm in a smiley tweet with the Auschwitz death camp as landscape is quite apart from being impervious to the hurtful consequences that tweeted selfie engenders.

The affect dimension that Berlant affirms and the clashing of public with private that Cvetkovich theorizes reverberate in the Breanna Mitchell selfie controversy. This case example, coupled with Shahak Shapira's Yolocaust project, illustrates how lack of (or ignorant disregard for) collective memory can mingle with self-promotion and morph into expressions of disrespect. There is a critical materiality component inherent to these self-crafted media bites that echo Haraway's cyborg and Lupton's assemblages that shape our object-driven worlds. The shaping, in part, is the personal and public intersection to what the smiley Auschwitz selfie communicates in the context of technologies of human rights work. Posted to social media, Breanna's selfie took on a "sticky" quality that cultural studies scholar Henry Jenkins (2009) defines as content that attracts and holds the attention of site visitors. Digital technologies such as like and share buttons transform sticky content to what Jenkins terms "spreadable," where, posted across a host of social media sites, it takes on a life of its own, signifying individual and group choices, preferences, and belief systems. Spreadable media is difficult to govern as it spirals from conceptual phenomena to embodied ideas and behaviors, reifying the material hybridity to digital data that Jenkins and Lupton et al. describe. The interactive platform to digital technologies, then, enables multiple permutations where users respond to but also modify original posts, adding onto and potentially altering meaning and import.

A high school senior's smiley selfie tweeted from the Auschwitz death camp may constitute one form of respective witnessing, but the sticky content of that selfie and the spreadable media storm that ensued inscribe codes of power and ethical formations that echo back to its Holocaust backdrop as a site of state-engineered mass genocide. Despite Ouellette's science of the selfie as context, preserving the origin and affect that ground Holocaust trauma evokes flies in the face of sanctioning the digitized and storied networks an Auschwitz selfie narrates. The intimate public to Berlant's affect world says that our survival relies on collective mediation, so we are not defeated by what is seemingly overwhelming (Berlant 2011, 222). Cyborg and digital assemblages engage this collective mediation as we navigate our way across multiple and often competing technologies where indiscretions collide with traumas.

Conclusion

The risks of contested trauma memories cannot be understated. Employing Hannah Arendt's (1963) notion of "the banality of evil," Gerard A. Hauser asserts, "People form their knowledge of the progressive possibilities of their histories from experiences that have endured as significant moments and that resonate with the current times. The preserved and shared past becomes a vernacular inscription of deeds and values. . . . Without cultural memory social actors are denied the very terms of which they may understand their own reflexivity in creating their identity. They are denied, as well, the precondition for confronting the past" (Hauser 1999, 156). Negotiating the landscape of trauma and memory in the context of new and emerging technologies brings a host of challenges as we infuse contemporary meaning into past human rights violations. Cvetkovich's analysis of Kron's *2.5 Minute Ride* provides a useful frame to interpret these challenges and to consider the tangible consequences of how and in what ways we engage with and archive memory of Nazi genocide.

In this chapter, we argue that technology intervenes, disrupts, and alters the public memory of Holocaust trauma. Kron's *2.5 Minute Ride* is salient to some of this disruption—particularly, much of the controversy surrounding the digital decorum of visitors documenting and sharing interactions with Holocaust memorials. On one hand, Cvetkovich reminds us of the competing narratives of trauma and banality inherent to Kron's performance, where we see a range of affect rise out of the dark and tragic corners of Auschwitz (Cvetkovich 2013, 22–23). Kron uses a roller coaster metaphor for her *2.5 Minute Ride* performance, a means to capture the peaks and valleys of Nazi trauma—her father's survival, her grandparent's murder—and the affective cushions we deploy to absorb suffering and pain. Cvetkovich also reminds us that stories about the Holocaust have become distant in time and commonplace to history, making some of the emotive power Holocaust testimony evokes ebb away (23). This resonates with the amnesic power of national culture that Cvetkovich articulates and, similarly, with the "cognitive prostheses" of digital record that Lupton theorizes (Lupton 2014, 33). What lingers, though, is the need to remember. Conversely, Cvetkovich affirms that Kron wants to jolt her viewers so that we react to Holocaust trauma outside expected parameters of shock and horror (Cvetkovich 2013, 23). Living under an umbrella of national trauma, as Berlant describes (226), Kron confronts her audience with a range of affect that in many ways helps us cope with archives of Nazi abuse that strip away at human dignity. For Kron, this includes performing "humor, the poignancy of everyday life, and the moral uncertainty of her father's claim that he was lucky" (Kron *2.5*).

In Cvetkovich's assessment of *2.5 Minute Ride*, then, we negotiate affective intersections with Holocaust trauma as we assemble and expand upon our own cultural memory. What seems taboo—a smiley selfie taken at the Auschwitz memorial, for example—might be a more authentic form of witnessing over what societal mores construct as appropriate concentration and death camp protocol. Even with this, Cvetkovich reminds us of the spilling over of trauma, as witnesses visiting Holocaust memorials circulate around unfolding national atrocities, and in these indirect but exposed roles, absorb the pain and suffering of the stories that surround them (Cvetkovich 2013, 3). The duality in Kron's and Cvetkovich's Holocaust analyses carries a poststructuralist element in that these divergent, culturally reproduced accounts with Holocaust affect elude representation. Cvetkovich affirms this textual disjunction, asserting that, despite a wide-reaching, instantly accessible digital palette, "living the horror of the Holocaust is quite apart from attempting to deconstruct that experience" (27). In Kron's *2.5 Minute Ride*, and in that smiley concentration camp selfie incident, we must distinguish between rhetorical yarns of tourists visiting a Nazi death camp as opposed to original testimony that reifies the atrocities Holocaust victims and survivors endured.

Ayse Gul Altinay and Andrea Peto, writing on gender, war, and genocide, assert that context and positionality of collective memories and movement of memory within and across geographies of time and place leave key questions regarding genocide and military intervention (Altinay et al. 2016, 5). The authors ask us to reflect on "traffic between different memory cultures and politics," particularly as these travel between "seemingly disparate sites" of nation-state and intimate public spheres (5). Thus, representing historical trauma against contending public and personal record requires us to stay mindful of the porous qualities that time and technologies imbue into memory practices. This poststructural complexity is evident in the shifting affect to Kron's *2.5 Minute Ride*, and it similarly manifests in the polysemic meaning making that visitors create at public sites that archive and memorialize Holocaust trauma. Salient to our argument, the performative, nonregulatory dimension to digital behavior impacts the restorative promise Holocaust memorials uphold. In this way, we call attention to ways diverse technologies can catapult yet also dichotomize human rights rhetoric aimed at unsilencing public histories of trauma.

Note

The authors wish to thank Hana Červinková and Juliet Golden, whose development of study abroad programs that explore the politics of memory in Central Europe served as a source of inspiration for this essay.

Works Cited

Altinay, Ayse Gull, and Andrea Peto. Introduction. 2016. *Gendered Wars, Gendered Memories: Feminist Conversations on War, Genocide, and Political Violence*, edited by Ayse Gull Altinay and Andrea Peto. New York, NY: Routledge, 2016.

Arendt, Hannah. 1963. *Eichmann in Jerusalem: A Report on the Banality of Evil.* New York, NY: Viking Press.

"Artist Shames Tourists Taking Inappropriate Selfies at the Holocaust Memorial Site in Berlin (NSFW)." *deMilked.* https://www.demilked.com/ holocaust-memorial-selfies-yolocaust-shahak-shapira/.

Berlant, Lauren. 2011. *Cruel Optimism.* Durham, NC: Duke University Press.

Blair, Carole, Marsha S. Jeppeson, and Enrico Pucci, Jr. 1991. "Public Memorializing in Postmodernity: The Vietnam Veterans Memorial as Prototype." *Quarterly Journal of Speech* 77 (August): 263–288.

Cronin-Furman, Kate. 2019. "Why Holocaust Comparisons Matter." *Slate.* July 3, 2019. https://slate.com/news-and-politics/2019/07/holocaust-museum concentration-camps-border.html.

Cvetkovich, Anne. 2003. *An Archive of Feelings: Trauma, Sexuality, and Lesbian Public Culture.* Durham, NC: Duke University Press.

Durando, Jessica. 2014. "Auschwitz Selfie Girl Breanna Mitchell Defends Her Controversial Picture." *USA Today.* July 23, 2014. https://www.usatoday.com/story/news/nation-now/2014/07/23/selfie-auschwitz-concentration-camp-germany/13038281/.

Edensor, Tim. 2001. "Performing Tourism, Staging Tourism: (Re)producing Tourist Space and Practice." *Tourist Studies* 1: 159–181.

Ellul, Jacques. 1964. *The Technological Society.* New York: Vintage Books.

Evans, Jennifer V. 2014. "Harmless Kisses and Infinite Loops: Making Space for Queer Place in Twenty-first Century Berlin." *Queer Cities, Queer Cultures: Europe Since 1945*, edited by Matt Cook and Jennifer V. Evans, 75–94. London, England: Bloomsbury Academic.

"Film inside the Memorial." *Memorial to the Homosexuals Persecuted under the National Socialist Regime.* https://www.stiftung-denkmal.de/en/memorials/memorial-to-the-homosexuals-persecuted-under-the-national-socialist-regime/film-inside-the-memorial.html.

"Gleis 17 Memorial, Berlin-Grunewald." *Information Portal to European Sites of Remembrance.* https://www.memorialmuseums.org/eng/staettens/view/338/Mahnmal-Gleis-17-%E2%80%93--Berlin-Grunewald.

Haraway, Donna. 1991. "A Cyborg Manifesto: Science, Technology, and Socialist-Feminism in the Late Twentieth Century." *Simians, Cyborgs and Women: The Reinvention of Nature*, 149–181. New York: Routledge.

Hauser, Gerard A. 1999. *Vernacular Voices: The Rhetoric of Publics and Public Spheres.* Columbia: University of South Carolina Press, 1999.

Hsu, Hua. 2019. "Affect Theory and the New Age of Anxiety: How Lauren Berlant's Cultural Criticism Predicted the Trumping of Politics." *The New Yorker*, March 25, 2019. https://www.newyorker.com/magazine/2019/03/25/affect-theory-and-the-new-age-of-anxiety.

Huyssen, Andreas. 1997. *Twilight Memories: Marking Time in Culture of Amnesia.* New York: Routledge.

Jenkins, Henry. 2009. "If it Doesn't Spread, It's Dead (Part Two): Sticky and Spreadable—Two Paradigms." February 13, 2009. http://henryjenkins.org/blog/2009/02/if_it_doesnt_spread_its_dead_p_1.html.

Katz, Eric. 2005. "On the Neutrality of Technology: The Holocaust Death Camps as Counter-example." *Journal of Genocide Research* 7, no. 3 (September): 409–421.

Keep, Dean. 2009. "The Portable Shrine: Remembrance, Memorial, and the Mobile Phone." *Australian Journal of Communications* 36, no. 1: 61–72.

Kron, Lisa. *2.5 Minute Ride.* https://www.lisakron.org/Lisa-Kron-theWorkOf-2.5MinuteRide.html.

Leventhal, Robert S. 1995. "Information and Technology in the Holocaust." http://www2.iath.virginia.edu/holocaust/infotech.html.

Lupton, Deborah. 2014. *Digital Sociology.* New York: Routledge.

Miles, William F. S. 2001. "Touring Auschwitz," *Midstream* (April): 11–12.

Ouellette, Jennifer. 2014. *Me, Myself, and Why: Searching for the Science of Self.* New York: Penguin Books.

Shapira, Shahak. *Yolocaust.* 2017. https://yolocaust.de.

Sharpley, Richard. 2009. "Shedding Light on Dark Tourism: An Introduction." In *The Darker Side of Travel: The Theory and Practice of Dark Tourism*, edited by Richard Sharpley and Philip R. Stone, 3–22. Bristol, England: Channel View Publications.

Sontag, Susan. 1973. *On Photography.* New York: Rosetta Books.

Sturken, Marita. 1997. *Tangled Memories: The Vietnam War. The AIDS Epidemic, and the Politics of Remembering.* Berkeley: University of California Press.

Wilke, Christiane. 2013. "Remembering Complexity? Memorials for Nazi Victims in Berlin." *International Journal of Transitional Justice* 7, no. 1 (March): 136–156.

Chapter Eight

Grieving, Breathing, Keeping Time

Rights, Sequences, and Sonnetic "Enfleshment"

HANNA MUSIOL

> Can't form . . . be a talisman against disintegration?
>
> —Rita Dove 1996, xiii

> At some point I realized . . . the thing I am really concerned with is measuring time.
>
> —Terrance Hayes 2018c, 175

> The nature of our trauma is that you actually have no recollection for it as a story . . . [It] is not about something you think or . . . figure out. This is about your body, your organism . . .
>
> —Bessel van der Kolk, in Tippett 2013, n.p.

The title of our volume, *Technologies of Human Rights Representation,* invokes registers often ascribed to art and humanities aesthetics and to social sciences and technology, respectively. In the context of human rights research and praxis, however, *technologies* and *representations* are fuzzy terms. Scattered across disciplinary geographies, they summon complex practices that are simultaneously collective, public or private, ironic, poetic, or explicitly political, juridical, instrumentally literal, technical, digital, mechanical. With proprietary technological design impacting rights access and experience across the world not just at unprecedented scale and speed but with extraordinary, penetrative, "monstrous intimacy" (Sharpe 2010), there is no denying that *new* technology is one of the urgently understudied areas of rights scholarship: eerily influential and still not fully legible as a rights-generating and suppressing instrument.[1] Yet, the resuscitative affordances of aesthetics, literature, art, and their complex violent legacies are also consequential and just as underestimated. Representing rights means different practices, after all, in different contexts of, say, a political science class, an art exhibit, a truth and reconciliation commission (TRC), a poetry reading, an International High Court courtroom, or a US Senate hearing. And when aesthetic objects, unruly as they are, represent rights in such different sites, they may do so disobediently, performing as investigative, evidentiary, communicative,[2] seductive, reflective tools, operating as technologies, "equipment for living" politically, corporeally, biosocially.[3]

Thus, while it would be logical to follow the new technology and rights trail of inquiry, as I do elsewhere (Musiol 2018), this chapter explores this complex entanglement of materialities and functionalities, effects and affects of art and technology somewhat counterintuitively, by turning to old *literary* technologies, to poetry and to the sonnet in particular. This approach to the literary form, of course, is not new in rights scholarship. Several literary genres—slave narrative, prison diary, memoir, sentimental novel, *bildungsroman,* and, now, cli-fi (climate fiction)—have been studied with attention to their narrative capacity to evidence violence and narrate rights, and earn simultaneous critical literary *and* legal recognition.[4] Prose may dominate in such rights scholarship, even if some see it as a "degraded form" of "closure" (qtd. in Hartman 2018, n.p.), but this chapter turns to a poetic form, the sonnet, in the context of violence, racialized afterlives of dispossession, and its anticipated violent futures. Specifically, it explores how in the hands of Marilyn Nelson and Philippe Lardy in *A Wreath for Emmett Till*, and Terrance Hayes in *American Sonnets for My Past and Future Assassin*, sonnets become receptacles of grief and resuscitative devices, assistive technologies for measuring, living through, and moving beyond violent time. Normative state and international rights have long been accused of resting on abstract notions of personhood,[5] disembodied, if not dismembered, even if, at the very least, they promise freedom from corporeal harm. Two sonnet sequence collections that I discuss deploy the poetic technology of the sonnet in ways that re-embody that specter of rights and "nourish" the body, which is at best ignored, and more often disappeared, by frameworks of legal justice. They become technologies of human rights re*presenting,* rematerialization, somatic actualization, for embodied "being and re/seeing" (Sharpe 2016, 21). In another sense, these sonnets are also what Christina Sharpe (2016) calls "enfleshed works" (21), poetic instruments for demanding the right to "public black grief" and the right to visceral critique of the structures that produce its conditions (Rutter et al. 2019, 14).

Reading, Grieving, Living

At a time of widespread sociopolitical rights crises, poetry remains a very "public language of grief" and is still being read, recited, and listened to with passion (Arsenijević et al. 2016).[6] Poet Laureate Tracy K. Smith (2018) in the United States and Donna Ferguson (2019) in the United Kingdom note poetry's "soaring" popularity, as if poetry were recognized as an unlikely antidote to violence-generating political newspeak,[7] and others believe it has the power to effect real change, to "stretch the sky," as Tony Medina (2016) does in his *Resisting Arrest* poetic anthology. Popular or not, poetry is, of course, always entangled with rights;[8] reading it aloud, performing, or memorizing it is just as important as writing it (Billington 2016, 86–114; Müller 2018; Rutter 2016; Austin et al. 2019). In this chapter, I turn precisely to its sonic, collective, performative affordances to engage with social traumas in often explicitly *non*-narrative, nonfigurative, but embodied ways. In other words, while officially poetry may be adopted to "picture politics" of states and social movements in more instrumental ways (Holmes 2008, 82), the poetic form is also a technology of smaller-scale, measured somatic consequences too, when it operates as a performative script, to be read, memorized, and spoken, enacted by and within the body of the reader; shared with others, or simply when breathed in and out on one's own, in private or in public.[9]

Research does not find automatic cause-and-effect links between a specific literary form and uniform social attitudes or interpretations,[10] but literary and cultural scholars explore how *communities* of readers themselves routinely assign specific cultural roles to poetry, and experience specific *affective* outcomes when engaging with specific art forms and poetic genres.[11] Trauma and narrative medicine researchers further emphasize the important role of performative and body art in the process of healing and coping with trauma (Billington 2016; van der Kolk, 1994; van der Kolk in Tippett 2013). Literature that emerges in the aftermath of violence or trauma, or is simply read in its aftermath, even if it does not elicit specific sociolegal outcomes, attends to enduring, psychosocial, cultural, and embodied affects—

grief, depression, shame, anxiety, anger, fear—for which juridical solutions, material or cultural rights to compensation or political recognition, or other forms of transitional justice, even when available (which they rarely are), offer too little relief.[12] Certainly, this assistive power of the literary resides not simply in the technology of form itself—as any genre plays with its form's limits—but also in the cultural and material context of its sharing, its accessibility, and the pre-existing condition of social understanding of its function. Commemorative, in the case of elegy, but different for other genres.[13] However, specific *poetic* forms are frequently used to generate very concrete kinds of social, physical, *and* bio- and psychosomatic responses and breathing patterns.[14] It is not surprising, then, that Annie Finch (2016) sees poetry as a "technology," whose meter and rhythm are "breathing" devices (1–4, 281–305) that impact the human "pulse rate" (542). To her, poetry is a "language *for* the body" (306; author's emphasis), as the *form* itself can instruct and help the body to breathe, or gasp for air, or help it keep time. It is, then, literally as much as culturally "enfleshed" (Sharpe 2016, 21).

The right to breathe is not a given, nor is the right to rights, as poets Marilyn Nelson, Terrance Hayes, and their readers know well. Nelson and Hayes turn to the sonnet, and specifically, to its serialized sequences in their works responding to the state-permitted terror against black bodies, to legacies of their dispossession, and in anticipation of more sociopolitical traumas of the flesh yet to unfold during Trump's presidency. In 2005, Nelson uses the crown (corona) chain sonnet in an elegy *A Wreath for Emmett Till* as a "protective device" of consolation, as an elegiac form whose rigid poetic rules keep the breath going, ensuring a return to wholeness, to making "hearts whole" ("How I Came to Write" *A Wreath*, n.p., Sonnet X). Hayes (2018c) also chooses the sequence sonnet explicitly. For him, it is a tool for "measuring" violent political "time" (175), for keeping score in the first two hundred days of Donald Trump's presidency in 2016, but also for settling the score with the reader.

Within a broader resurgence of black elegy devastatingly documented in *Revisiting Elegy in the Black Lives Matter Era,*[15] the sonnet is a peculiar tool for dealing with "extreme violence" and "extreme emotion" (Grunebaum 2002, 307). The sonnet is, after all, a strict verse form of fourteen lines, often with one or two stanzas in iambic pentameter (verse lines of five metrical feet/beats of stressed and unstressed syllables), which carry a theme through a varying rhythm schema, often from a more reiterative octave and a sestet or three quatrains and a couplet, via a volta (a rhetorical or dramatic turn), toward a resolution. These rhythmical patterns, syntactical contortions, and spatio-sonic distributions of the arguments, thoughts, and breaths within stanzas, fourteen lines, and poetic beats may feel unsuitable for the contemporary tenor of violence. Yet even if its "unusual syntax [employed] in service to landing on appropriate meter or rhyme [may] sound deeply artificial to our modern ear" (Peake 2007, n.p.), the sonnet is far from being a "belated" form (Timothy Yu in Finch 2016, 539), too stale, or too "bombastic" (Peake 2007, n.p.). In fact, despite "being associated with the European heritage and white cultural privilege," it's a "transgressive," dialectical tool frequently and defiantly used by African American poets for "black annotation and redaction" (Müller 2018; Sharpe 2016, 131).[16] It is also a remarkably multimodal instrument.[17] Sonnets are spatial, "percussive," sonic and corporeal notation and narrative devices, after all. The argumentative and logical shifts in them depend on phonic, spatiotemporal, nontextual "accelerations" in "thought," "mood," and "feeling" (Preminger and Brogan 1993, 1168), with rhyme or voltas often deployed as instruments of sonic, somatic, and spatial impacts, rather than simply conduits for logocentric cognition.[18] This is important in the context of trauma, which, in a more clinical sense, Bessel van der Kolk reminds us, is antinarrative; it is "about [the] body," and "has nothing to do with cognition" (in Tippett 2013, n.p.).

Nelson's award-winning collection[19] *A Wreath for Emmett Till* is an immersive, elegiac sonnet collection, mourning racial violence. It was written, as Nelson (2005c) put it, at a time of overwhelming personal and collective, chronic grief, desperation, and "breathlessness" (n.p.).[20] The book focuses on Emmett Till's lynching in 1955, its aftermath, and its violent, mediatized, and visceral "postmemory," but also on the silence, the public disavowal of such loss, violence, and traumatic grief that haunt generations of young black Americans (Hirsch 2012; Jenkins et al. 2014; Patton 2014).[21] Illustrated by Philippe Lardy, the sonnet collection is designed with children and young readers in mind (Nelson 2015a) and is structured as a poesivisual wreath of chained Petrarchan sonnets. It is framed by telling invocations of Shakespeare—the opening lines of the first and last poem in the book, "Rosemary for remembrance, Shakespeare wrote," echoing *Hamlet*'s famous scene in which Ophelia uses herbarium references as a symbolic code for her grief and as an admonition to others to remember (Nelson 2005c, Sonnet I, X; figure 8.1). Nelson then turns to other artists and keepers of American memory—Paul Laurence Dunbar, Billie Holiday, Walt Whitman, Lorraine Hansberry, abolitionists (Sonnets II, X, XIV). She also borrows from Inger Christensen's "fantastically beautiful" heroic crown sonnet,[22] seeing the regal beauty of the crown as a *consoling* aesthetic for her young readers ("How I Came to Write," Nelson 2005c, n.p.).

Figure 8.1. The opening sonnet and image of "Rosemary for Remembrance, Shakespeare wrote" from A WREATH FOR EMMETT TILL by Marilyn Nelson, illustrated by Philippe Lardy. Text copyright © 2005 by Marilyn Nelson. Illustrations copyright © 2005 by Philippe Lardy. Reprinted by permission of Houghton Mifflin Harcourt Publishing Company. All rights reserved. Photo by Karolina Gorzelanczyk. Reprinted by permission.

Traumatic grief, trauma specialists explain, involves the embodied experience of loss when bereavement turns physical and "psychobiological," often disablingly so, and they point out that embodied traumatic grief in children demands a "multimodal" therapy approach (Dyregrov et al. 2015, 26; van der Kolk 1994; van der Kolk in Tippett 2013). On a small scale, Nelson works multimodally across narrative, poetic, somatic domains, against the flatness of the text, brutality of the language, the hypervisibility, and the silence. First, having drawn from a recognized elegiac and tragedy motif,[23] Nelson places black children's trauma within a recognizable cultural frame, and centers on it, while searching for a new language for bereavement and remembrance in her work, settling on symbolic plants to use in her wreath—"mandrake" and "rue, yew, cypress. / Forget-me-nots"—and a very old Petrarchan form to write about racial violence and loss for the twenty-first-century's grieving young readers (Nelson 2005c, Sonnet I). Then, she *weaves* her poetic wreath in literal ways by chaining fifteen sonnets together, the last line of each poem being the first line of the next, and concludes with a crown sonnet XV, composed exclusively of repeated first lines of all fourteen preceding poems. She also makes the reading spatially complex, as the final sonnet is also an acrostic, and reads the first letters of each line, down, vertically, to say "RIP Emmett L. Till" (Nelson 2005b, 1). This enables two spatio-affectively competing ways of reading the poem: laterally, preserving the circularity of the narrative consolation, and the focus on the reader, and vertically, offering a final line to Emmett Till.

Emily Rutter (Rutter et al. 2019) writes that "contemporary elegies carve out a public space for black grief, while decidedly resisting the turn toward consolation that often characterizes the poetic form" (14). Others note a similar move away from consolation in trauma poetry more broadly (Armstrong 2020, 302). And yet, *A Wreath* is as dedicated to commemorating and devictimizing Till and to a scathing political critique of the "country with Janus face . . . / thy nightmare history and thy grand dream" (Sonnet XI) as it is to posttraumatic collective recovery, and to consoling the body, and, especially, the bodies of young readers of color (Nelson 2005a). When she was writing *A Wreath*, Nelson reveals, she was grappling with her own depression tied to Till's death, "whose name still catches in [her] throat" (Sonnets III, IV, XV). "[T]he strict form become a kind of insulation, a way of protecting myself from the intense pain of the subject matter," she explains, "allow[ing] the Muse to determine what the poem would say" (Nelson 2005c, n.p.). Nelson's sonnet sequence and the final poem, the most sonically reiterative poem, attends then to collective and personal embodied grief, rehearsing rituals of remembrance, witnessing, mourning, *and* consolation. In that sense, the sonnet sequence as a rigid form becomes "a talisman against disintegration" (Dove 1996, xiii), which can contain grief. But it can also liberate time, which traumatic grief immobilizes, or distorts. The sonnet distorts time too, but also measures breaths, and it can contract, speed up, and expand time deliberately and meaningfully via the arrangements of poetic feet, voltas, repetitions, enjambments.

If one of the goals of restorative justice practices in public storytelling responses to trauma is producing a space for witnesses and "acknowledging listener[s]" (Grunebaum 2002, 307), *A Wreath* addresses this inexcusable narrative violence, this inexcusable absence: children, and children of color in particular, are rarely attended to as witnesses, listeners, targets, and as grieving subjects deserving of rights and consolation.[24] Nelson and Lardy understand the complex situatedness of young readers, who may identify with the subject of this elegy, simultaneously enveloped by memories of Till's brutal murder or other murders like his, besieged by the belatedness of the public apology, retraumatized by ongoing spectacles of racial violence, and in constant danger of becoming the "targets-subjects" of such impending violence themselves (Katz 2019; Musiol 2016). Nelson's expanded sequence of fifteen sonnets affords more time for an extended crown sonnet wreath. The immersive and multisensory project is then breathtaking and breath-giving, and spatiotemporal. As Nelson and Lardy create a ceremonial *space* for readers to navigate the different stages of pain, grief, outrage, and resistance, the poet consoles and transfers the oxygen from the page to the mouth, to the lungs of readers-speakers, insisting on their right to breathe, on their right to live.

The sonnetic wreath is also carefully "scored" by the atmospheric, delicate floral illustrations that assist the reader through the elegiac process of confronting the violence, grieving, and militancy, and of contemplating the future (figure 8.1). Lardy's images provide "hushed" decorative, narrative accompaniment to the louder poetic composition of death and insurrection, and the artist reclaims the rich tradition of commemorative visual art without violating the young adult (YA) aesthetics codes of children's books (Nelson 2005, "Artist's Note" n.p.). Nelson, on the other hand, is more explicit in her depictions of the violence inflicted on Till, the subsequent suffering of his mother, and the comparisons the poet draws between his lynching, 9/11, and twentieth-century genocides in Europe and Rwanda. The opening title line of her Sonnet III, for instance, bolded by the large black stylized cursive typeface, "Pierced by the screams of a shortened childhood"; or the direct invocation to Till in Sonnet VI, when she tries to reimagine and replace the image of his body—"Mutilated boy martyr, if I could / I'd put you in a parallel universe"—offer haunting descriptions of the attack and the harm inflicted on Till, his family, and the poet herself. Just a young boy, a "wormhole history passed through" (Sonnet VI), is "a running boy," chased by "five men in close pursuit / . . . five pale faces in the moonlight. / Noise, silence, back slaps. One match, five cigars" (Sonnet III). Lardy adds visual echoes and highly symbolic references to plants and flowers, and the interlinked visual and textual components move the sonnets not simply across pages but also across liminal stages and modalities of grief. Lardy also adds a progressive visual structure to the poetic composition, by dividing the book into the prelude, the murder, and the aftermath, "the interlude, mourning, and the lessons" in his words, marking each book section with a shift in color scheme, first dominated by greens, then reds and browns, and, finally, yellow and orange, more hopeful, hues (Nelson 2005, "Artist's Note," n.p.).[25] He contrasts the "interlude" and "mourning" sections visually without using any literal images of Till's mutilated body in a casket,[26] freeing Till from the never-ending cycle of visual rebrutalization. Nelson's work is then not a return to explicit literariness of violence, although iambic pentameter can and does reactivate what may be a traumatic repetition and rhyme pattern. Nelson admonishes us that the violence must be confronted and should not be forgotten, so it is part of the design—"*Rosemary for remembrance,* Shakespeare wrote," she reminds us (Sonnets IX, XI, and XIV). But the five-beat (iamb) poetic meter, alliteration, rhymes, denaturalize, disturb the descriptive speech, the prosaic normativity of violence, disturb the pleasure that white spectators, including children, draw from the lynching spectacle, unsettle the banality of the scene, especially in the most brutal Sonnet IX:

> The crowds standing around like devil choirs
> The children's eyes lit by the fire's gleam
> Filled with the delight of licking ice cream,
> Men who hear hog screams as a man expires
> Watch-fob good-luck charms teeth pulled out with pliers, . . .

There and elsewhere, literal descriptions of violence as spectacle are held together but also subverted by artificial syntax, rhythm, and rhyme; the logic of violence disrupted by punctuation, or its absence, followed by aberrant capitalization; the violence undone by language and verse structure, condemned by rhyming repetitions, or pivoted via enjambment of a poetic line or a volta toward resistance and consolation. The crown sonnet forces the reader to breathe in and out, to keep on going, to anticipate patterns, to dread and seek refuge in the poetic rota, but the sonnet verse form also keeps the literal violence in check. And to ensure such a progressive, consoling understanding, such a spatiovisual-sonic *sensation*, Nelson and Lardy include brief, conversational, extrapoetic explanatory addenda in the preface and final sections of the book: "How I came to Write This Poem," Who Was Emmett Till?," "Sonnet Notes," "Artist's Note," "References," as well as public readings, and teachings (Nelson 2005a, 2005b, 2005c).[27] This is to help young readers decode and *feel* the complex visual and poetic techniques, to assign a sensation to the symbolic references in poetic and visual design, the notation of the language and cadence of a heroic crown sonnet, and numerous allusions to works of the English and specifically African American literary and oral elegy tradition.

In her work on mourning and precarity, Judith Butler (2004) sees "loss" as a shared human experience, which, if recognized as such, could make "a tenuous 'we' of all of us" (20). Yet, even though "the condition of black life is one of mourning" (Rankine 2015), and the experience of "loss and traumatic grief" among black children is widespread (Jenkins et al. 2014), such grief rarely generates collective recognition and empathy, is offered a "public" space and "language" (Arsenijević et al. 2016; Patton 2014; Katz 2019). Sonnet XIV speaks to the particular nonspace of the children's experience of loss and the violent regulations of "public expressions of black grief" in the context or racial terror (Rutter et al. 2019, 14). Thus, in the wreath, Nelson attempts to craft this "tenuous" poetic grief community, to embrace young readers, especially when she switches to a collective voice: "we are whole, . . . We can speak now . . ." in Sonnet XIV. Ultimately, the heroic crown sonnet form, as restrictive as it is, aids the work of "rememory," which Toni Morrison (2019) describes not simply as a process of "recollecting and remembering" but also as the daunting and difficult task of reconstituting the bones, "*reassembling* the members of the body, the family, the population of the past" (324). As such, *A Wreath* is a restorative project, "enfleshing," re*presenting* children's rights to breathe, becoming a poetic breathing machine: for strained, gasping breath, which it resuscitates, evens, and breathes out, line after line, poem after poem, and in a cadenced, ceremonial ritual (Sharpe 2016, 21).

Measuring Time, Settling the Score

While Nelson and Lardy use an ekphrastic wreath to create a mixmedia poetic and somatic object, embracing children in a shared consoling ritual, the National Book Award–winning collection *American Sonnets for My Past and Future Assassin,* by Terrance Hayes (2018a), might be the ekphrastic object itself of the American racialized political economy, and the technology for measuring the pulse of the American racial "necropolitics" (Mbembe 2019). Hayes's sonnet sequence is as equally visceral, preoccupied with the leitmotif of racial violence, as Nelson's, but it demonstrates little faith in the sonnets' consoling, resuscitative power, and more, in their controlling, dangerous grip. In fact, the very first poem announces: "In a second I'll tell you how little / Writing rescues" (5). What follows are seventy-six untitled unrhymed sonnets, all gathered under the same heading as "American sonnet for my past and future assassin," including, among them, readers; their relationship with the poet, dangerous, deadly, is mediated by the writing, which traps, "that sheds a noise so lovely it is sung at sunset / Weddings, baptisms, & beheadings henceforth" (Hayes 2018a, 46).

The premise behind the project seems archival at first: Hayes writes one sonnet each day in the first two hundred days of Donald Trump's presidency and then selects seventy-seven unedited ones for the book. The symbolic and literal import of Trump's presidency is obvious: Trump's election marks a retreat from social justice and human rights discourse, promptly followed by that of domestic and international policy, and thus the first months are a time of grief for domestic social justice advocates, for communities of color, sexual/gender dissidents, migrants, the poor, and women—all apprehensive of what exact devastation his tenure might bring.[28] Yet, Hayes does not spend time documenting *Trump's* America day by day in a tidily historical fashion, and, if anything, Trump haunts the collection, Caligula style, "too flaky / To be the villain," at the center of the story (10, 42). Besides, "history is beyond me," the poet will say later in the book (Hayes 2018a, 58). Hayes knows that the clock of the presidency is a catastrophic metronome that will regulate the heartbeat and pulse of some and stop that of others; and it did *trigger American Sonnet*. But its clockwork had been wound-up long before—"antiblackness" has long been "the Weather" (Sharpe 2016, 21)—so its feel and tempo are familiar, and so is mixing with ghosts, the undead, and the living, not unusual for those for whom living means living razor-thin-close to dying. And since the drum of the metronome of the sonnet precedes 2016, it is a dangerous device, "a meat / Grinder" in Hayes's hands, too (Hayes 2018a, 11). The poet announces himself as less a historian, then, and more a "Time Lord" (Hayes 2018a, 40, 77), a black "Doctor Who . . . who knows no god / [and] is more powerful than time" (77); one who "speaks for the dead" (17) and plans to "leave / A record of [his] ruptures" (6) in his sonnets. The rigid form "gives shape" to words "we all share" (Hayes 2018b), but it can keep time *and* settle the score.

To proceed with his dangerous project, the poet "brace[s] in a small stall" of the sonnet and in contemporary America. He is anxious because he is always a target of "half-studies, misreads & night / Mares" (Hayes 2018a, 6) but is also ready to "time travel & doctor" himself, an essential skill "when a knee or shoe stalls against his neck" (77). Then, he continues to grapple with an "existential jambalaya" (9, 39) of what it means to be and create "in the land of a failed landlord with a people of color / Complex"[29] (31). While Nelson (2005c) speaks of the rigid form of the sonnet as a "protective" instrument against "intense pain" ("How I Came to Write" n.p.), for

Hayes (2018a), fitting this "existential jambalaya" (39) in the sonnet is like "breakdancing in a straitjacket against yourself" (Hayes 2018b). The form constrains the dance but does not stop it, and each day of the presidency is a chance to break-dance a bit more in a tighter space, in a company with disobedient, often violent, ghosts, "willful" dead and undead (Ahmed 2014; Hayes 2018a, 50), staging spectral performances of devastating, morbidly funny, or poignant resurrections of Prince, Langston Hughes, Jesus's sister, the wine maker, Phyllis Wheatley, Jimi Hendrix, Ginuwine, Trinidad James, Miles Davis, Aretha Franklin, Emmett Till, Toni Morrison, Maxine Waters, James Baldwin, Sylvia Plath, and Elizabeth Dickinson, and other ghosts, children, murderers. Haunting, carousing together, brooding, masturbating, threatening, torturing, seducing, loving, reminiscing, humming. Also, gnawing at each other, dying, and becoming alive.

Unlike Nelson's Petrarchan sonnet sequence, explicitly linked by repeated opening and closing lines and the chronological structure of her narrative, Hayes's American sonnets are connected in different ways. For one, they offer no simple chronology, narration, or progression, and each sonnet is a self-contained story, a vignette, a list of things that kill, a vivisection, a love letter, a tribute, an elegy, a manifesto. However, they are all linked and haunted in less literal ways by the recurrent meditations on art, loss, dread, men, blackness, violence, and frequent returns to a murder scene—Chicago, Baltimore, Ferguson, Charleston (12, 81)—by repeated motifs of trauma and defiance, by surprising visitations by literary figures, friends, lovers, and family members, harassed by white supremacists and metaphors, connected by timed conditions of their writing, by echoes of the American cultural soundtrack. The lingering specter of brutality, just as present and pervasive as the denial of it, referred to as "a black hysteria" (Hayes 2018a, 26, 55, 76). And just as dangerous, "as if you are not being hunted," . . . "as if your death is never death. / You appear, you appear to disappear, you disappear" (76).

Hayes's sonnetic technology is also American in form, abandoning the strict rhythm and rhymes rules of the Italian classic, even if it retains the rhythmical complexity and voltas for narrative and somatic impacts. The poet credits Wanda Coleman's influence for "jazzing" the form of American sonnet (Hayes 2018a, 91), tributes other unruly American sonneteers—Whitman, Hughes, Plath, Bishop, Baraka, cummings (Hayes 2018b)—but also other nameless artists: "the chorus of history" (Hartman 2018, n.p.), "all the poetry weirdoes & worriers, warriors, / Poetry whiners & winos falling from ship bows, sunset / Bridges & windows" (Hayes 2018a, 5). At the same time, the sonnet form is not *just* a form, but the "procedural," the allegory, with the technology of and the story itself, using "the compass / of language" dangerously, "like a tangle of wire endowed / With feeling (Hayes 2018a, 46), "hold[ing] its own storm & drum" (46). His American sonnet restricts, echoes, reverberates, transforms, and mirrors; it repeats *and* resists, confronts, and transmutes, within the fourteen lines and across pages.[30] The spatial affordances of the form and the time allotted to the creation of each poem—one day and no revisions—set spatiotemporal limits; the sonnet, its inherited, ghostwritten, in a sense, form, yet becomes the technology of *literary* insurrections, of political theory, a reclamation of literary and cultural space and time. In Hayes's hands, this serialized time-keeping becomes a gothic kind of archiving, with the sonnet a ghostly *social* literary media, and a space "of ruptures" seized by American ghosts, a time created, not just counted (Hayes 2015a, 6).

If the sonnet is not unlike the algorithmic tracking—"insufficient" but inescapable, always finding you, "flashing grins and money . . . / Before [you] were ghosts" (56)—the assassin can be a target, too. In the collection, poetry stars and "winos," family and friends mingle with the "past and future assassins," among them George Wallace (69), the notorious Jim Crow architect, "constituents / Of Midas," Caligula, readers (32), this lethal "kindhearted white woman" included (15). Ultimately, his sonnets address and confront, in the collection title, and headings on each page, and in many poems, the "serial killer," the "past and future assassin," as the readers themselves. Hayes frequently and mockingly explores complex relationships he has developed with them: reminiscing on his getting close to and becoming friends with "white boys who grew into assassins" (50, 55); proclaiming to not hold grudges, because "I ain't mad at you, Assassin" (63); probing the assassin's psyche, as in "Assassin, you're a mystery" (65). Yet, even though he says that he is "old enough to know the drum, though beaten, is not an instrument of violence" (74), *American Sonnet* also aims to settle the score with the reader, throughout the sequence form and in several single sonnet-contained confrontations, when the poet, a poetic persona, a political chronicler, reverse-deploys the political sonnet against his "assassins," promising "a pinch of serious poison for [them]" (Hayes 2018a, 12).

Sonnet VII opens with a direct declaration: "I lock you in American sonnet," which the poem's speaker describes as "part prison / Part panic closet" in a house ablaze (Hayes 2018a, 11, lines 1–2). He reinforces the declaration with four additional repetitions, spell-like, present-tense promises to the reader-assassin: "I lock you in a form that is part music box, part meat / Grinder" (line 3), "I lock your persona in a dream-inducing sleeper hold" (line 5), "I make you both gym & crow here" (line 7), "I make you a box of darkness . . ." (line 11), trapping in both reader and poet. Then, a scripted performance is extracted from the assassin in a ritual of racial violence and torture: chillingly described as a "beautiful catharsis." Hayes commits to using little more than the poetic tools of torture, "voltas of acoustics," alliterations, puns, metaphors, and the prescribed fourteen lines. In the end, the poet meditates on what is enough for the assassin, once the sonnetic "meat grinder" has "separate[d] the song of the bird from the bone," separated the bad "from the better self," concluding the poem with the ambiguous statement that the "voltas of acoustics" might not be enough, but neither is "lov[ing]" the assassin, or "want[ing] them destroyed" (11).

Nelson's explicitly circular poetic wreath enables a ritual of grieving and breathing in order to move beyond, to break the grip and circle of violence, to craft a future outside the wreath. Hayes's (2018a) sequence, which pretends chronology, development, cause and effect, ultimately undermines the chronological progression, re-enacts violent repetitions, waiting to trap the assassins who, the poet knows, always return to the scene of the crime to wreak more devastation. But it also *sonnets* new octaves of trauma feelings and expressions, in a form whose "notes must tear & tear" and be a "record of witness and daydream" (46).

Poetic Rights Instruments

Rights violations and solutions to them are still often spoken of in urgent tones, represented in crisis management genres, accounted for in categories of acceptable loss, narrated in disciplines of grief recognition. Poetry's impact factor, in contrast, seems low in rights and trauma studies alike (Armstrong 2020), even when rights advocates remind us of poetry's remarkable critical, affective, and political force.[31] Yet, if human rights are predicated on the "disappearance" of the body, of the skin, of the child's grief, and now have officially ended anyway (Hopgood 2013), perhaps this ghostly absence-presence can be addressed by the "somatics of literature," of poetry, precisely because poetic forms narrate *and* "enflesh" and re-*present* the body (Robinson 2008; Sharpe 2016, 21). In other words, poetic procedurals, ekphrastic objects, sonnetic sequences, "tender" and violent narrative and poetic rituals they engender (Tokarczuk 2019) make us *experience* time, hear the clock of "the trauma of the routine" (Onwuachi-Willig 2016), account for "quotidian catastrophic events," or racialized, mundane, chronic violence that seem like "total climate," or the "atmosphere" (Sharpe 2016, 20, 21). But poetry also makes *sense* from what it means to "suffer from political despair, from despair about the *organization of things*" (Moten 2003, 93; emphasis mine). The sonnets, like other poetic forms, are, then, biosocially "mnemonic" (Armstrong 2020, 296). As *biocultural* fossils, they are material archives of cultural memory and someone else's breath, which they "remember" in the form. When read aloud, or performed together, the sonnet is also a more real-time corporeal tool. It engages the body of the reader-speaker and can, thus, expand a *sensorium*, not simply cognition, of embodied justice (Billington 2016). In that, it can "enflesh" and make public anguish, pain, grief, trauma, when expressing them in a more representational, or "narrative form" might be more expedient but might make less present-time corporeal *sense* (Arsenijević et al. 2016; Sharpe, 2016, 21; Winning 2020).

Thus, Hayes's *American Sonnets* resurrect the sequence sonnet not only as a cultural graveyard filled with bodies and disobedient ghosts, or as a recording technology for the routinization of violence, of the brutal touch of American "necropolitics" (Mbembe 2019; Moten 2003; Onwuachi-Willig 2016). In repeated fourteen lines, Hayes's sonnets keep track of rights violation but also capture and captivate the reader to settle the score. Neither is Nelson's and Lardy's sonnetic wreath *about* evidencing racial violence only. It does so too, but it also helps readers inhale and exhale, maintain their breathing in extended poetic, corporeal rituals of mourning, and guide them via text and image toward political consciousness and embodied, felt consolation. These poetic breathing, grieving, and time-keeping technologies might seem but meager human rights instruments. And yet, sonnets do "enflesh," rematerialize the ghostliness of human rights, and articulate an immersive "resistance to th[e] imposition of non/being" (Sharpe 2016, 21). Those who live as "no-citizen[s]," Sharpe (2016) argues, "with no state or nation to protect" them, "with no citizenship bound to be respected," must "think and be and act from that preposition" (22). Hayes and Nelson do so. They demonstrate precisely how breathing and rights are woven together and how reclaiming breath in a sonnet can be political, a mode of resistance. Ultimately, they show that "the healing is heroic," defiant, *and* poetic (Hayes 27015a, 7) by offering "the language for the body" that is missing (Finch 2016, 306).

Notes

I thank James Dawes and Alexandra Schultheis Moore and anonymous reviewers for their thoughtful feedback; Elizabeth Rutter and Charles Armstrong, for generously sharing their then yet unpublished work; Atle Dyregrov and Jo Winning, for responding to my last-minute requests for material; Gulabudin Sukhnawar and Minh Chau Nguyen Pham, for their research assistance; and Kristen Ebert-Wagner, for her editorial help.

1. New technology re-"engineers inequity," re-establishes new (neo)colonial domini and political assassination targets, and creates new zones of inaccessibility, of environmental, econopolitical, and epistemological sacrifice (Benjamin 2019, 49; Algorithmic Justice League 2020).

2. Artistic research and art are recognized knowledge disciplines in Scandinavia and are incorporated in the largest EU and EAA *research*-funding schemas. Their strategic practitioners, the Forensic Architecture group (2019), for example, blend art-based investigative research practice with ambitions of litigation in the international courts.

3. See Burke (1973); Billington (2016); Felski (2008); Felski (2020); Berlant (2011); Holmes (2008); Slaughter (2008).

4. Climate-destabilization critics often invoke the transformative power of bio art, environmental storytelling, and climate fiction for public opinion and public environmental policy (Armiero and De Angelis 2017; Nixon 2011; Stengers 2018). Also, see Slaughter (2008).

5. I draw from Russ Castronovo's (2002) discussion about disembodied citizenship predicated on the "disappearance" of the body and "material differences" (118). The disembodied abstractions shape citizenship and normative human rights personhood alike. Also, see Katz (2019).

6. A viral and global response to Amanda Gorman's 2021 presidential inaugural poem recitation testifies to this phenomenon.

7. See similar trends in the US (Iyengar 2018). I thank Rutter et al. (2019) for pointing me to these sources.

8. Poems by Carolyn Forché or Claudia Rankine are some of many examples.

9. For classic work on literature or art as "equipment" or "device," see Burke (1973); Shklovsky (1990); Felski (2008); as a technology of politics and a medium of theory making, see Stengers (2018); Musiol (2020); as a generator of somatic responses, see Budelmann et al. (2017); Robinson (2008); for "poetry of witness" and of trauma, see Forché and Wu (2014); Armstrong (2020); for its use in trauma and pain treatment, see Billington (2016, 86–114).

10. Suzanne Keen (2007) critiques linking a specific literary form to a particular kind of empathetic reader-response and politically prosocial behavior. For challenges to the humanizing, "curative" power of literature, see Berlant (2011); Miller (2005); and, partially, Billington (2016).

11. See Keen (2007), on empathy and the novel; on attachment and art forms, see Felski (2020); on literature and empathy and self-reflection, see Koopman and Hakemulder (2015); on tragedy and endorphins, see Budelmann et al. (2017); on literacy and childhood trauma, see Dernikos (2018); on writing, children, grief, and mass trauma, see Dyregrov et al. (2015, 4). On psychosocial and somatic entan-

glements of literature, art and the body in medical humanities, narrative medicine, and art therapy, see Billington (2016); Winning (2020).

12. Transitional justice measures such as TRCs or other public performances of accountability are not adopted frequently, and if they are, often belatedly.

13. The aesthetic form is a contextual code hard to test in a lab setting.

14. Josie Billington, notes, for instance that poetry read aloud by patients was "*sensed* [author's emphasis]" by readers as "almost physical events" (2016, 90).

15. Austin et al. (2019) examine contemporary elegiac works by Tony Medina, Angela Jackson-Brown, Anne Lovering Rounds, Patricia Smith, Aja Monet, Fred Moten, Sequoia Maner, Shane McCrae, Paula Bohince, Claudia Rankine, and others.

16. See, also, the entire 2019 special issue on poetry and race of *New Literary History* (Ramazani 2019).

17. While Dyregrov et al. (2015) discuss the need for a mixture of therapeutic approaches to children's grief and mass trauma (5), their calls for "multimodal" responses are pertinent to the discussion of the elegiac sonnets; they are also most consistent with the pioneering research of van der Kolk (1994).

18. When a thought is developed in fourteen prescribed lines toward a resolution via a "volta," the reader senses, experiences, hears this sudden "sonic" and poetic "turn of thought" and meaning before understanding the words (Preminger and Brogan 1993, 1168).

19. It won the 2005 Boston Globe–Horn Book Award, and was a 2006 Coretta Scott King Honor Book, a Michael L. Printz Honor Best Nonfiction Book for Young Adults, and a Lee Bennett Hopkins Poetry Award Honor Book.

20. Pages in *A Wreath* are unnumbered; subsequent references include sonnet numbers only.

21. Note that even within trauma studies, the racial trauma of children within the Global North occupies a tenuous place; see Onwuachi-Willig (2016); Katz (2019).

22. By activating the "heroic" crown sonnet, Nelson also alludes to Till's martyrdom already being a heroic part of the national narrative, as the protests against the acquittal of his murderers played a role in igniting the civil rights era.

23. Austin et al. (2019) list twenty-nine other African American elegies for Emmett Till (253–54).

24. Cindi Katz (2019) notes that while the abstract "child" is often invoked in scholarly praxis, it is rarely the child that "the racialised state violence [. . .] kills, maims, and incarcerates young people of colour at staggeringly disproportionate rates in the US, Canada, and elsewhere" (41).

25. Elsewhere, Lardy opts for other allusive symbols: colors; live, cut, and wild plants; thorns; the mandrake under the cut tree as a metaphor for death and execution; ravens as symbols of murder; the wreaths to carry out the meaning-making work (as symbols of love, mourning, peace, suffering, death, beauty, or innocence).

26. In a double spread between Sonnets IX and X, many open caskets and bodies to commemorate Till appear, but the caskets are filled with flowers instead

of corpses. Till's casket is empty but for one white bloodroot flower. The image of his face graces the side of the coffin, but it is the image not of a brutalized victim but of a pensive teenage boy.

27. Nelson also reiterates these instructions in the poems themselves.

28. The US commitment to international human rights had, of course, been questioned by scholars, policy makers, and activists before. See Stephen Hopgood's *The Endtimes of Human Rights* already in 2013. Yet, beginning in 2016, the "endtimes of human rights" became official foreign policy, with a deliberate scraping of human rights from domestic and foreign policy considerations and the literal scraping of "human rights" language from official documents.

29. This line, without enjambment, closes Sonnet 31 ("[On some level . . .]"), concluding an uneasy asymmetry, a black homeless man "dancing on the subway pole," and the self-referential and indulgent "white girls" "taking selfies of themselves taking selfies" (Hayes 2018a, 31).

30. For a conversation about his sonnets' echoes, textures, and poetic polyphony, see Share and Garbutt (2017).

31. See Arsenijević et al. (2016), Billington (2016); Mauro-Flude (2019), Medina (2016), and Rutter et al. (2019). The Electronic Disturbance Theater (EDT) co-founder Ricardo Dominguez emphasized, for instance, that the work of EDT on behalf of undocumented migrants online was not technological and activist but poetic. "We're not activists, we are artists," he insisted when describing EDT's modality of sociocultural electronic intervention (30). "Our interest," Dominguez explained, "is not GPS global positioning systems but global poetic systems" (30).

Works Cited

Ahmed, Sara. 2014. *Willful Subjects.* Durham, NC: Duke University Press.

Algorithmic Justice League. 2020. https://www.ajlunited.org/.

Armiero, Marco, and Massimo De Angelis. 2017. "Anthropocene: Victims, Narrators, and Revolutionaries." *South Atlantic Quarterly* 116, no. 2: 345–62.

Armstrong, Charles. 2020. "Trauma and Poetry." In *The Routledge Companion to Literature and Trauma,* edited by Colin Davis and Hanna Meretoja, 296–304. Abingdon, Oxon: Routledge.

Arsenijević, Damir, Jasmina Husanović, and Sari Wastell. "A Public Language of Grief: Art, Poetry, and Transitional Justice in Post-Conflict Bosnia" in Vlad Beronja, and Stijn Vervaet, eds. *Post-Yugoslav Constellations: Archive, Memory, and Trauma in Contemporary Bosnian, Croatian, and Serbian Literature and Culture.* De Gruyter, 2016. 259–77.

Austin, Tiffany, Sequoia Maner, Emily Ruth, and darlene anita scott, eds. 2019. *Revisiting the Elegy in the Black Lives Matter Era.* New York: Routledge.

Benjamin, Ruha, ed. 2019. *Captivating Technology: Race, Carceral Technoscience, and Liberatory Imagination in Everyday Life*. Durham, NC: Duke University Press.

Berlant, Lauren. 2011. *Cruel Optimism*. Durham, NC: Duke University Press.

Billington, Josie. 2016. *Is Literature Healthy?* Oxford: Oxford University Press.

Budelmann, Felix, et al. 2017. "Cognition, Endorphins, and the Literary Response to Tragedy." *The Cambridge Quarterly* 46, no. 3: 229–50.

Burke, Kenneth. 1973. "Literature as Equipment for Living." In *Philosophy of the Literary Form: Studies in Symbolic Action*, by Kenneth Burke, 293–304. Berkeley: University of California Press.

Butler, Judith. 2004. *Precarious Life: The Powers of Mourning and Violence*. London: Verso.

Castronovo, Russ. 2002. "Souls That Matter: Social Death and the Pedagogy of Democratic Citizenship." In *Materializing Democracy: Toward a Revitalized Cultural Politics*, edited by Russ Castronovo and Dana D. Nelson, 116–44. Durham, NC: Duke University Press.

Dernikos, Bessie P. 2018. "'It's Like You Don't Want to Read It Again': Exploring Affects, Trauma and 'Willful' Literacies." *Journal of Early Childhood Literacy*. https://doi.org/10.1177/1468798418756187.

Dominguez, Ricardo. 2011. "The Art of Crossing Borders: Migrant Rights and Academic Freedom [an Interview with Ricardo Dominguez]." By Louis Warren. *Boom: A Journal of California* 1, no. 4: 26–30.

Dove, Rita. 1996. *Mother Love*. New York: Norton.

Dyregrov, Atle, Alison Salloum, Pål Kristensen, and Kari Dyregrov. 2015. "Grief and Traumatic Grief in Children in the Context of Mass Trauma." *Current Psychiatry Reports* 17, no. 6: Article 48.

Felski, Rita. 2008. *Uses of Literature*. Malden, MA: Blackwell.

Felski, Rita. 2020. *Hooked*. Chicago: University of Chicago Press.

Ferguson, Donna. 2019. "Poetry Sales Soar as Political Millennials Search for Clarity." *Guardian*, January 21, 2019. https://www.theguardian.com/books/2019/jan/21/poetry-sales-soar-as-political-millennials-search-for-clarity.

Finch, Annie. 2016. *A Poet's Craft: A Comprehensive Guide to Making and Sharing Your Poetry*. Ann Arbor: University of Michigan Press.

Forché, Carolyn, and Duncan Wu, eds. 2014. *Poetry of Witness: The Tradition in English, 1500–2001*. New York: Norton.

Forensic Architecture. 2019. "About Forensic Architecture." Goldsmiths, University of London, November 18, 2019. https://forensic-architecture.org/about/agency.

Grunebaum, Heidi. 2002. "Talking to Ourselves 'among the Innocent Dead': On Reconciliation, Forgiveness, and Mourning." *PMLA* 117, no. 2: 306–10.

Hartman, Saidiya. 2018. "On Working with Archives: An Interview with Saidiya Hartman." By Thora Siemsen. *The Creative Independent*, April 18, 2018. https://thecreativeindependent.com/people/saidiya-hartman-on-working-with-archives/.

Hayes, Terrance. 2018a. *American Sonnets for My Past and Future Assassin.* New York: Penguin Poets.

Hayes, Terrance. 2018b. "Politics and Prose [conversation]." July 16, 2018. https://www.politics-prose.com/event/book/terrance-hayes-american-sonnets-my-past-and-future-assassin.

Hayes, Terrance. 2018c. "Shakespeare and Scooby-Doo: An Interview with Terrance Hayes." By Jeffrey J. Williams. *Iowa Review* 48, no. 1 (Spring): 169–87, 196.

Hirsch, Marianne. 2012. *The Generation of Postmemory: Writing and Visual Culture after the Holocaust.* New York: Columbia University Press.

Holmes, Brian. 2008. "Liar's Poker: Representation of Politics, Politics of Representation." In *Unleashing the Collective Phantoms: Essays in Reverse Imagineering,* by Brian Holmes, 81–94. Brooklyn, NY: Autonomedia.

Hopgood, Stephen. 2013. *The Endtimes of Human Rights.* Ithaca, NY: Cornell University Press.

Iyengar, Sunil. 2018. "Taking Note: Poetry Reading Is Up—Federal Survey Results." *Art Works Blog,* National Endowment for the Arts, June 7, 2018. https://www.arts.gov/art-works/2018/taking-note-poetry-reading-%E2%80%94federal-survey-results.

Jenkins, Esther J., Edward Wang, and Larry Turner. "Beyond Community Violence: Loss and Traumatic Grief in African American Elementary School Children." *Journal of Child & Adolescent Trauma* 7, no. 1 (2014): 27–36.

Katz, Cindi. 2019. "Children and Childhood." In *Keywords in Radical Geography: Antipode at 50,* edited by the Antipode Editorial Collective, 41–44. Hoboken, NJ: Wiley-Blackwell for the Antipode Foundation Ltd.

Keen, Suzanne. 2007. *Empathy and the Novel.* Oxford: Oxford University Press.

Koopman, Eva Maria, and Frank Hakemulder. 2015. "Effects of Literature on Empathy and Self-Reflection: A Theoretical-Empirical Framework." *Journal of Literary Theory* 9, no. 1: 79–111.

Mauro-Flude, Nancy. 2019. "Technās Tranquil Submission: On Being Spoken," In *Anywhere III,* edited by S. Lowry and S. Douglas. Parsons School of Design, The New School, and Victorian College of the Arts, University of Melbourne: Project Anywhere.

Mbembe, Achille. 2019. *Necropolitics.* Durham, NC: Duke University Press.

Medina, Tony, ed. 2016. *Resisting Arrest: Poems to Stretch the Sky.* Durham, NC: Jacar Press.

Miller, Richard E. 2005. *Writing at the End of the World.* Pittsburgh: University of Pittsburgh Press.

Morrison, Toni. 2019. *The Source of Self-Regard: Selected Essays, Speeches, and Meditations.* New York: Knopf.

Moten, Fred. 2003. *In the Break: The Aesthetics of the Black Radical Tradition.* Minneapolis: University of Minnesota Press.

Müller, Timo. 2018. *The African American Sonnet: A Literary History.* Jackson: University Press of Mississippi.

Musiol, Hanna. 2016. "Willful Targets of Rights." In *Discursive Framing of Human Rights: Negotiating Agency and Victimhood,* edited by Jonas Ross Kjærgård and Karen-Margrethe Simonsen, 148–66. London: Routledge.

Musiol, Hanna. 2018. "Metaphors of Decryption: Designs, Poetics, Collaborations." In *Decrypting Power,* edited by Ricardo Sanín Restrepo, 157–78. London: Rowman and Littlefield.

Musiol, Hanna. 2020. "Toxicity, Extinction, and Rights: Political Imagination in Mixmedia, Literary, and Cinematic Futurescapes." In *Writing Beyond the State: Post-Sovereign Approaches to Human Rights and Literary Studies,* edited by Alexandra S. Moore and Samantha Pinto, 330–57. Cham, Switzerland: Palgrave Macmillan.

Nelson, Marilyn. 2005a. " 'Emmett Till': A Poem of Sorrow, and Hope" [Nelson's reading of the collection]. Interview by Farai Chideya. *NPR,* August 29, 2005, 12:00 a.m. https://www.npr.org/templates/story/story.php?storyId=4818586&t=1574422308824.

Nelson, Marilyn. 2005b. "An Interview with Marilyn Nelson" [Transcript]. Interview by Andrea Davis Pinkney. *TeachingBooks.net,* 2005. https://www.teachingbooks.net/content/Nelson_qu.pdf.

Nelson, Marilyn. 2005c. *A Wreath for Emmett Till.* Illustrated by Philippe Lardy. Boston: Houghton Mifflin.

Nixon, Rob. 2011. *Slow Violence and the Environmentalism of the Poor.* Cambridge, MA: Harvard University Press.

Onwuachi-Willig, Angela. 2016. "The Trauma of the Routine: Lessons on Cultural Trauma from the Emmett Till Verdict." *Sociological Theory* 34, no. 4 (December 2016): 335–357.

Patton, Stacey. 2014. "In America, Black Children Don't Get to Be Children." *Washington Post,* November 26, 2014. https://www.washingtonpost.com/opinions/in-america-black-children-dont-get-to-be-children/2014/11/26/a9e24756-74ee-11e4-a755-e32227229e7b_story.html.

Peake, Robert. 2007. "The Trouble with Sonnets." *RobertPeake.com,* July 16, 2007. https://www.robertpeake.com/archives/336-tactics-for-contemporary-sonnets.html.

Preminger, Alex, and Terry V. F. Brogan, eds. 1993. "Sonnet." In *The New Princeton Encyclopedia of Poetry and Poetics.* Princeton, NJ: Princeton University Press.

Rankine, Claudia. 2015. "The Condition of Black Life Is One of Mourning." *New York Times,* June 22, 2015. https://www.nytimes.com/2015/06/22/magazine/the-condition-of-black-life-is-one-of-mourning.html.

Robinson, Douglas. 2008. *Estrangement and the Somatics of Literature: Tolstoy, Shklovsky, Brecht.* Baltimore: Johns Hopkins University Press.

Rutter, Emily Ruth. 2016. "Contested Lineages: Fred Moten, Terrance Hayes, and the Legacy of Amiri Baraka." *African American Review* 49, no. 4: 329–42.

Rutter, Emily Ruth, Sequoia Maner, Tiffany Austin, and darlene anita scott. 2019. "Introduction." In *Revisiting the Elegy in the Black Lives Matter Era,* edited by Tiffany Austin, Sequoia Maner, Emily Ruth Rutter, and darlene anita scott, 9–26. New York: Routledge.

Share, Don, and Lindsay Garbutt. 2017. "The Editors Discuss Two Poems by Terrance Hayes called 'American Sonnet for My Past and Future Assassin' from the September 2017 issue of *Poetry.*" *Poetry Magazine* Podcast, September 11, 2017. https://www.poetryfoundation.org/poetrymagazine/poems/143917/american-sonnet-for-my-past-and-future-assassin-598dc83c976f1.

Sharpe, Christina Elizabeth. 2010. *Monstrous Intimacies: Making Post-Slavery Subjects.* Durham, NC: Duke University Press.

Sharpe, Christina Elizabeth. 2016. *In the Wake: On Blackness and Being.* Durham, NC: Duke University Press.

Shklovsky, Viktor. 1990. "Art as Technique." In *The Theory of Prose,* translated by Benjamin Sher, 1–14. Elmwood Park, IL: Dalkey Archive.

Slaughter, Joseph R. 2007. *Human Rights, Inc.: The World Novel, Narrative Form, and International Law.* New York: Fordham University Press.

Smith, Tracy K. 2018. "Poetry Is Hot Again: The Poet Laureate Explore How, and Why." *New York Times,* December 18, 2018. https://www.nytimes.com/2018/12/10/books/review/political-poetry.html.

Stengers, Isabelle. 2018. "Reclaiming Imagination: Speculative SF as an Art of Consequences." Interview by Casper Bruun Jensen and Line Marie Thorsen. *NatureCulture,* 2018. https://www.natcult.net/interviews/reclaiming-imagination-speculative-sf-as-an-art-of-consequences/.

Tippett, Krista. "Bessel van der Kolk: How Trauma Lodges in the Body" 2013, updated in 2019. https://onbeing.org/programs/bessel-van-der-kolk-how-trauma-lodges-in-the-body/.

Tokarczuk, Olga. 2018. "Tender Narrator: A Nobel Prize Lecture." https://www.nobelprize.org/uploads/2019/12/tokarczuk-lecture-english-2.pdf.

van der Kolk, Bessel A. "The Body Keeps the Score: Memory and the Evolving Psychobiology of Posttraumatic Stress." *Harvard Review of Psychiatry* 1, no. 5 (1994): 253–65.

Winning, Jo. 2020. "Trauma, Illness and Narrative in the Medical Humanities." In *The Routledge Companion to Literature and Trauma,* edited by Colin Davis and Hanna Meretoja, 266–77. Abingdon, Oxon: Routledge.

Chapter Nine

The Right to Securitization

PETER HITCHCOCK

Throughout rights discourses questions of security, safety, sanctuary, and protection are central to the maintenance of personal and communal viability before crisis. Within these broad parameters the precarity of mobile populations—in particular, migrants, refugees, asylum seekers, and displaced persons—have given focus to a gamut of legal and institutional protections. Many of these have attempted to address key material constraints of our time around borders and boundaries, sovereign individual and state rights, the imperatives of global circulation and the conditions of upheaval including, but not limited to, state failure, civil war, environmental collapse, and numerous symptoms of combined and uneven development across the planet. The following will address a specific condition of contemporary logics of movement, one which represents a structural antinomy not just for rights discourses but also for the maintenance of socioeconomic hierarchization. The obvious point is that securitization is a shared concept between the desire to protect vulnerable populations and the wish to safeguard economic activities. The more complicated element is what is actually being shared and whether a structural incompatibility now assumes the force of material contradiction, where no amount of reform can secure the securitization of either. Could it be that securitization in this sense names not only a contemporary regimen of desire but a security to come, one based precisely on the irresolution of its given forms in the present? This larger theoretical and political question will haunt the discourse below, one that seeks to fathom the intersections of rights and technology that exist in contemporary systems of securitization.

If the futurity of security is characterized by a certain divisibility in the present, such a condition is usually read as logical and necessary. The drive for securitization among human rights scholars/activists is overdetermined by an intensification of its lack; however, it is one that is produced paradoxically by states strengthening security as a primary if not primordial dispositif. This is particularly evident in Europe and North America after 9/11 when terrorism was quickly linked to specific groups of migrants deemed to be a security threat over and above individuals profiled as "terrorist." To a great extent, the contradiction between aims and imperatives is also informed and shaped by the terms of globalization and the nostrums of neoliberalism that predate the security crises around terrorism as such. The freeing and opening of circulation—of people, capital, goods, and services—as a general principle has been qualified by and subjected to specific demands of individual state integrity, especially when sovereignty is asserted against a background of waning social security in general. This, however, is only one more measure of antagonism at or around contemporary border epistemology. Whereas global security might be securitized by law and convention in the hands of human rights advocates before state and inter-state institutions (including, most obviously, the UN), "in-state" security is securitized by countries via, on the one hand, rapid development of biometric and surveillance technology and, on the other, developing revenue streams through and in tandem with financial instruments bound by a not altogether congruent securitization in capital markets. This is where what Saskia Sassen terms the unbundling of sovereignty (1996, 31) meets the bundling of risk in financialization. If neither the terminological coincidence nor the logical inconsistency is shocking in histories of "capitalist democracy" (for some an obstinate oxymoron of modernity) or in the shorter ones of neoliberal reconfigurations of the state, how might one begin to track such infernal imbrication today?

Securitization strains within and across three processes simultaneously: the state, financial logic, and the enforcement of international order. The forms of incommensurability securitization produce reveal both the desire for stability and the calculation of acceptable risk specific to each process. Within the expanding field of migration studies, much research focuses on challenging the logic of the state in its attempts to regulate, impede, or reject at-risk mobile populations. Under the rubric of "securing twenty-first century societies," for instance, Anna Hayes and Robert Mason jump scales in their analysis in order to help elucidate the importance of innovation in the organization of *local space* as a viable alternative to state-based security. In terms of hospitality (which, for instance, can be critically considered via a Derridean idea on acknowledgment) any cosmopolitan extension must be wary of maintaining the historical memories of both in-place and migrant communities yet also can be read as a fluid identification consonant with mobility itself. Essays in the Steiner/Hayes/Mason collection, *Migration and Insecurity* (2013), for example, emphasize a cultural citizenship over a legally defined one which we would stress is an epistemological challenge rather than a necessarily practical one before a border officer, for whom legal definitions are paramount. The line between securitization and defensiveness on the part of states is also becoming fluid, again paradoxically, to the point where it assumes a nationalistic and often ethno-centric absolutism. To counter this, security has often been redefined as human, using the UNDP (United Nations Development Program) definition of 1995, and critiques focus on freedom from fear and want. The idea is to validate the individual security of the migrant rather than reinforce that migrancy is somehow always in itself disruptive or "illegal" for the state. The violation of human rights as individual security is particularly prevalent toward refugee populations and irregular migrants often already traumatized by the loss of home, family, community, and assets. This is not necessarily because states are bound to elide benevolence, but because the rhetoric of security itself has transformed in the last forty years. Using the human as the basis of security usefully redefines major protocols around population safety and sustainability. A significant problem, however, lies in restricting this ground as a contrast to the demonstrable machinations of state self-identity. A complex of forces negotiates the articulation of borders and regulates, if not prescribes, the ways in which security can be thought. This is not to challenge the sentiments behind long-term belonging, but it is to question how the assertion of human security might undo the securitization of the world system as such.

The friends of human security also have the means to fragment it, to reconstellate it as various mechanisms of control, extraction, and efficiency. Technologies of securitization are not just dual use, but the constitutive undecidable of long-term belonging in the contemporary period. I refer here not only to the abstractions of big data, but also to algorithmic decision and the mobility of capitalist securitization. This leap, not of faith, but of theory, within the right to securitization will need clarification below, where I will consider the technologies of investment in risk as a conduit for the production of border security itself. Here, the accentuation on human security as a precondition of rights recalls a quandary well noted in Hannah

Arendt's thoughts on the right to have rights, as a right separable from those assumed to be the harbor of nation-state citizen subjects. Recall that Arendt would entertain a deep skepticism about the possibility of reparative rights in the wake of nation state collapse by the end of the Second World War. The stateless refugee was a clear symptom of aporia in the possibility of security per se. Who or what would be the medium of the right to rights in the absence of any state guarantee? We are in an age of even greater statelessness (another seeming paradox, as the proportion of states themselves has multiplied), yet one in which the state itself is held with incredulity regarding safe harbor or resort. But surely this is not a claim that data has emerged as the locus of rights protection, as the salve that saves states and statelessness in equal measure? If the first qualification is about the edge of rights in what secures the human, the second is about the right to secure and sublate borders within the same logic. This is where the right to rights is confronted by the right to securitization in actually existing globalization.

Whereas border control might offer securitization coupled with state humanitarianism, itself an ideological miasma of what Aradau (2004) has called a politics of risk and pity, securitization has a long-standing function in articulating economic borders between law and market. This is not just a coda to political economy around, for instance, Thomas Piketty's highly influential analysis of twenty-first-century capitalism (in which, from Marx, he discovered capital and, more recently, ideology) but a comment on the materialization of the border through financialization itself. What Seyla Benhabib (2007, 445)) calls "democratic iteration" in the right to have rights limns, or iterates, alongside the right to accumulation, in which the human assumes a new form of "groundlessness" (Balibar 2007, 730). What then is securitization in this declension? Obviously, securitization in finance is not the same as securitization of immigrants at some putative border, yet the logic of rights is coterminous with the technological emergence of the modern state. Basically, securitization is a form of financialization that trades on a business relationship—it commoditizes it. Ostensibly, the idea is to manage the risk of the relationship as, for example, an MBS (mortgage-backed security) "manages" a mortgage-based asset by covering its risk in a securities market. Importantly, the right here is in commoditizing itself over and above the claims of the mortgagee in their relation to a lender. The lender's risk is tradable: the debt obligation, however, can become primarily personal (accepting that the mortgagee, as itself a tradable entity, can be depersonalized via hybridized legal forms, like an LLC, "limited liability company"). It is true that lineaments of such tradability have a long history in capitalism. The difference now is in the scale and intensity of transactionalized relations, processes deepened not just by technological infrastructure (fiber optic cables, microwave communications, and the pursuit of light speed exchange) but by the regulative matrix that guarantees the circulation of risk to be secured. The right to securitization is a linchpin of the contemporary economic order and yet, as de Goede (2010, 104) has suggested, financialization has nevertheless normalized "spectacular *in*security in economic life."

If we think of borders as articulated contact zones rather than as only physical divisions, real or imagined, the specific subjectivation of the migrant and financialization are co-constitutive of rights securitization. Again, this does not mean that the logic of rights is identical but that transactionality mediates the possibility of the right to rights in Arendt's sense. Should we be surprised then, as Amoore (2011) has pointed out, that UK border practices deploy algorithmic formulae heavily "derived" from derivative metrics (a point to which I will return)? Or that the corporation, Unisys, not only has contracts to develop surveillance protocols that identify migrants at the border, but it also produces software suites that enable business entities to transact anonymously? One difficulty, then, is to challenge what de Goede calls the "chains of securitization" (2010, 100) without also breaking the very foundations of rights as security themselves.

The agonistic confluence of humanitarianism and political economy in the articulation of borders is symptomatic of broader concerns about the extent to which the fields of international relations and international political economy can productively speak to one another (Boy 2015; Boy et al. 2017). Conceptualizations of rights across discursive modes both provide an important epistemological context but not necessarily the political grounds in their antinomy (the stark contrast between being humane and pricing humanity). The frame is less to enhance the conversation and more to probe its meaning for a materialist understanding of the confluence. Put another way, if risk mediates the contingency of financial instruments, this can assume an allegorical level in contemporary materialism whereby the efficacy of contingency (against, for instance, instrumentalization) can be cynically read as risk aversion before embedded processes of hegemony (a difference between enhancing the struggle with ambivalence and being ambivalent about struggle). The politics of theory around securitization appears to mime the precarity that provokes its articulation. To some extent this is broadly symptomatic of the deconstruction of arrogation in theoretical decision. Thus, while declarations of resistance may be made, they can be qualified and undermined by knowing allusions to the wayward signifier that accentuate emphatic reflexivity. When Marx comments on capitalist revolution by noting "all that is solid melts into air, all that is holy is profaned," he is referring both to structure and structuration, or the logic of relations. Such "melting" is common across politics, and no more so than in its theorization. This is undeniably a good thing because it can open up radical rethinking before norms and normativity. Yet the political forms it takes are not beyond regulating risk as immanent to the theory (hesitant heuristics and theorizing as its own reward), one that produces a hermeneutics of hedging as an end in itself. Even at the level of theory, then, the right to securitization might be a condensation of such protocols where contravention and confirmation compulsively intertwine.

Pertinently, such insistence (as hedging) is prominent in contemporary theorizations of the border. Quoting Saskia Sassen (2007, 214) on "the actual and heuristic disaggregation of 'the border,'" Mezzadra and Neilsen note: "The multiple (legal and cultural, social and economic) components of the concept and institution of the border tend to tear apart from the magnetic line corresponding to the geo-political line of separation between nation-states" (2013, 3). This is demonstrable and is a powerful mode of unthinking the prescriptive logic that has girded the form of the nation since at least the Peace of Westphalia. Yet at soon as one creatively opens the border to "heterogenization," the conceptual tools themselves cleave closely to their object, as in "the radically equivocal character of borders and their growing inability to trace a firm line between the inside and outside of territorial states" (2013, 7). Borders, Mezzadra and Neilson argue, "regulate and structure the relations between capital, labor, law, subjects, and political power even in instances where they are not lined by walls or other fortifications" (2013, 8). Again, this is an appreciable and necessary intervention: the border is always and never only at the border, but to combine method and description in such sentences leaves us with something akin to regulative equivocation, or an "inability" akin to the contradictory rule of risk as management. When Mezzadra and Neilsen describe their approach as "relational," it is both eminently adequate to the general principle of shifting borders and consanguine, methodologically, with those for whom all manner of equivocation, instability, ambiguity, hesitancy, contingency, and provisionality are risk opportunities for capital accumulation (especially in relation to the "borders" of taxation). Securitization, the commoditizing of relations, is meant to secure the risk in transactionality while at the same time profiting from risk itself. Fungible borders are not a constitutive limit on capital accumulation; indeed, such liquidity is fundamental to financialization as such. Borders are certainly an investment venture. The ends of political economy between these models are, of course, radically incommensurate. The point is to register that the conceptual metaphors deployed are not in themselves a break from a capitalist logic, which, in the boardroom of, say, Founders Fund, is used to reconfigure or otherwise make relational borders constantly. If indeed the border (subject to securitization) is primarily an "epistemological viewpoint" revealed by technological and theoretical sophistication, can one undo its effects within risk assessment and the right to relational transformation?

The chief advantage of border as method in this regard is that, in addressing the making (and "scissions") of subjectivity, and particularly political subjects, it draws attention to the limits of the human and humanitarianism in security as right. The emphasis on "unstable configurations" (Mezzadra and Neilson 2013, 20) not only advances a critique of governmental race and gender prescriptions at the border (the ordering in bordering) but also questions how humanitarianism becomes an extension of "migration management" (24). Since this provides perspective on securitization between the production of subjectivities and the impress of financialized subjectlessness it is worth considering in more detail. For instance, Vicki Squire's (2015) work on the Mexico/US border examines the ways in which the positive effects of humanitarian activism can be countered and contravened when based narrowly on the human in humanitarianism, and that the challenge to security in this sense is also in reading the de-privileging of this centered subject. For the most part, what Squire means by "more than human" or "post-humanitarian" in her fieldwork comes down to "more than victim" in the presumptive assignation of migrant agency or the lack thereof. Rather than absent migrants in their movement as simply an effect of state management, Squire wants to extend their presence by including, for instance, an important stress on the materialization of the border as an arena of "things and places" (2015, 4). The focus on a place, the Sonoran Desert in Squire's primary example, or things, like migrant belongings discarded en route, is not interested in discounting the mobility of actual people but looks to deprivilege the ethics of care and pity mediating humanitarian engagement of a specific border crisis. In effect, Squire's approach highlights how the border configures the terms of humanitarianism while a host of alternative practices (including economies of recycling and gifting) challenge the matrix of live and let die. Yet if security is a legal demand across and through the "placing" of a border, does this overdetermine what counts as humanitarian, despite the solidarity with and among migrants on the move?

On one level, the paradox of securing migrant safety through a humanitarianism that also structures the production of "illegality" is as unsurprising as it is insistent. Regimes of care simultaneously determine risk and juridical status even when intention might wish to suspend the priorities of the latter. Nicholas De Genova (2006), for instance, has pointed to the slide between the maintenance of legal procedure and the idea of "deportability" at the Mexican/US border, an entanglement aided by long-standing racialization. When the US Immigration Act of 1917 sought to bar all immigration from Asia, Mexican labor was encouraged to cross the border as a political, economic, and racial exigency. The flexibility of racial quotas and racism does not free humanitarian concern from strategies of exclusion, and historicizing a specific national border throws into relief the complex ideological matrix that can make this so. De Genova accentuates that the legal institution of documentation, defining admissible from deportable, has been used to turn functionally open borders into a "revolving door," one that manages labor and othering as a national (and nationalist) priority. If the humanitarian concern mediates the personal risk from border crossing "without documents," its conventions of securitization are thus subject to securitization as sovereign demand, or what De Genova calls the "the legal production of Mexican/migrant 'illegality'" (2006, 61). More recently, of course, and again within conditions of socioeconomic crisis, the legislation of irregular migration has been extended to at risk populations from Central and South America who have both reconfigured the US/Mexico border and the meaning of securitization in the region.

The moment of the border (in its multiplication, again, particularly notable given the historical production of the US state vis-à-vis Mexico) can be used to obfuscate the logic of securitization in play. Individual metrics might point to the extent of undocumented Mexican migrants, 4.7 million people from the 1960s on, 85% of whom migrated in the 1990s. Surely such largesse at the US southern border proves that despite sovereign demand, actual demand (especially for relatively cheap labor selectively delinked from worker rights) demands mobility over and above the stability of nation state self-identity? In fact, the scale of migration proves the opposite: that the documentation divide underlines the extent to which the state will risk legal protections for "efficiencies" in labor supply. The historical specificity of "crisis" is still valid; the regime of risk, however, the systemic logic of securitization, cleaves to alternative measures of document and decision.

This is evident in several ways, some of which have already been indicated, yet conventional metrics often elide the concrete experiences of migrant communities themselves, whose assertion of rights is securitization in a different key that appeal both to what is extant in the discourses of security across borders and to a potential that appears logically unfulfilled in such frameworks. Alison Gerard (2014), for instance, has studied Somali transnational migrants, especially the experiences of women fleeing famine and the violence of civil war and ethnic conflict who enter the EU through Malta. Her research shows how the EU has attempted to securitize against such migration by putting the emphasis on development, peacekeeping, and relief programs in the Horn of Africa rather than on the settlement of refugees and asylum seekers. Exit decisions for the Somali women interviewed were complicated by several factors, including but not limited to, the age of their children, the location of husbands (whether they had emigrated first), and the conditions of local livelihood. During the civil war in particular, incidences of rape and other violence against women and children were not uncommon and compounded experiences of trauma for those seeking safe haven. The dangers of everyday life spurred departure, even when the risks of extended travel and the possibilities of detention also loomed large. Carrier sanctions (i.e., the production of a functional border at the airport of a country of origin) have often discouraged an exit, but because of the level of precarity refugees have sought alternative routes that embody their own dangers (for instance, overcrowded or ill-equipped boats have claimed thousands of lives). For the most part, the securitization of the migrant according to the EU means deterrence and exclusion, where risk assessment is guided by the security of the destination, not the insecurity of those who have fled war, famine, and gendered violence. These are not absolute divisions, yet the question of the right of mobility is riven by the priorities and privileges of security that overdetermine the right to rights as a geopolitical reflex.

The securitization within migrant communities is complex and demonstrable and stands as a challenge to the claims of state sovereignty over mobility itself. It is also mediated by the financialization of and through mobility, which figures rights as a calculation of risk, as an integer of the precarity of profit. There are several ways to elaborate this range of determination and infrastructural intersectionality, but let us ponder how this might look within a border zone that links security studies with the transactional logic of securitization. As noted, there is a pivot between two versions of spatial fixes—one driven by the weakening of states through social, economic, political, and environmental crises that foster mobile populations large and small within and across national borders; and another, connected but discrete, that constitutes a financial approach to the limits of capital itself at a world scale. Both are materializations of displacement, condensations of the changed dynamics of the globe and globalization that have a longue durée and more immediate symptoms.

One inflection point is clearly the financial crisis of 2007–2008, which in many respects is a crisis of and in securitization. The history around this has been much discussed, but few commentators doubt the role that financial instruments, specifically derivatives like mortgage-back securities, played in the run up of asset prices. Because mortgage risk was bundled or tranched through separate tradable practices, for instance, the underlying debt of the asset appeared to have been "swapped" for the returns on trading contracts themselves (including fees). Rather than examine the complexities and obscurantism of derivative risk, market participants seemed to believe speculative desire would always overcome the more toxic and predatory elements of loan origination in the mortgage business (helped, of course, by the merging of retail and investment bank interests—with one providing capital for the other). The pooling of securities would normally be read to spread risk and minimize the effects of price fluctuation in underlying assets, or even in the movement of relevant interest rates. The returns, however, because abstracted from the risk in the loan terms, encouraged greater speculation, especially when the agencies meant to rate the instruments helped to inflate the level of quality in the bundle of assets as a whole (the bald corruption in such synergy continues to astound). This, coupled with rising and reset adjustable interest rates in the mortgage market at the time, led to a cascade of default and an inability to cover basic financial obligations. Collateral was skewed in favor of cash, and banks stopped lending (to each other) in any other way. There was also a collective realization that a huge part of financial activity had emerged with little or no institutional oversight or meaningful regulation. Securitization had not been securitized.

As de Goede has pointed out, it was President Obama who seemed to offer a new way to think the breakdown in securitization when in October 2008 he noted that the financial debacle was one of the greatest national security crises facing the nation. Against a backdrop of potential institutional collapse, the liquidity crunch was reframed in terms of the kind of state instability that had necessitated or rationalized the war of terror (again, the bundling of risk was now deemed synonymous with the unbundling of sovereignty). De Goede underlines that "Securitization, in this sense, refers to the discursive and political processes through which societal phenomena become understood and addressed as security issues" (100). In other words, for security studies, transactionality itself, under specific conditions, may ground risk rather than its remedy. In truth, of course, as Randy Martin (2007) had reminded us the year before Obama's pronouncement, the political meaning of security has long been braided with finance, and for Rudolph Hilferding, whom Martin quotes, its monopolistic tendencies take the form of making special claims for national security, including those of an imperialist suasion (Martin usefully characterizes this as an "empire of indifference"). The right to secure borders includes the right to secure them well beyond the national (and nationalist) border at stake, and the edge of finance, especially during crisis, finds new borders all over the world.

The processes through which securitization was securitized in the bailout to the financial upheaval of 2007–2008 are also instructive. If the language of war was often used to characterize the task at stake, cleaning up the mess clearly meant casualties (Lehman Brothers, the financial services company, being the most obvious). Sacrifice was invoked, and the Emergency Economic Stabilization Act of 2008 required a great deal of it. The Troubled Asset Relief Program (TARP) alone cost over $700 billion and the total cost to the U.S. government has been measured up to $29 trillion (easily surpassing the total outlay for all of U.S. warfare in the last hundred years). While some of this cost is notional and a collateralization of last resort (the Federal Reserve), few doubt that the extraordinary measures underline the importance of finance to the security of the state itself.

Traditionally, as Nina Boy (2015) has noted, security studies has respected the relative autonomy of securitization in finance from the interests of state security found, say, in international political economy. The effects of the financial crisis are many and continuing but include various calls to integrate the logic of finance and financial instruments much more forcefully into the "futures" of security itself. Boy has argued for an elaboration of "sovereign safety" not just in the sense of safe haven (the Fed's role in unwinding debt positions in the financial crisis) but as public credit, as various forms of liquid government bond, and as a risk-free asset. The long history of pledges signifying sovereign right has been complicated by financialization because, as the example of mortgage-backed securities makes clear, "safety" is continually mediated by the circulation of contracts at some remove from realization in the initial asset. Indeed, if a Foucauldian *dispositif* might find sovereign security in the control of circulation, then networks of exchange and, in particular, technological transformations in transactional speed, represent financial sovereignty as collateralized contingency. This does not mean the role of central banks, for instance, has been vacated by the wizardry of algos and high-frequency trading. Far from it. In fact, the emergence of a fully integrated yet volatile financial network has placed more emphasis on the function of monetary policy, payment security, and the appropriate regulation of banks and banking in the world system. Of course, the power of central banking is relative to the state that nurtures it, but the idea is that the right to modulate financialization is an accepted horizon of economic activity, not least because, as the financial crisis proves, the infrastructural power of state can articulate safety mechanisms when the market appears unable or unwilling to do so. One issue is whether financialization can pursue profligacy precisely because state sovereignty constitutes a power to reward it. Yet even if or because the power of state and finance move symbiotically, the question of securitization points to the possibility of involution in both and that shifting borders are also changes in the forms of socialization they might otherwise wish to command.

The specter of change overdetermines the production and meanings of migration in this regard. The right to securitization in the mobility, in particular, of at-risk populations figures the deepening dilemmas of security in socialization and the extent to which political economy as global capitalism can continue to be both a primary source and solution to such contradictions. Again, the monetization of interstate migration has an extensive history both in the practices of individual states and in various manifestations (sanctioned or otherwise) of "middlemen." If one has substantial financial means, several countries offer "citizenship by investment" programs. One can also purchase "elite residency," although, since this is based primarily on special visas, it can be more easily revoked. Internal migration can also be monetized, especially if a state modulates movement through residency permits of some kind. Critically, of course, poor and working people find it much harder to secure mobility financially, and an unofficial network can quickly grow to capitalize on precarity at or around specific borders against a background of social upheaval. Credit from institutions is possible, but the cost of moving is often based on family, family connections, and community experience. For refugees and asylum seekers even basic economic security may not be possible, and this accentuates the role of states and NGOs in answering primary needs. How can financialization be read into the constructions of border and rights of passage? Does this shape in some way the manner in which the right to securitization can be figured at these scales?

There are several ways that finance capital and the financialization of global networks affect border security and the securitization of the migrant. The financial crisis itself, for instance, while slowing migration in some instances, saw a notable impact on remittance payments to "developing" countries (in part because the origin of the crisis was in the North). Remittances in general remained resilient, but not without increasing hardships for those providing them. Undocumented migrants, in particular, are proportionately more vulnerable in economic downturns because social safety nets may not be accessible. One of the key reasons undocumented migrants tend to stay in place, however, is the fear that re-entry into their host country may not be feasible once the upheaval has passed. If a distinct hardening of borders in the "developed" world occurred in light of the attacks and aftermath of 9/11, technological advances in financial trading that helped produce the crisis were also active in securing borders after it.

Amoore has investigated the use of algorithms in the UK's "e-border" program, "a risk-based system that deploys processes of data mining and analytics in order to derive a risk score or flag for individuals entering or exiting the UK" (2011, 25). In the United States, the DXC Technology subsidiary, Unisys, who previously aided CBP (Customs and Border Protection) with contracts for fingerprinting and facial scanning, now has developed an AI suite called LineSight, that can cross-reference airline ticket information (including passenger history), cargo manifests, and Interpol reports to profile likely "threats." At the border, the system uses live video (passive biometrics) to generate facial recognition matches. Unisys also produces a biannual security index that offers both financial and national security assessments. Meanwhile, Unisys' Stealth software, originally developed for the U.S. Defense Department, can now hide two-way communications on corporate servers. Whereas one element of its security interests is primed to profile and reveal, another, Stealth, facilitates disappearance and anonymity. Using the tagline, "You can't hack what you can't see," the latter can be used to thwart monitoring of many kinds. Both security projects hinge on discourses of preemption, the technological production of rights articulated with rights curtailed built in. In business parlance this is called "micro-segmentation," and the challenge is to link it across modes of securitization.

Much is made of the fact that over 30 years after the fall of the Berlin Wall, seen as a key symbol of walls and walling, resources are being prioritized for new ones. The monetizing of border security, however, spreads digital demarcation at and beyond the production and reproduction of physical boundaries. While hard borders place greater restrictions on the displaced and undocumented, the privilege of being biometrically profiled (with fees themselves as a pertinent barrier) permits a level of borderless dedocumentation (with important equivalents in shipping too). Variations of the concept are already in development and include digital travel tokens that combine trust and verification. Other investment opportunities abound. Since the wall is constituted as a space of interdiction, Palmer Luckey, of Oculus VR headset fame, has started a new company, Anduril. Heavily funded by Peter Thiel's venture capital concern, Founder's Fund, and with a staff that includes former members of Palantir, the data-crunching surveillance company, Anduril has distinct market advantages, even against proven border securitization interests like the Israeli company Elbit Systems. Anduril's project, pitched to DHS, features portable surveillance technology, including towers topped with radar, communications antennae, and laserguided cameras that can detect and identify motion within a two-mile radius. The system, "Lattice," has been described as "a general platform for geographic near-omniscience" and offers the cost efficiencies of technology to wall the US/Mexico border electronically. In a trial run, Lattice aided CBP in interdicting over 50 "unauthorized border crossings." Monitoring the border from above (drones) and below (subterranean fiber optic cables like OptaSense) enables walling, but the point is such "invisible boundaries" are not outside the technological and infrastructural logic of the bordered borderlessness of securitization as an internal dynamic of contemporary capitalism.

We would like to think that these two forms of right are simply and irrevocably antithetical, and yet they are symptomatically entwined. Here I would underline that securitization currently composes a contradiction in the world system as such and that in large part what produces mass mobility also creates the techné of security as a financial claim on social being. When Marx was considering the working day and the disjunct rights of labor and capital, he wondered about the endgame in such a scenario:

> The capitalist maintains his rights as a purchaser when he tries to make the working-day as long as possible, and to make, whenever possible, two working-days out of one. On the other hand, the peculiar nature of the commodity sold implies a limit to its consumption by the purchaser, and the laborer maintains his right as seller when he wishes to reduce the working-day to one of definite normal duration. There is here, therefore, an

> antinomy, right against right, both equally bearing the seal of the law of exchanges. Between equal rights force decides. (1976, 341)

Obviously, the securitization of the migrant does not pivot simply on the logic of work and the working day, and the law of exchange in financialization has a "peculiar nature" all of its own. And yet the production of rights across these discourses bears more than a little compulsive consanguinity, as the Mezzadra/Neilson "border" methodology implies. The question is not to dissolve one into the other but to come to terms with the logics of securitization in the current conjuncture, one in which state and regional crises accelerate the movement of refugees and asylum seekers while stronger states contend that citizen security must come first. Meanwhile, technological financialization can move much faster than a migrant and yet just as easily secure the border that securities otherwise cross. However we prioritize human rights in migrant crises, forces of finance and sovereignty seek securitization in their own image, even if their specific modes of transactionality might actually undermine the security at stake. Are such forces decisive within securitization or is migrancy a power of contention? There is a certain unity of purpose in conventions around human security but, while there are many proactive groups who defend and advance the rights of migrant communities, their force as a whole does not move securitization in principle to the point of transformation. In the spirit of Mark Fisher's (2009, 81) "capitalist realism" we might proffer that "the tiniest event can tear a hole in the grey curtain of reaction," and yet part of the realism at stake requires addressing the fabric of securitization itself. This might mean not only deconstructing the relative autonomy of finance and state security as noted by Boy above, but also interrogating the logic of securitization as systemic. The migrant now reveals this logic if not the exact form of security in socialization to come.

Works Cited

Amoore, Louise. 2011. "Data Derivatives: On the Emergence of a Security Risk Calculus for Our Times." *Theory, Culture and Society* 28, no. 6: 24–43.

Aradau, Claudia. 2004. "The Perverse Politics of Four-Letter Words: Risk and Pity in the Securitization of Human Trafficking." *Millennium* 33, no. 2: 251–277.

Arendt, Hannah. 1973. *The Origins of Totalitarianism.* New York: Harcourt Brace.

Balibar, Etienne. 2007. "(De)Constructing the Human as Human Institution: A Reflection on the Coherence of Hannah Arendt's Practical Philosophy." *Social Research* 74, no. 2 (Fall): 727–738.

Benhabib, Seyla. 2007. "Democratic Exclusions and Democratic iterations: Dilemmas of 'Just Membership' and Prospects of Cosmopolitan Federalism." *European Journal of Political Theory* 6 (October): 445–462.

Boy, Nina. 2015. "Sovereign Safety." *Security Dialogue* 46, no. 6: 530–547.

Boy, Nina, John Morris, and Mariana Santos. 2017. "Introduction: Taking Stock of Security and Finance." *Finance and Society* 3, no. 2: 102–105.

De Genova, Nicholas. 2006. "The Legal Production of Mexican/Migrant 'Illegality.' " In *Latinos and Citizenship: The Dilemma of Belonging*, edited by Suzanne Oboler, 61–90. New York: Palgrave, 2006.

De Goede, Marieke. "Financial Security." In *The Routledge Handbook of New Security Studies*, edited by J. Peter Burgess, 100–109. London: Routledge, 2010.

Derrida, Jacques. 2000. *Of Hospitality: Anne Dufourmantelle Invites Jacques Derrida to Respond.* Stanford: Stanford University Press.

Fisher, Mark. 2009. *Capitalist Realism: Is There No Alternative?* Zero Books.

Gerard, Alison. 2014. *The Securitization of Migration and Refugee Women*. New York: Routledge.

Hayes, Anna, and Robert Mason. 2013. "Securing twenty-first century societies." In *Migration and Insecurity: Citizenship and Social Inclusion in a Transnational Era*, edited by Niklaus Steiner, Robert Mason and Anna Hayes, 3–16. New York: Routledge.

Martin, Randy. 2007. *An Empire of Indifference: American War and the Financial Logic of Risk Management*. Durham: Duke University Press.

Marx, Karl. 1976. *Capital (Volume One).* Trans. Ben Fowkes. London: Penguin.

Mezzadra, Sandro, and Brett Neilson. 2013. *Border as Method; or, The Multiplication of Labor*. Durham: Duke University Press.

Piketty, Thomas. 2017. *Capital in the Twenty-First Century.* Trans. Arthur Goldhammer. Cambridge, MA: Belknap Press.

Sassen, Saskia. 1996. *Sovereignty in an Age of Globalization*. New York: Columbia University Press.

Sassen, Saskia. 2007. *A Sociology of Globalization*. New York: W. W. Norton.

Squire, Vicki. 2015. *Post-Humanitarian Border Politics Between Mexico and the U.S.* London: Palgrave.

Steiner, Niklaus, Robert Mason, and Anna Hayes, eds. 2013. *Migration and Insecurity: Citizenship and Social Inclusion in a Transnational Era*. New York: Routledge.

Contributors

David Cingranelli is a professor of political science at Binghamton University, SUNY (USA) and codirector of the university's Human Rights Institute. He and his students developed some of the earliest quantitative measures of national human rights practices. He has written widely on human rights, democracy, governance, and the scientific study of human rights. His 2007 book with Rodwan Abouharb, *Human Rights and Structural Adjustment* (Cambridge UP), demonstrated the negative human rights impacts of World Bank and IMF program lending in developing countries. He is a former president of the Human Rights Section of the American Political Science Association. Until 2012, he served as the codirector of the Cingranelli and Richards (CIRI) Human Rights Data Project, the largest and most widely used human rights data set in the world. Presently, he, Mikhail Filippov, and Brendan Skip Mark are codirecting a successor to the CIRI project, which is called the "CIRIGHTS" data project.

James Dawes, professor at Macalester College (USA) is the author of *The Novel of Human Rights* (Harvard UP, 2018), *Evil Men* (Harvard UP, 2013), *That the World May Know: Bearing Witness to Atrocity* (Harvard UP, 2007), and *The Language of War* (Harvard UP, 2002).

Elizabeth A. DiGangi is a New York native who earned her bachelor's degree in anthropology and history and master's in biological anthropology from the State University of New York at Buffalo. She then attended the University of Tennessee in Knoxville to pursue studies in bioarchaeology and forensic anthropology. For five years, she worked as a senior forensic advisor in Bogotá, Colombia, offering a variety of training courses for the country's professional forensic scientists in addition to collaborating on lab design. It was a research methods course developed by her and a colleague for Colombian anthropologists that led to the publication of her coedited volume (with Dr. Megan Moore): *Research Methods in Human Skeletal Biology* (Academic Press, 2013). Her most recent book (with Susan Sincerbox) is *Forensic Taphonomy and Ecology of North American Scavengers* (Academic Press, 2018). Dr. DiGangi is currently associate professor of anthropology at Binghamton University. She is board certified by the American Board of Forensic Anthropology and works on cases for local and state law enforcement in addition to teaching and mentoring undergraduate and graduate students. Her research interests in forensic anthropology include improving trauma analysis, critiquing ancestry analysis via use of Critical Race Theory, and human rights.

Ulic Egan is a PhD Candidate and Swansea University Research Excellence Scholar (SURES) at the Hillary Rodham-Clinton School of Law, where he is undertaking a sociolegal intersectional analysis of the role of technology in the investigation of conflict-related sexual and gender-based violence. He is also a program manager for the Institute for International Criminal Investigations (IICI) in The Hague. He is an attorney and holds a Bachelor of Civil Law degree from the National University of Ireland, Galway, and an LL.M. in International Criminal Law from the Irish Centre for Human Rights.

Mikhail Filippov is an associate professor of political science at Binghamton University (SUNY; USA). He holds a PhD from California Institute of Technology. His research, focusing on comparative federalism, post-Soviet integration, and human rights has appeared in journals such *APSR, Journal of Politics, British Journal of Political Science, Journal of Human Rights and Public Choice.* He coauthored (with Peter Ordeshook and Olga Shvetsova) *Designing Federalism: A Theory of Self-Sustainable Federal Institutions* (Cambridge University Press 2004). He is codirector of the CIRIGHTS human rights dataset, which measures respect for over 20 internationally recognized human rights in all countries of the world.

Jamie Grace is a senior lecturer in law in the Department of Law and Criminology at Sheffield Hallam University, UK. Jamie was course leader of both the MA and LLM in applied human rights courses in his department for four years. He has been appointed as vice-chair to the Data Analytics Ethics Committee established by the West Midlands Police and crime commissioner. Jamie also serves on the West Midlands Police general force ethics committee. Jamie held a Visiting Fellowship at the Institute of Advanced Legal Studies (University of London) in the summer of 2020, contributing to the work of the Centre for Information Law and Policy at the institute.

Peter Hitchcock is professor of English at the CUNY Graduate Center and Baruch College of the City University of New York (USA). He is also on the faculty of women's studies and film studies at the Graduate Center. He is the associate director of the Center for Place, Culture, and Politics at the Graduate Center. His books include *Dialogics of the Oppressed*; *Oscillate Wildly: Space, Body, and Spirit of Millennial Materialism*; *Imaginary States: Studies in Cultural Transnationalism*; *The Long Space: Transnationalism and Postcolonial Form*; and, most recently, *Labor in Culture, or, Worker of the World(s)*. He has also coedited two essay collections, *The New Public Intellectual: Politics, Theory, and the Public Sphere* and *The Debt Age*. Recent essay publications include "History and Class Struggle," "Resistance Is Futile: The Cultural Politics of Transformation in the Digital Age," "Kant at the Federal Reserve," and "The Speed of Place and the Space of Time: Toward a Theory of Postcolonial Velo/city." Books in progress include "The World, The State, and Postcoloniality," "Trading Objects: Finance, Commodities, and Culture," and "Serial, Seriality, and Serialization."

Alexa Koenig, PhD, JD, MA, is executive director of UC Berkeley's Human Rights Center (winner of the 2015 MacArthur Award for Creative and Effective Institutions), cofounder of the center's Investigations Lab, and a lecturer at Berkeley Law (USA). She is a member of AAAS's Committee on Scientific Freedom and Responsibility, as well as cochair of the International Bar Association's Human Rights Law Committee and the International Criminal Court's Technology Advisory Board. She has won multiple awards for her work, including the United Nations Association-SF Global Human Rights Award and the Mark Bingham Award for Excellence. Recent books include *Digital Witness: Using Open Source Information for Human Rights Investigation, Documentation and Accountability* (Oxford UP 2020) and *Hiding in Plain Sight: The Pursuit of War Criminals from Nuremberg to the War on Terror* (UC Press 2016).

Donna M. Kowal, PhD, is professor emerita in the Department of Communication at SUNY Brockport (USA). Her research centers on the rhetoric of social movements and representations of gender, ethnic, and class in public discourse. She is author of the award-winning book *Tongue of Fire: Emma Goldman, Public Womanhood, and the Sex Question* (SUNY Press, 2016).

Barbara LeSavoy, PhD, is associate professor in the Department of Women and Gender Studies (WGS) at SUNY Brockport (USA). Her research and publication areas include women's global human rights, identity politics in literature and popular culture, and historical to contemporary perspectives on gender equality. Her most recent scholarship includes a coauthored book chapter on Seneca Falls and a feminist politics of relation. Dr. LeSavoy serves as lead faculty for a global classroom linking SUNY Brockport students with students at Velikiy Novgorod State University in Russia, and she has taught WGS seminars for several summers at the NY Institute for Linguistics, Cognition, and Culture (NYI) in St Petersburg, Russia.

Brendan Skip Mark is an assistant professor of political science at the University of Rhode Island (USA). He conducts research exploring the intersections between human rights, political economy, collective dissent, and empirical methodology. His research focuses on questions related to the domestic consequences of International Monetary Fund conditionality, contentious politics, labor rights, economic rights, protest behavior, repertoires of repression, remittances and migration, economic crisis, and the interrelationships between human rights. His work highlights the ways in which measurement and modeling choices affect what we know about these relationships. He is codirector of the CIRIGHTS human rights dataset which measures respect for over 20 internationally recognized human rights in all countries of the world. He is also codirector of the Center for Non-violence and Peace Studies at the University of Rhode Island.

Alexandra S. Moore is codirector of the Human Rights Institute and the Kaschak Institute for Social Justice for Women and Girls, and professor of human rights and the humanities, Department of English, at Binghamton University (USA). She also serves as chair of the university's Citizenship, Rights, and Cultural Belonging Transdisciplinary Area of Excellence. She has published two monographs, *Vulnerability and Security in Human Rights Literature and Visual Culture* (2015) and *Regenerative Fictions: Postcolonialism, Psychoanalysis, and the Nation as Family* (2004). In addition, she has coedited six volumes, most recently: *Writing Beyond the State: Post-Sovereign Approaches to Human Rights to Literature and Culture* (2020), *Witnessing*

Torture: Perspectives of Survivors and Human Rights Workers (2018); and *The Routledge Companion to Literature and Human Rights* (2015). Her current work focuses on human rights violations in the war on terror.

Hanna Musiol is an associate professor of English and a founding member of NTNU ARTEC and Environmental Humanities at the Norwegian University of Science and Technology. Her research interests include American literary and cultural studies, transmodal storytelling, critical theory and pedagogy, with emphasis on human rights, migration, and political ecology. Musiol has published on literary and transmedia aesthetics and justice (in *Writing Beyond the State, Environment, Space, Place, Digital Humanities Quarterly, Oil Culture, Human Rights and Literature, Journal of American Studies*, and *Discursive Framing of Human Rights*), and she collaborates regularly with grassroots initiatives and nonacademic institutions in Europe and the United States on city-scale curatorial, public humanities, global classroom, and civic engagement projects.

Ş. İlgü Özler is a professor of political science and international relations at SUNY New Paltz (USA). She is the founder and director of the SUNY Global Engagement Program in New York City. Her previous research focused on civic engagement as it relates to political parties, nongovernmental organizations and social movements. She has conducted research in Turkey, Mexico, and Chile. Her most recent work focuses on human rights and global governance at the United Nations. Her publications appeared in various academic journals including *Sociological Perspectives, Ethics and International Affairs, Representation, Journal of Civil Society, Democratization, Latin American Perspectives, Global Environmental Politics, Mexican Studies,* and *Turkish Studies.* Her teaching has incorporated innovative experiential learning in courses related to the United Nations and global engagement through civil society organizations. She has been active in the United Nations Association and Amnesty International in various capacities. She served as an officer on the Board of Amnesty USA (2017–2020) focusing especially on global strategic planning and policy work. Özler received her PhD in political science from University of California, Los Angeles (2003).

Christiane Wilke is an associate professor in the Department of Law and Legal Studies at Carleton University (Ottawa, Canada). She received her PhD in political science from the New School for Social Research and has published on transitional justice, human rights and memory, state violence and visualities. She is a coeditor of *Sensing Law* (GlassHouse, 2017) and volume 4 of the collected works of Otto Kirchheimer (Nomos, 2019). Her research project on counting and accounting for airstrikes is supported by a grant from the Social Sciences and Humanities Research Council (SSHRC).

Index